Loris Malaguzzi and the Reggio Emilia Experience

Kathy Hall, Mary Horgan, Anna Ridgway,
Rosaleen Murphy, Maura Cunneen and
Denice Cunningham

Continuum Library of Educational Thought
Series Editor: Richard Bailey
Volume 23

continuum

Continuum International Publishing Group
The Tower Building, 11 York Road, London SE1 NX
80 Maiden Lane, Suite 704, New York, NY 10038

www.continuumbooks.com

© Kathy Hall, Mary Horgan, Anna Ridgway, Rosaleen Murphy, Maura Cunneen and
Denice Cunningham 2010

British Library Cataloguing-in-Publication Data
A catalogue record for this book is available from the British Library.

ISBN: 978-1-8470-6105-8 (hardcover)

Library of Congress Cataloging-in-Publication Data
Loris Malaguzzi and the Reggio Emilia experience / Kathy Hall ... [et al.].
   p. cm. – (Continuum library of educational thought ; v 23)
 Includes bibliographical references.
 ISBN 978-1-84706-105-8 (hardcover)
 1. Malaguzzi, Loris, 1920-1994. 2. Educators–Italy–Biography. 3. Reggio Emilia approach
(Early childhood education) I. Hall, Kathy, 1952– II. Title. III. Series.

 LB880.M3152L67 2010
 370.92–dc22
 [B]

2009020436

Typeset by Kenneth Burnley, Wirral, Cheshire
Printed and bound by CPI Group (UK) Ltd, Croydon, CR0 4YY

Loris Malaguzzi and the Reggio Emilia Experience

Contents

Series Editor's Preface

Education is sometimes presented as an essentially practical activity. It is, it seems, about teaching and learning, curriculum and what goes on in schools. It is about achieving certain ends, using certain methods, and these ends and methods are often prescribed for teachers, whose duty it is to deliver them with vigor and fidelity. With such a clear purpose, what is the value of theory?

Recent years have seen politicians and policy makers in different countries explicitly denying *any* value or need for educational theory. A clue to why this might be is offered by a remarkable comment by a British Secretary of State for Education in the 1990s: 'Having any ideas about how children learn, or develop, or feel, should be seen as subversive activity.' This pithy phrase captures the problem with theory: it subverts, challenges and undermines the very assumptions on which the practice of education is based.

Educational theorists, then, are troublemakers in the realm of ideas. They pose a threat to the status quo and lead us to question the common-sense presumptions of educational practices. But this is precisely what they should do because the seemingly simple language of schools and schooling hides numerous contestable concepts that in their different usages reflect fundamental disagreements about the aims, values and activities of education.

Implicit within the *Continuum Library of Educational Thought* is an assertion that theories and theorizing are vitally important for education. By gathering together the ideas of some of the most influential, important and interesting educational thinkers, from the Ancient Greeks to contemporary scholars, the series has the ambitious task of providing an accessible yet authoritative resource for a generation of students and practitioners. Volumes within the series are written by acknowledged leaders in the field, who were selected both for their scholarship and their ability to make often complex ideas accessible to a diverse audience.

It will always be possible to question the list of key thinkers who are represented in this series. Some may question the inclusion of certain thinkers;

some may disagree with the exclusion of others. That is inevitably going to be the case. There is no suggestion that the list of thinkers represented within the *Continuum Library of Educational Thought* is in any way definitive. What is incontestable is that these thinkers have fascinating ideas about education, and that, taken together, the Library can act as a powerful source of information and inspiration for those committed to the study of education.

RICHARD BAILEY

Birmingham University

Foreword

Loris Malaguzzi and the Reggio Emilia Experience by the University College Cork team of Kathy Hall, Mary Horgan, Anna Ridgway, Rosaleen Murphy, Maura Cunneen and Denice Cunningham, is an erudite and challenging study, providing fresh insights into the 'Reggio Experience'.

As the authors state, Reggio Emilia's early childhood education has become world renowned, a shining example we are all exhorted to emulate in principle but not to duplicate. Leading scholars from many countries have written ringing endorsements of practice in the nurseries in this area of northern Italy. And Reggio's own proponents have produced books, as well as providing travelling exhibitions and study visits, which have added to both Reggio's prestige and funding to further supply the nurseries with exciting resources and materials. One has no doubt that the late Loris Malaguzzi, Reggio parents, local politicians and all the professional colleagues involved, acted on their deeply held beliefs about young children, their families and community, and about interdependence.

However, the Reggio Experience, despite promulgating the view of adults as joint learners in the enterprise and encouraging teacher development through the study of a much wider range of ideas and philosophies than might be the case in other parts of the world, does not offer explorations of the work of the 'giants on whose shoulders they stand', perhaps because they fear that they will then be 'pigeonholed'. They are also clear that dialogue, thinking and the study of new ideas need to be continuous processes. Malaguzzi himself related how he had been influenced by many writers, such as Dewey for example, and Kathy Hall and her colleagues provide us with thoughtful accounts of the links they have found by analysing both the explicit predecessors of the Reggio philosophy and those they detected through their document research and study visits.

This book's illuminating historical account of the political background to Reggio's development adds greatly to our understanding of why and how the area came to be famous for its early childhood provision. More than a decade ago, a small group of us attended a seminar in London to discuss the possibility of initiating a Reggio Experience in England. My anxiety then was that we would be unable to transcend the constraining political context in which we found ourselves. Reading this book has made me reflect on my own career, particularly my time in the area in England known as the Potteries, during the 1970s and 1980s. There the legacy of R.H.Tawney and the Workers' Educational Association was congruent with the political will to provide nursery education in an area traditionally associated with very high, skilled, female employment. Further, I was privileged to be guided by Gwen Stubbs, then the local nursery inspector, whose vision was Reggioesque before any of us had heard of the Reggio Experience, and by the late Dr Corinne Hutt, whose insightful interest in play and young children's learning has fired me ever since. Within the last year, a group of nursery schools in that Stoke-on-Trent area have been deemed excellent by school inspectors – so have they submitted to the 'managerial concepts such as delivery, quality, excellence and outcomes'[1] or somehow subsumed (or subverted) such demands within their own strong traditions? My involvement in the Organization for Economic Co-operation and Development's (OECD, 2006)[2] recent study of early childhood services in 20 countries, together with observations in Chinese kindergartens and reading work by Chinese academics, has further convinced me that it is impossible to simply transplant nursery systems or curricula, because history, traditions and political contexts maintain powerful influences (which brings us back to another of Malaguzzi's cited giants – Urie Bronfenbrenner). It is obvious that Chinese politicians and practitioners are taking home ideas from many countries. But what is exciting about China is the way in which, like Reggio, they are adopting both a *social constructivist* and a *social constructionist* perspective. They too seek to 'make sense' of their own proposed innovations by developing practice in ways which fit with their traditions.

This text is an eloquent study, acknowledging both the lack of research into the effects of the nurseries and the fact that Reggio advocates would argue that such research would be contrary to Reggio philosophy. The Cork team's publication will enable a deeper dialogue and deeper reflections by practitioners on provision in their own countries and settings, wider exploration of the theories of favored 'giants' and challenges to some of the simplistic pronouncements of politicians.

Members of the University College Cork Early Childhood team are already internationally recognized for their innovative undergraduate and postgraduate degree work. Under Professor Francis Douglas and Dr Mary Horgan's leadership their Early Childhood Studies courses and research have acted as a spur to professional and academic education in this field. Now the fruits of that work and the collaboration with Professor Kathy Hall, one of the most respected and intellectually rigorous colleagues I know, have resulted in a book which will instigate higher levels of thinking and debate in the field of Early Childhood Education and Care – I anticipate future publications from this group with great relish!

TRICIA DAVID

Emeritus Professor of Education, Canterbury Christ Church University and Honorary Emeritus Professor of Early Childhood Education, University of Sheffield.

Deal, Kent, July 2009

Notes

1 Gunilla Dahlberg and Peter Moss (2006) Introduction. In C. Rinaldi, *In Dialogue with Reggio Emilia*. London: Routledge, p. 2.
2 OECD (2006) *Starting Strong II*. Paris: OECD.

Acknowledgments

We would like to thank Greenwood Publishing Group for permission to use quotations from pages xv, xvi, xvii, 3, 8, 15, 34, 36, 58, 63, 68, 70, 74, 78, 57–8, 83–4, 114, 118–19, 149, 189–190, 240, 264, 276, and 285–6 of the published work *The Hundred Languages of Children*, edited by Carolyn Edwards, Lella Gandini and George Forman. Copyright © 1998 by Ablex Publishing Corporation. Reproduced with permission of Greenwood Publishing Group, Inc., Westport, CT.

We would also like to thank Taylor & Francis for permission to use quotations from pages 8, 20, 17, 26, 27, 40, 46, 58, 66–7, 73, 81–2, 93, 123, 125, 131–2, 155–6, 181, and 196 of the published work *In Dialogue with Reggio Emilia*, by Carlina Rinaldi. Copyright © 2006 by Routledge. Reproduced by permission of Taylor & Francis Books UK.

Finally we acknowledge the support of a grant from University College Cork in completing this book.

To the memory of the Reggio Women, 1945–63

Introduction

For many in the field of early childhood education Reggio Emilia is synonymous with ideal practice. Its principles and methods have been endorsed by eminent scholars in education and particularly in the field of early childhood. Early-years educators in Europe, the US and beyond have embraced its tenets and have sought to align practices in their own settings with those they have observed in Reggio Emilia preschools or read about in Reggio Emilia literature. Despite the fact that its founder Loris Malaguzzi wrote little about his philosophy of childhood education, there is now a considerable literature on the 'Reggio Emilia Experience' as well as significant interest in its practices on the part of early-years educators and policy makers, as evidenced by the many study visits made to Reggio schools and childhood centers.

Much of what is written about the Reggio approach is extremely positive, ardent even, with few challenging voices and critical accounts. How does one explain the international appeal of what is termed the 'Reggio Emilia Experience' and what many claim is 'unique' in the field of early childhood? Those writing from 'inside' Reggio, those who claim to know Malaguzzi's mind and who see themselves as responsible for disseminating its principles and practices, have been reluctant to associate themselves with any one theoretical orientation, keen to distance themselves from being pigeon-holed into a single particular perspective. What then are the sets of ideas, ideologies, assumptions, principles, theories – explicit and implicit – underlying Reggio thinking and practices?

This volume explores the construct of Reggio Emilia. It draws on a range of conceptual lenses to interrogate its assumptions, theories and perspectives on learning, children, professionals, knowledge and community.

The book is divided into three parts. Part 1, 'Socio-cultural Context and Intellectual Biography', has one chapter and this offers an historical account of the Italian contexts, events and structures that originated and shaped the Reggio Emilia movement. The life and work of Loris Malaguzzi, its key architect, is also described in this chapter which, overall, provides an essential background to the detailed description and discussion of the Reggio principles and practices that feature in subsequent chapters.

Part 2, 'Critical Exposition of the Reggio Emilia Experience', has four chapters, each dealing with aspects of Reggio thinking and practice and drawing on different perspectives to illuminate its fundamental ideas and methods.

Chapter 2 examines the experiences of children in a Reggio Emilia preschool, focusing on the roles of the teacher, *atelierista* and *pedagogista* as well as the expectations of children, staff and parents. Based on existing literature as well as participation in an International Study Group visit to Reggio Emilia, it analyses the fundamental tenets and practices in Reggio Emilia settings, highlighting Reggio understanding of such features as project work and examining links with Gardner's multiple intelligences.

Chapter 3 develops this aspect further in elaborating on the nature of parental partnerships in toddler centers and preschools. How partnerships are enacted is the theme of the chapter, while the notion of a pedagogy of relationships, social management, inclusion and integration, and the pivotal role of documentation, are all Reggio elements that are explained.

Chapter 4 delves further into the values underlying Reggio Emilia principles and practices, this time foregrounding theories of curriculum and pedagogy and interrogating Reggio in the context of different theoretical perspectives. The purpose is to explicate the versions of curriculum, pedagogy and childhood embedded in Reggio thinking.

There is little that could be described as systematic research on Reggio practices and, to our knowledge, there are no longitudinal studies of processes or impact. In this regard, an analysis of the ways in which Reggio ideas are represented in the literature was considered to be a valuable direction to take in this volume. Drawing on a poststructuralist perspective, Chapter 5 offers an analysis of the dominant discourses in Reggio texts along with an account of the rhetorical devices used to convince the reader of the legitimacy of those discourses.

Part 3, 'The Relevance of Reggio Emilia', has one chapter and this deals with issues of quality provision in early childhood settings and the extent to which Reggio thinking conforms to contemporary perspectives on effective provision.

In sum, the volume presents a full account of the philosophical pedagogy of Reggio Emilia. It explicates dimensions of Reggio that heretofore have remained implicit, taken for granted, and therefore, unexamined. This, in turn, has allowed tensions and contradictions that stem from the different cultural legacies that are variously endorsed in the literature to emerge. The book offers reflections on the appeal of Reggio approaches and their relevance for early childhood education.

Finally, a note about our approach to writing this book. We were mindful from the beginning of this project of the difference between the focus of this volume and others in the series, in particular the fact that we were not writing about the life and work of one particular educator or writer. Rather our attention was on a movement, a way of thinking about early childhood, and this required a different framework for communicating the ideologies and practices associated with that movement. Moreover, the limited nature of empirical or conceptual research studies of Reggio practices meant that a synthesis of reviews and evaluations of its effectiveness was not an option for us. We were dependent therefore on the substantial literature that was primarily descriptive in orientation and primarily commendatory in message. All this pushed us to do more than describe and review the field of publications; we felt obliged to analyse, critique and evaluate assumptions underlying Reggio thinking as well. In sum, we sought to provide the reader with an accessible and authoritative account of the Reggio Emilia Experience.

Part 1

Reggio Emilia and Loris Malaguzzi: Socio-cultural Context and Intellectual Biography

It was based on the initiative of women who had developed their awareness through all the terrible experiences of war and through the struggle for liberation, through the resistance . . .

(Barsotti, 2004, p. 11)

Chapter 1

The History and Context of the Development of the Reggio Emilia Experience

Introduction

Reggio Emilia is a town in the northern Italian region of Emilia Romagna. This region of Italy is wealthy and has become a model of economic development for the rest of the country due to the presence of 45,000 small- and medium-sized enterprises which are involved in manufacturing, food production and processing. Many towns are known for their own specialities, such as Parma for ham, Modena for Ferrari cars and machinery, and Reggio Emilia for cheese (Richards, 1995). However, Reggio Emilia has also become noted for its development of an early-years system of education known as the 'Reggio Experience' which has been epitomized by the following elements:

> Young children are encouraged to explore their environment and express themselves through all of their available 'expressive, communicative, and cognitive languages'. . . . From the beginning, there has been an explicit recognition of the relationship or partnership among parents, educators, and children. . . . The approach provides . . . new ways to think about the nature of the child as learner, the role of the teacher, school organization and management, the design and use of physical environments, and curriculum planning that guides experiences of joint, open-ended discovery and constructive posing and solving of problems.
>
> (Edwards et al., 1998, pp. 7–8)

The Reggio Experience contains the elements now seen as crucial to the development of child-centered educational facilities suited to young children. These include parental involvement, close collaboration between home and school, viewing education as part of the wider social context, seeing young children as competent learners, providing an environment that interests and challenges them and allowing children to experience and explore their surroundings. Children are considered as having rights, not as adults in the making, but as people with their own needs and interests.

In relation to understanding how the Reggio Experience came into being, it is necessary to understand the political philosophies which underpinned Italian society prior to the Second World War, for, if any system of education can be said to have grown out of the political landscape of a country, it is that of Reggio Emilia. In the case of Reggio Romagna and its population, the two opposing ideologies of Socialism/Communism (which was generally approved) and Fascism (which was generally abhorred) were fundamentally important to what was eventually to become known as the Reggio Experience.

Socialism/Communism

'Socialism', as generally understood, is a much broader concept than 'communism', . . . Socialists believe that capitalistic production is a system which tends to produce large divisions between rich and poor, and which can develop only in an erratic way . . . Like Soviet Communism, socialism presumes the idea of economic management – it is in opposition to the unfettered rule of markets.

(Giddens, 1993, pp. 666–7)

The upheavals in Europe following the French Revolution of 1789 resulted in the evolution of Socialism as a political theory in the nineteenth century. The Industrial Revolution also caused many to question the injustices and inequalities which arose as a consequence of the *laissez-faire* market economy. In the first half of the nineteenth century, Socialist theory emerged mainly from France and Britain, with its proponents including Henri de Saint-Simon, Pierre-Joseph Proudhon, Charles Fourier, Louis Blanc and Robert Owen. These theorists advocated the egalitarian redistribution of wealth and the abolition of private property accompanied by the establishment of small, collectivist communities.

In 1848, Karl Marx and Friedrich Engels produced the *Manifesto of the Communist Party* in which they outlined their theories of social reform. This 'scientific Socialism' advocated the abolition of bourgeois property and considered class struggle to be the basis upon which all societies had been formed. They believed that only a revolution by the proletariat, i.e. the working class, to secure the means of production and wealth (capital), would transform society. This Marxist theory, as it became known, considered Socialism to be a transitional stage between capitalism and Communism. A Communist society would be characterized by the end of both the class system and class warfare, the collective holding of the means of production and the redistribution of wealth, 'From each according to his ability, to each according to his needs' (Marx, 1875). Thus, according to this theory, people would no longer feel alienated from society as they both contributed to, and benefited from, being part of the co-operative means of production and might then be in control of their own destiny (Giddens, 1993).

According to Williams (1976) religion influenced the descriptive use of the words 'Socialist' or 'Communist' in that the latter was perceived to be more atheistic than the former. Furthermore, Engels (1888 [2002]) noted that Socialism was considered more 'respectable' than Communism, due to the latter's association with working-class movements. In the last 30 years of the nineteenth century, social democratic parties were founded in many parts of Europe, including Italy.

In the Italian context, the Italian Socialist Party (Partito Socialista Italiano, PSI) was founded in Genoa in 1892 and adhered to the Socialist principles as outlined above. As a consequence, the party suffered greatly at the hands of successive governments in its early years. However, electoral gains were made in the early years of the twentieth century. At that time, the PSI contained two divisive factions, the Reformists and the Maximalists, led by Filippo Turati and Benito Mussolini respectively. Turati was supported mostly by the unions and the parliamentary group, while Mussolini looked to the international group of Socialist parties of the Left. This division caused many difficulties for the PSI.

The First World War (1914–18) caused even greater problems for the PSI, as its refusal to support Italy's entry into the war caused Mussolini and his faction to leave the party. Many ex-PSI members eventually joined Mussolini and his newly formed Fascist party. Following the Russian Revolution of 1917, the PSI supported the Communist government's call for the overthrow of the bourgeoisie.

During the years 1919–20 there were many violent clashes between the Fascists and Socialists and, in 1921, the radicals in the PSI split to form the Communist Party of Italy. Following the assassination of the Socialist, Giacomo Matteotti, in 1924 and the establishment of a Fascist dictatorship, the PSI, along with all other political parties, was banned and its leadership remained in exile during the Fascist era.

The Communist Party of Italy (Partito Communista d'Italia) was founded in 1921 having resulted from a split with the Italian Socialist Party (PSI). It supported the principles of Communism outlined by Marx and Engels and, as a result, was banned by the Fascist government and was subject to violent assault from elements of that party. In 1926, the Communist Party of Italy was disbanded and subsequently re-formed under the name of the Communist Party of Italy, Section of the Communist International, a title it retained until 1943 when Stalin dissolved the Communist International. However, Partito Communista d'Italiano (PCd'I) was the name by which the party was generally known. In these early years, the Communist Party had three main factions, the Left, the Right and the Centre, whose leaders were Amadeo Bordiga, Angelo Tasca and Antonio Gramsci respectively. The ideological differences among these groups caused some difficulties for the party; however, structures were put in place for its national organization. These structures included provincial federations, union groups and an organization (Ufficio Primo) for engagement with armed Fascist groups. During the Fascist era, the Communist Party was banned, and the Communist Left went into exile (Piccone, 1983).

In the north of Italy, including the Emilia Romagna region, where parties of the Left would have been the popular political parties of choice, then (as now) both Socialists and Communists suffered greatly during the time of the Fascist regime. The ideologies they supported were in direct opposition to those of the government and, as a consequence, members of these parties became targets of Fascist attack. During the Second World War, many of the partisans who fought were members of the PSI or the PCd'I. The experiences of living under the Fascist regime and the events of the Second World War changed the views of many as regards the principles under which people ought to live, work, raise and educate children. In the case of Reggio Emilia, this history resulted in parents, in particular, searching for a radically different way to educate their young children.

Fascism

In post-First World War Italy, Fascism took root at a time of great economic hardship with mass unemployment and high inflation. Fears of a Bolshevik revolution, strikes and violence in the years 1919–20 brought both Gabriele d'Annunzio (1863–1938) and Benito Mussolini ((1883–1945) to prominence. d'Annunzio, a writer and fervent nationalist, created 'myths' and elaborate ceremonies which brought to mind the glories of Ancient Rome and its legionaries. It was he who introduced the 'Roman salute' and the black shirts which were to become so identified with Mussolini's Fascists. Many considered d'Annunzio as being likely to play a leading role in the future of Italian politics, but this was not to be. Instead, emerging from the radical Right of Italian politics was one Benito Mussolini, who had been named after the Mexican revolutionary Benito Juarez, whom his parents admired. He was a former Socialist and one-time editor of the Milanese Socialist paper *Avanti*. He advocated Italy's entry into the First World War on the side of the Allies, which infuriated the Socialists. In 1915, he founded his own paper, *Il Popolo d'Italia* and, when Italy joined the war against Germany, he enlisted and reached the rank of Corporal before being discharged in 1917 due to shrapnel wounds. By 1919, Mussolini was disenchanted with post-war Italy and its economic and social difficulties, and on 23 March 1919 in Milan, along with others, founded the Fasci di Combatti (Groups for the War Veteran) whose members became known as Fascists (Griffiths, 2005).

Fascism was (and is) an extreme right-wing ideology that glorifies a nation or race above all other loyalties. It is hostile to Marxism, liberalism and conservatism, and rejects, as threats to national or racial unity, the principles of workers' internationalism or class struggle. Fascism rejects representative government, yet may use such channels to gain power (Lyons and Berlet, 1996). The program of the Italian Fascists in these early years was a combination of doctrines of both the Left and Right and included proposals such as seizure of church property, abolition of the monarchy, abolition of the Senate, 85 percent tax on war profits, nationalization of the munitions industry, worker participation in management, universal suffrage, an eight-hour working day and a minimum wage. The Fascist organization was paramilitary in nature, and was not averse to using violence against its opponents. Also, Fascism opposed the parliamentary system of alliances, yet, in 1921, Mussolini negotiated an electoral alliance with the then Prime Minister, Giovanni Giolitti, and won 33 seats in the May election of that year. By 1922, a quarter of a million people were members of the party, and in August, the Left called for a general strike, and issued an ultimatum to the government calling on them to prove that within 48 hours they could assert authority or else the Fascists would assume power. The strike collapsed, but civil unrest continued with Communist power bases being destroyed by the Fascists.

Following on from this event, the Fascists came to believe that normal parliamentary procedures could never ensure implementation of their program. As a consequence, the 'March on Rome' was organized on 24 October 1922. The Fascists occupied public buildings throughout Italy and approached Rome from three different directions. The King, Victor Emmanuel III, offered Musssolini the Prime Ministership on 28 October and Fascist troops entered Rome two days later. By these means, Benito Mussolini and his Fascist Party came to power in Italy.

Within a very short time of assuming power, the Fascists discarded some elements of their earlier program. No longer did they seek to seize church property, tax war profits, introduce a minimum wage or universal suffrage (Italian women did not achieve the right to vote on an equal basis with men until 1945) (Giddens, 1993). Fascist violence and intimidation against opponents, particularly parties of the Left, continued unabated, with the complicity of both the police and the army.

In the election of April 1924, the Fascist Party won 374 of the 535 seats in the Italian Parliament, but in June, Fascists killed the Socialist, Giacomo Matteotti. This caused outrage to which Mussolini responded by making a speech in Parliament accepting responsibility and suggesting that the only way by which Italy could overcome such civil unrest was the institution of a dictatorship. On 25 December, a law was passed giving Mussolini complete control of the government of Italy. Thus, the dictatorial power of 'Il Duce' became absolute (Griffiths, 2005).

Within a very short time of having assumed control of Italy, Mussolini introduced the following measures: political parties and trade unions were banned, a free press was abolished, increased powers of arrest and detention were introduced, the death penalty was extended to apply to actions taken against the Fascist authorities, special courts were set up to deal with political crimes, and a secret police force was created. On the economic front, Mussolini advocated the doctrine of the Corporate State. According to this policy, a group composed of workers, employers and state representatives would oversee the nation's economic activities for the betterment of all. However, this policy resulted in high taxes, direct control of major industries, protectionism and ultimate economic stagnation.

Mussolini's attitude towards the Catholic Church changed radically with the signing of the Lateran Treaty of 1929, wherein the Vatican became a sovereign and independent State. The Church still retained a level of support among the population, particularly among the traditionalists of the south of Italy, an area in which Fascism made very little progress. Also, the Church's control of education remained a very important aspect of Italian life (Griffiths, 2005).

On the foreign policy front, throughout the 1920s, Mussolini obtained Fiume from Yugoslavia, declared a protectorate over Albania, invaded Corfu and Ethiopia, and crushed a revolt in Libya. In 1936, Mussolini allied himself with Germany's Adolf Hitler (1889–1945) in the Rome–Berlin Axis. On the 22 May 1939, Mussolini signed the Pact of Steel with Germany and became its ally during the Second World War which began on 1 September that same year. However, by 1943, Italy was losing the war and, in July, Mussolini was deposed by his own Fascist Grand Council and the very King who had appointed him, Victor Emmanuel III. Allied troops landed in Sicily, and Italy surrendered on 8 September. Mussolini was arrested but was rescued by the Germans, and escaped to German-held northern Italy. He was captured by partisans near Lake Como and executed in April 1945.

The legacy left by Fascism on Italian society was extremely divisive. Its treatment of parties of the Left resulted in the alienation of vast sections of the population in areas of the country in which there were strong Socialist/Communist sentiments. This was particularly so in the area of Reggio Emilia and its hinterland. Rectifying past injustices and creating a better future for their children became the founding principles upon which the system of early-years education was developed. Thus the Reggio Experience came into being.

The Reggio Emilia preschools and the Reggio Experience grew out of a particular social milieu and philosophy at a time in Italy when great change was occurring. They are unusual in that they did not emanate from educators, but from parents who sought a secular system of education for their young children. In the history of Italian education it is quite unique.

Educational and Historical Developments in Italy

It is believed that Indo-European peoples began to migrate to Italy in about 2000 BC. The Etruscans dominated this area until overthrown by the Romans in the third century BC. The Romans conquered all of Italy south of Cisalpine Gaul and retained control until the Fall of the Empire in AD 476. In Classical Rome, education was considered of great importance. At this time, higher education consisted of the trivium (the three-part curriculum: grammar, logic, rhetoric) and the quadrivium (the four-part curriculum: geometry, arithmetic, astronomy, music). However, early-years education was not entirely ignored, as rhetorician, Marcus Fabius Quintilianus (Quintilian) (AD 35–96), in the *Institutio Oratoria,* emphasized the importance of the first seven years of a child's life. He stressed the vital necessity of parental involvement in education, abhorred the use of corporal punishment, opposed academic pressure being applied at a young age and recognized the value of play.

> Nor am I so ignorant of the capacities of different ages as to think that we should straightaway place a grievous burden upon tender minds . . . For one thing especially must be guarded against, viz. lest one who cannot yet love studies come to hate them . . . Let this first instruction be in the form of play; . . .
>
> (Smail, 1938, p. 16)

The conversion of the Roman Emperor Constantine in 312 accelerated the growth of Christianity and, following the Council of Nicaea in 325, the theory and practice of Christian education emerged which influenced educational provision throughout Europe in the succeeding centuries. However, in 410, Alaric (a Visigoth) laid siege to Rome and, in succeeding years, it was attacked by hordes of Vandals, Suevi, Huns, Franks and Alemanni, resulting in the Fall of the Roman Empire in 476 (Roberts, 1997).

The Dark Ages which followed the collapse of the Roman Empire saw the ransacking of libraries, the destruction of museums and the neglect of education. However, on Christmas Day, 800, Charlemagne was crowned Holy Roman Emperor, and education, particularly Christian education, was once again considered of great value.

In the late thirteenth century, Italian states such as Florence, Venice and Milan began to amass great wealth, due to the expansion of trade. Italian superiority at sea enabled these city states to develop lucrative trade routes to England, Flanders and the Black Sea. In 1307, Dante Alighieri (1265–1321) began to write the *Divine Comedy* and, in 1341, Petrarch (1304–74) was crowned Poet Laureate in Rome. In 1348–51, the Black Death ravaged Europe, and Boccacio (1313–75) included a graphic account of plague in the 'Decameron'. Europe slowly recovered from the devastation caused by the plague and trade resumed among countries. In 1397, the Medici Bank was founded in Florence and, as wealth accumulated, Florence made a contribution to the Renaissance which was unparalleled by any other state.

The subsequent age of exploration and discovery expanded European interests to unimaginable degrees. In 1487, Diaz (1450–1500) rounded the Cape of Good Hope and Vasco da Gama (1469–1524) reached the East Indies. In 1492 Columbus (1451–1506) discovered America. These explorers opened up European societies and an age of 'rebirth' began in Europe. The rediscovery of the learning of Ancient Greece and Rome and the explosion of knowledge in the arenas of art, literature, medicine and science were the hallmarks of the Renaissance (Painter, 1973).

> The Renaissance was an age of reformers. They wanted to reform education, correct the errors of medieval scholarship, improve the translations of legal and religious texts, enrich the content as well as the style of literature, recover the wisdom of the ancients, recapture the order and simplicity of nature . . .
>
> (Jensen, 1992, p. 2)

The fifteenth century saw the Medici family rise to power in Florence, and from 1434 to 1494 they became patrons of the artists Uccello, Botticelli and Michelangelo. The Medici family also encouraged scholars to collect and study the writings of Ancient Greece and Rome and they built palaces, villas and churches. However, the opulence and luxury of Florentine life did not please all its citizens. Discontent grew and found a spokesman in the person of Girolamo Savonarola (1452–98). He wished for a return to the simplicity of the life of Christ and objected to the rise of humanism – especially the writings of Plato and Aristotle. In 1494 he became ruler of Florence. He proceeded to burn many books and paintings and, in so doing, accumulated many enemies (including Pope Alexander VI). Savonarola was sentenced to death and was burned at the stake in 1498 (Jardine, 1996).

Savonarola had attempted to halt the inexorable tide of progress and strenuously objected to the education of girls, claiming that their ingenuousness had been completely lost by the age of 20! His worry was needless, as the education of girls and women was not a high priority in any part of Europe in those years. In 1466, Florentine Guilds made it a rule that all of their officials should be literate – all except women. Noble girls were sent to convents at eight or ten years of age and were taught spinning and weaving, reading and writing. This type of education was to prepare them for marriage or the Church.

At this time, boys were taught the basic subjects of grammar and arithmetic, which prepared them for a life in trade. Classical studies were considered unimportant for the education of future merchants. The Guilds provided their own pupils with a practical education, but very little regulation by the governments of different states was evident with regard to the curriculum followed or the teaching methods employed.

One of the rare exceptions to these types of school was that run by Vittorino da Feltre (1378–1446), whose house at Mantua (Giocosa), i.e. Happy House, taught girls as well as boys and rich as well as poor. His pupils examined the works of Virgil, Cicero, Demosthenes and Homer, which were used as an introduction to grammar. They then proceeded to study dialectic and rhetoric, followed by mathematical studies of arithmetic, geometry, astronomy and music. The pupils who completed this course of learning were then allowed to study Plato and Aristotle. This type of instruction was exceptional at this period and, in the case of girls, quite singular (Gage, 1968).

During the eighteenth and nineteenth centuries, war became one of the defining features of Italian life. Milan, Naples and Sardinia were lost to the Hapsburgs of Austria after the War of the Spanish Succession in 1713. Napoleon Bonaparte crowned himself King of Italy in 1800 but, following the Congress of Vienna in 1815, Austria once again became the dominant power in Italy and crushed uprisings in 1820–21 and in 1831. As a result of these defeats, Giuseppe Mazzini, a liberal nationalist, organized the Risorgimento (Resurrection) which laid the foundation for the eventual unification of Italy. Italians looked to the House of Savoy for leadership and found it in the person of Count Camille di Cavour (1810–61) who, in 1859, aided France in their war with Austria and gained control of Lombardy in northern Italy. In the south of Italy, Giuseppe Garibaldi (1807–82) had conquered Sicily and Naples and turned them over to Victor Emmanuel II (1820–78), King of Sardinia, who was proclaimed King of Italy in 1861. Venetia and Papal Rome were annexed in 1866 and 1870 respectively, resulting in the total unification of Italy under a constitutional monarch (Holmes, 1997; Hearder, 1991).

Throughout the nineteenth century, despite its difficulties, interest in education had remained a feature of Italian life. During the 1820s, daycare centers, custodial in nature, had been opened. In 1831, Abbot Ferrante Aporti founded a children's home in the city of Cremona. This establishment had an explicitly educational approach, with play often being replaced by domestic activities for girls and crafts for boys (Della Peruta, 1980). Froebel's Kindergartens began to be established in Italy from 1867 onwards. Towards the end of the nineteenth century, the Catholic Church provided out-of-home care for disadvantaged children. During this century, legislation concerning education was also passed. The Casati Law (1859), which emanated from the Piedmont State, outlined the provision for the organization of compulsory 'lower' primary education (a first and a second class) and 'higher' primary school (a third and a fourth class). Such education was to be the responsibility of the Municipalities. Following the Unification of Italy, it was noted that Victor Emmanuel II had a particular interest in education, including that of the very young, and the provisions of the Casati Law were introduced in the whole of Italy. In 1877, the Coppino Law introduced a compulsory (two years) primary school attendance period.

As the twentieth century dawned, progressive educators became involved in early-years education. In 1907, Maria Montessori (1870–1952) established the first Casa dei Bambini in Rome. Furthermore, the Agazzi sisters had developed a new method and philosophy for the education of young children. Meanwhile, a teacher-training school was established to prepare those who were to educate young children (Edwards et al., 1998). During the First World War, the Milanese commune recognized the needs of working mothers and established its own preschool program.

However, after the war, Italy's economy lay in ruins, thousands were without employment and, on 23 March 1919, Benito Mussolini (1883–1945) and others formed the National Fascist Party. In Italy, due to the economic situation and the growing popularity of the Fascists, Mussolini was elected to the Chamber of Deputies in 1921. In October 1922, King Victor Emmanuel III asked Mussolini to form a government and appointed him Prime Minister. Thus, 'Il Duce' (Mussolini), supported by the Fascists, assumed control of Italy which he retained until he was deposed in 1943.

In 1923, Mussolini's government instituted the Gentile reforms to the education system which was now to include the Scuole Maternae (pre-primary schools catering for children between the ages of three and six years wherein attendance was not compulsory) as well as primary and secondary schools. However, the Ministry of Education did not expand pre-primary provision and this sector became the province of the Catholic Church with few exceptions and Fascist approval. The Fascists did not encourage Montessori Education, but did encourage that of the Agazzi sisters.

Rosa (1866–1951) and her sister Carolina (1870–1945) Agazzi formulated their theory of early-years education in the Momprano (Brescia) nursery school in which Rosa was teacher. The Agazzi Method emphasized children's natural ability at expressing themselves in spontaneous and natural ways in home-like surroundings. The Agazzi sisters considered that the natural environment in which a child should be educated should be based on the home, with family life and the mother being of prime importance. Thus, they believed that the didactic material should be as home-like as possible, as it would be familiar to the children. They considered social education of great value and, therefore, older children were each to be given the care of younger ones. The Agazzi Method found favor throughout Italy and accounted for 74 percent of all existing preschools in the early to middle twentieth century. As a consequence, the Agazzi method of teaching young children, favored by the Church, was taken as the official state policy in that area (Edwards et al., 1998).

Also, in 1925, a law entitled the 'Protection and Assistance in Infancy' was passed which provided for the establishment of the National Organisation for Maternity and Infancy (OMNI). This organization set up a system of state-run services for the care and support of large families, in keeping with Mussolini's aim of increasing the population. It is interesting to note that the 604 OMNI centers officially transferred to city administrations only in 1975 (Lucchini, 1980).

In 1946, a year after the end of the Second World War, a republic was proclaimed and the monarchy rejected in Italy. The Italian Constitution of 1948 introduced radical changes to the school system including that of the pre-primary, although control of that sector remained largely in the remit of the Catholic Church. During the 1950s, post-war Italy became a founder member of the European Economic Community (now known as the European Union) following the Treaty of Rome in 1957, and a member of NATO (the North Atlantic Treaty Organization).

In the 1960s, initiatives in relation to education were undertaken by the Italian government. Law 444, passed in 1968, provided national funds for pre-primary schools and proclaimed the right of Italian children aged three to six years to such education. This decree not only led to the development of a state-run Scuole Maternae system, it also formulated the Tripartite (State, Municipality-Region, Private) type of early-years education and care. The latter is a feature of pre-primary provision up to the present day. In 1971, under Law 1044, Asili Nidi (Infant–Toddler Centers for children aged four months to three years) officially became part of national legislation under the management of local authorities and the twenty regional governments. As a consequence of this law, municipal governments were given the responsibility of overseeing the standards, regulations, funding, construction and organization of these centers.

In the year 2000, under Law 30, the school cycles were reorganized and the title of pre-primary was changed from Scuole Maternae to Scuole dell'Infanzia (infant schools, more generally called preschools). Finally, in 2003 (Law 53) and 2004 (Decree 59), Scuole dell'Infanzia became fully part of the education system of Italy.

Developments in Reggio Emilia

Reggio Emilia is the town where, on 7 January 1779, the Italian tricolor was first unveiled. Emilia Romagna, the region in which Reggio Emilia is situated, is the richest agricultural and industrial region in Italy, after Lombardy. It is centered in what is known as Italy's 'Red Belt', the area of Italy which supported the Socialist and Communist Parties, having led the resistance to German occupation during the Second World War. Following the end of the war, the region received Italy's highest honor, a Gold Medal for Military Valor. Thus the political philosophy of the population of this region would have been in complete opposition to that of the ruling Fascist ideology at this time. In fact, in the villages surrounding Reggio Emilia, partisan uprisings and anti-Fascist activity were among the highest in any area of Italy during the Fascist era. Thus, the end of Fascism and the Second World War were pivotal moments in the history of Reggio Emilia and its people and, since then, Communists (now known as the Party of the Democratic Left) have been in control of local government, either alone or in coalition (Richards, 1995).

The Socialist principles with which this region identified (and identifies), particularly in regard to the necessity of providing an egalitarian social community (Giddens, 1993), influenced their view of children, their rights and the education they should receive. As Socialist philosophy completely rejects Fascism and its tenets, the system of education which eventually emerged in Reggio Emilia considered children from their earliest days as being competent learners deserving of every opportunity to fulfill their potential:

> What the people wanted was a school that immediately set out to free the children from an age-old subjection by the official schools, which had always awarded the privilege of birth and sooner or later expelled the students of humble origins . . . The students who only spoke the local dialect, who, even having learned to read and write, would be destined to the barns and fields and the workshops where their fathers labored, who were as willing to work hard as they were uneducated.
>
> (Barazzoni, 2000, p. 18)

In order to realize this ambition, within a few days of the end of the Second World War, a group of women, members of the GDD (Groups in Defense of Women and in Assistance to the Freedom Fighters), began what has since become known as the Reggio Emilia Experience. On 19 June 1945, women members of UDI (Union of Italian Women) sought subscriptions from the public towards the establishment of a nursery school. Fundraisers included dances, lotteries and theatrical events. The members of the UDI were motivated by a deep sense of social solidarity and were focused on the future which they hoped would be a better one for their children. The fact that it was women, in the main, who spearheaded this initiative, is notable due to the fact that, at that time and in Italy, women would not have been in positions of power to any great extent. In fact, they only received the right to vote in that same year, yet they felt impelled to improve the lives of the population for the following reasons:

> In 1945, the most pressing problem for a population that had just come out of a war was that of rebuilding, materially, socially, and morally . . . the people also felt the need to overcome the ideological divisions that had lasted for two decades. . . . The groups organized to fight against the dictatorship, the German occupation, and injustice, and for emancipation, social equality, progress, and a better future (for which these groups were subjected to a bona fide persecution) saw in their children the scope of their commitment. The children would be the inhabitants of that 'new world' that was rapidly being built. It was thus entirely

natural that the C.L.N. (Comitato di Liberazione Nazionale) would concern itself with early childhood.

(Reggio Children, 2002, p. 6)

In the village of Villa Cella, women salvaged bricks and sold an abandoned German tank, trucks and horses which raised 800,000 Lira for the local Committee of National Liberation (CLN). This money was invested in the school building project. Land was donated by a local farmer, and parents worked at night and at weekends to build the school. A local building co-operative offered its services as well as its machinery.

Families worked at weekends and holidays loading up sand and gravel, collecting bricks, beams, doors and window frames from buildings bombed during the war. Other families brought food to the workers or raised money by gathering hay or selling bundles of sticks. Eventually, after eight months of hard work, the school was opened by the Mayor of Villa Cella, Cesare Campoli. On 13 January 1947, the Superintendent of Education signed the official authorization allowing the school to open to its first 30 students and to its teacher, Elena Zanni, and cook, Leontina Brugnoli-Tita. The new project committee for the school included both women and men such as Ideale Friggeri, Anna Spaggiari, Paolino Mantelli, Omero Lanzi, Eliseo Bertolini, and Giuseppe Ghinolfi (Barazzoni, 2000).

The first school was named April 25th School, in honor of the day on which the Allies liberated the region. The plaque outside the school bears the following inscription: 'Men and women working together, we built the walls of this school because we wanted a new and different place for our children. May 1945' (Fraser and Gestwicki, 2002, pp. 7–8).

People in other villages, such as Sesso, also began to look to the future and envisioned a preschool which would serve the needs of all children. The preschool in Sesso was called the Martiri di Sesso Nursery School (now known as the Martiri di Sesso Centro Verde Preschool), in honor of the 33 people executed there between 1943 and 1945. It is ironic to realize that this preschool found a home in the Casa del Fascia (local Fascist headquarters) until 1959 when it was forced to move to the Casa del Popolo (local Communist headquarters) where it remained until 1971. For some years after its establishment, equipment was scarce in the preschool and the children brought sugar, flour and butter from home, and the cook, Attila Orsini, used vegetables from the garden and the international aid packages of powdered milk, canned meat, pasta, rice and oil to cook meals for the children (Reggio Children, 2002).

Women were also actively involved in the survival of the Sesso preschool. One woman strongly identified with this preschool is Rosa Boni Galeotti who became director of the local branch of the UDI in 1947–48. She remembers gathering kindling, eggs and fruit for the children, and fundraising to ensure that the preschool could continue to function. Other members of the UDI strongly involved with the struggle to keep the pre-school functioning at Sesso during the 1940s and 1950s included Rina Bianchini Bonezzi, Laura Bianchi, Ernesta Gamberelli, Bice Bertani, Gerbella Segalina and Bianca Manfredi, Ione Bartoli, Rosa Galeotti, and Piera and Bruna Gamberelli. During the 1950s, funding for the preschool was applied for from the Municipal and Provincial Administration, the Pre-fecture and the Ministry of Public Education – but none was granted (Reggio Children, 2002).

The women of the UDI and the people of Reggio Emilia continued to undertake fundraising as they felt it was vitally important that the preschools remain open. This sense of communal responsibility with which the people worked to fulfill their dream, now allied to Socialist principles, is

. . . not of recent origin, but rather traced back to the craft guilds and communal republics of the 12th century; . . . Clearly, ideas about partic-ipatory democracy and civic community are fundamental to what edu-cators in Reggio Emilia feel about their educational vision and mission.
(Edwards et al., 1998, p. 8)

Ideals such as these would have been in stark contrast to Fascist ideology and would not have been elements of the philosophy of the main provider of pre-primary education at that time, the Catholic Church.

Following the Liberation, other schools were established under the auspices of the Committee of National Liberation (CLN), the Union of Italian Women (UDI) and the co-operatives of Reggio Emilia. These schools were as follows: those of San Maurizio and Massenzatico founded by the CLN in 1946, and those of Villaggio Foscata, San Prospero Strinati and Bainsizza were also established in the same year. The sister school of Villa Cella, established in 1945, Santa Croce Esterna, had been supported by factory workers of the Reggiane, but, as it was sited on state property, it was eventually closed down. While five of these schools were recognized by scholastic authorities, three were not, namely, those at Sesso, Bainsizza and Massenzatico.

Throughout the 1950s and early 1960s, funding of the preschools con-tinued to be a problem. However, such was the strength of feeling among the people that these preschools should survive that the following tasks were undertaken in Villa Cella:

. . . men and women carried on, for the sake of their children, what they had done to help the Partisans; they gleaned fields, cut the grass banks of the ditches, collected paper, scrap metal, wood, and rabbit skins. They checked coats at parties and dance halls, and bicycles at the bicycle depots . . . The help of shopkeepers and the consumers' cooperatives was also necessary . . . The children themselves helped in raising funds, both with a monthly fee of 250 lira, and by putting on theatrical productions . . .

(Barazzoni, 2000, p. 21)

In 1960, the UDI and the people of Sesso sought municipal management for their school – but it was not granted. However, three years later the authorities decided on the following course of action: they would set up 'two prefabricated schools', one of which was to be known as the Robinson Preschool and was to be the first-ever city-run school for young children. It was given the name Robinson in deference to the author Defoe's character, and was housed in a wooden building. This was a truly significant event, both in an historical and educational context, as Edwards et al. (1998, p. 52) note:

For the first time in Italy, the people affirmed the right to establish a secular school for young children: a rightful and necessary break in the monopoly the Catholic church had hitherto exercised over children's early education. It was a necessary change in a society that was renewing itself, changing deeply, and in which citizens and families were increasingly asking for social services and schools for their children.

As a consequence of this event, throughout the 1960s much pressure was brought to bear on the municipal authorities to secure the future of the parent-run schools. Eventually, in 1967, these schools were brought under the administration of the Municipality of Reggio Emilia. This was a momentous event, as it was part of the larger, country-wide political struggle for publicly supported secular schools. The number of pre-primary classes run by the Municipality grew very quickly: in 1968 there were 12 classes, in 1973 there were 43, in 1980 there were 58 catering for three- to six-year-olds. In 2003, 21 preschools (catering for 1,508 children) and 13 infant–toddler centers (catering for 835 children) were supported by the Municipality (Boyd-Cadwell, 2003). With regard to children under three years, the first infant–toddler center was opened in 1970 in the Municipality of Reggio Emilia, in advance of Law 1044 (1971). Many of the preschools and infant–toddler centers are named after artists, scientists, poets, writers and thinkers such as Michangelo, Paolo Freire and Pablo Neruda (Thornton and Brunton, 2007).

In March 1970, a national conference was held in Bologna entitled, 'For a Public School for Children Between the Ages of 3 and 6' to discuss provision for this age group. That same month in Reggio Emilia a conference was held concerning children under three and their requirements and was called 'The Movement for Infant–Toddler Centers as Social Services Run by Local Authorities'. As a result of the latter conference, a petition relating to the needs of children under three was sent to Sandro Pertini, President of the House at that time (Reggio Children, 2002).

By 1972, such was the influence of the Reggio Emilia preschools that the rules and regulations which governed them were accepted by the entire City Council and the Catholic minority-run preschools. This was an historic event for the people and preschools of Reggio Emilia. It was the culmination of many years of work beginning with the establishment of the Robinson preschool in 1963. The 1972 City Council meeting had been preceded by a

'constituent assembly' that lasted eight months and requested twenty-four drafts of the text. It involved (in a collegial effort carried out at various levels) the Council Supervision Committee, all the teaching and auxiliary staffs, the City-School Committees, the presidents of the Neighborhood Councils, the Unions, the U.D.I. and C.I.F. Women's Associations, and a number of functionaries of the Municipality, including Loris Malaguzzi.

(Reggio Children, 2002, p. 33)

In that same year, 1972, the poet and writer, Gianni Rodari, dedicated his book *The Grammar of Fantasy* to the children of Reggio Emilia preschools.

In 1974, due to the economic situation in Italy, funding of the Reggio Emilia preschools was affected. A week of protest was organized from 16 to 21 December entitled 'A week of initiatives for the defense and development of the infant-toddler centers and preschools'. Demonstrations were held and petitions delivered to local and national government. In the following year, 1975, a national conference was held in Bologna, Emilia Romagna, 'The Child as Subject and Source of Rights in the Family and Society', wherein the experiences of the previous year informed the discussion.

However, in November 1976, there began a seven-day onslaught on the Reggio Emilia schools on the radio program of Gustavo Selva (Barazzoni, 2000). He attacked the education model of the schools and considered that it constituted a harassment of the existing private, Catholic schools. As a result, it was decided to invite the local Catholic clergy to a debate on the Reggio schools. These public discussions lasted for five months, at the end of which all parties emerged with a better understanding of each other (Edwards et al., 1998).

A new development occurred in 1980, with the establishment in Reggio Emilia of 'The National Group of Infant–Toddler Centers and Preschools', an independent body consisting of teachers, university professors and researchers. The aim of this body is the in-depth study of issues related to infant–toddler centers and matters relating to early childhood. In 1981, the Reggio Emilia exhibition 'The Hundred Languages of Children' was taken to the Stockholm Museum of Modern Art. Thus began a relationship with Sweden which has been maintained to the present day (Dahlberg, 2004). In fact, it is possible to undertake a module on the Reggio Emilia approach to early-years education as part of teacher education programs in Sweden. Also in the 1980s, Howard Gardner visited and, subsequently, conducted research involving Project Zero and Reggio Emilia schools. Visitors to Reggio preschools included, among others, Urie Bronfenbrenner and Jerome Bruner.

In 1990, in Reggio Emilia, the international conference 'So Who Am I?' was held with the aim of sharing knowledge and experiences so as to enhance the status, rights and potential of children and adults. Politicians, academics and researchers attended, including David Hawkins, Paolo Freire and Mario Lodi (Reggio Children, 2002). Also, in 1991, it was stated in *Newsweek* magazine that the Diana preschool in Reggio Emilia was considered to be one of the ten best in the world. This article aroused much interest among those involved in education in other countries. In subsequent years, educators from many places have visited the Reggio schools, and its approach to early-years education has been adopted in countries such as the United States, the United Kingdom, New Zealand and Australia.

In 1994, the National Conference of Local Authorities was held in Reggio Emilia entitled 'Investing in the Future: choices and resources, subject to a national policy for the rights and potential of children'. At this conference, discussions were held on the preschools of the area and others around Italy and the promotion of the knowledge of the region experience further afield. As a consequence, the Municipality of Reggio Emilia constituted a company which became known as 'Reggio Children – the International Center for the Defense and Promotion of the Rights and Potential of All Children'. Members of the company include public authorities, parents, school staff, individual community members and private agencies. The purpose of this company is the promotion of the practices of the

Reggio Emilia preschools, through seminars, publications, study tours and international exchanges (Reggio Children, 2002).

Red Vienna

When investigating the development of provision in Reggio Emilia and the Socialist philosophy which underpins it, an analogy can be made with developments which occurred in Vienna in the years 1918–34. After the First World War, German Austria was proclaimed a Republic on 12 November 1918. At the city parliament elections of 4 May 1919, all adult persons (for the first time ever) voted, and the Social Democratic Party gained absolute power in Vienna, earning it the title of 'Red Vienna'. The National Parliament declared Vienna the ninth Austrian Bundesland (State) on 1 January 1922.

At the end of the First World War, refugees, former soldiers, middle classes who were now poor, and a short food supply made life very difficult. Tuberculosis and the Spanish Flu were raging and inadequate housing conditions were features of life at that time. The election of the Social Democrats seemed to portend a new beginning for the city. Yet, for all its ills, Vienna had intellectual 'greats' the like of whom would not be seen in one place again such as Hans Kelsan, Karl Buehler, Sigmund Freud, Arthur Schnitzler, Karl Kraus, Adolf Loos, Arnold Schoenberg and Ernst Mach (Janik and Toulmin, 1973).

Immediately upon election, the Social Democrats considered public housing to be a priority. The Tenant Protection Act of 1917 froze the rent for housing at 1914 levels which made it unprofitable to undertake private housing projects. This situation enabled the administration in Vienna to plan for extensive public housing. Between 1925 and 1934 over 60,000 new housing units were built in what were known as 'Community Buildings'. This distinctive type of architecture is to be seen in Vienna to this day.

In relation to health and social services, Red Vienna provided free medical care, and recreation holidays and sports facilities were made available to enhance fitness and general health. The Municipality also provided an affordable gas and electricity supply and refuse collection which was beneficial for the health of the population. As a result of these measures, tuberculosis cases dropped by 50 percent and infant mortality dropped below the Austrian average at that time. Services for parents and children included the provision of kindergartens, after-school care and children's spas. This facilitated the return to work of mothers, and children benefited both from an educational and health point of view. Parents also got a 'clothes package', so as to ensure that their children were adequately dressed.

The Catholic Church did not look favorably on Red Vienna. It has been noted by Gunther (1940, p. 379) that '. . . Vienna was Socialist, anti-clerical, and, as a municipality, fairly rich. The hinterland was poor, backward, conservative, Roman Catholic, and jealous of Vienna's higher standard of living.'

Unfortunately for Vienna, in 1932 Chancellor Englebert Dollfuss of the Christian Social Party came to power and in 1933 his cabinet ceased the functioning of the parliament and the following year created a one-party state based on the philosophy of AustroFascism and with the tacit agreement of the Catholic Church. The same tenets underscored the Austro-Fascist political viewpoint, as did those of Mussolini's Fascism. Immediately upon seizing power, the state took complete control of all regions of the country, including Vienna. Thus, the social experiment that became known as 'Red Vienna' came to an end.

It is interesting to note the similarities and differences between the experiences of Red Vienna and those of Reggio Emilia. Both faced Fascist dictatorships with ultra-right-wing ideals, backed by the Catholic Church. Both introduced health and education services, and physical environments for the benefit of all. However, they differed in the fact that Red Vienna and its philosophies did not survive beyond 1934 and Reggio Emilia did not begin its struggle until 1945 but eventually was successful.

Loris Malaguzzi (1920–94)

If any one person above all others is instantly associated with Reggio Emilia and the Reggio approach to early-years education, it is Loris Malaguzzi. He was born in Correggio, near Reggio Emilia, in 1920. He grew up under the rule of the Fascist dictatorship of Benito Mussolini. He enrolled in a teacher-training institute in 1939 and qualified as a primary teacher and, in 1946, went to Rome to study psychology (the first post-war course of its kind) at the National Center for Research (CNR). He worked in a state primary school for seven years. While mostly known for his work in education, Malaguzzi was also a sportsman, theater director and a journalist who, from 1947 to 1951, directed the editorial office of *Il Progresso d'Italia* (Hoyuelos, 2004). On his return to Reggio Emilia, he worked for the Municipality in a mental health center for children experiencing difficulties at school. In 1958, he was to become director of preschools in Reggio Emilia where he would spend the remainder of his working life until his death in 1994.

In 1945, having heard of the attempts of parents to build their own school in Villa Cella and being intrigued by the idea of parents taking control of their children's education in such a direct manner, Malaguzzi cycled out to the village to investigate the situation. Thus began a relation-ship with preschools, parents and children, not only in Villa Cella but in the other preschools which followed, which was to last a lifetime. He con-tinued working during the morning at the mental health center, and spending the afternoon and evenings at the preschools (Edwards et al., 1998). He built up a relationship with the women, who in most instances were the driving forces behind the projects. In an interview conducted with Carlo Barsotti in 1993, Malaguzzi had this to say about the development of the preschools:

> It was based on the initiative of women who had developed their aware-ness through all the terrible experiences of war and through the struggle for liberation, through the resistance . . . Without these women we would never have seen not just the birth, but the survival of this kind . . .

During the 1950s and 1960s, many parents and educators realized that there was a very great need for the provision of better early childhood edu-cation in Italy. New ideas from the 'popular school' movement in France and the writings of Celestin Freinet and John Dewey were gaining influence in the country. The Movement of Co-operative Education (MCE) was set up in 1951, led by the educator, Bruno Ciari. He was asked by the left-wing administration of Bologna in Reggio Romagna to administer their school system. Through the meetings which he organized in Bologna to discuss educational innovations, Ciari influenced and inspired Malaguzzi and the two became great friends. Furthermore, Ciari advocated the development of a close relationship between educators and parents, and believed that two teachers should work in each classroom, that children should be grouped by age for part of the day and that the physical environment was of particular importance (Ciari, 1961, 1972). Malguzzi incorporated these ideas into what eventually became known as the Reggio Experience.

When, in 1963, the Municipality opened the first preschool under its direct control, Malaguzzi described it as a 'decisive achievement'. In the years which followed, to find their identity and acceptance as early-years educators, Malaguzzi proposed taking the preschool children into town, putting on exhibitions of their work and teaching school in the open air. It had the desired effect: it got people talking and aroused their interest. Such ventures also alerted Malaguzzi to the need for adaptation of ideas to take advantage of situations as they arose. Every event provided new experiences for both adults and children and encouraged the development of new educational strategies.

In 1968 a symposium was organized to study the relationship of the disciplines of psychiatry, psychology and education with regard to young children, while children's graphic expression was the subject of a later meeting which was held among biologists, neurologists, psychologists and educational experts (Edwards et al., 1998).

In 1971, a national meeting for teachers was organized at which 200 participants were expected. In fact, 900 attended, which gave an indication of the level of interest in the area of early-years education. This meeting led to the publication of two pieces of work relating to early childhood education: *Experiences for a New School for Young Children* (Malaguzzi, 1971a) and *Community-based Management in the Preprimary School* (Malaguzzi, 1971b). As knowledge of the Reggio Emilia preschools spread, a government agency, the National Teaching Center, invited Malaguzzi to their meetings.

In 1980, the National Group of Infant–toddler Centers and Preschools was established, with Loris Malaguzzi as president. Following this event, the journal *Zerosei* (Zero to Six, 1976–1984), now called *Bambini*, was begun, with Malaguzzi as director. According to Carla Rinaldi, Pedagogical Director of the Municipal Infant–toddler Centers and Preschools:

> These two initiatives were not limited to pedagogical elaboration and a sharing of daily experiences and scientific contributions. They were also a means of contact and direct dialogue between persons working in the schools, of comparison, and of spreading the word about what was being elaborated and realized in Reggio Emilia . . .
>
> (Reggio Children, 2002, p. 39)

Also during the 1980s, 'The Hundred Languages of Children' exhibition, incorporating examples of children's work, began to travel the world. Four versions of this exhibition have gone to many countries up to the present day.

It has been said that Malaguzzi wrote very little in the field of pedagogy (Hoyuelos, 2004). Yet, with regard to the educational philosophies and theorists who influenced his thinking, Malaguzzi included the following: Jean Piaget, John Dewey, Henri Wallon, Edward Chaparede, Ovide Decroly, Anton Marenko, Lev Vygotsky, Erik Erikson, Urie Bronfenbrenner, Pierre Bovet and Adolfe Ferriere. He stated that the following psychologists, philosophers and theoreticians also influenced his approach to education: Wilfred Carr, David Shaffer, Kenneth Kaye, Jerome Kagan, Howard Gardner, David Hawkins, Serge Moscovici, Charles Morris, Gregory Bateson, Heinz Von Foerster and Francisco Varela. With regard to influence of the above-named individuals on the Reggio Experience, Malaguzzi stated:

The network of the sources of our inspiration spans several generations and reflects the choices and selections that we have made over time . . . And, overall, we have gained a sense of the versatility of theory and research. But talk about education (including the education of young children) cannot be confined to its literature. Such talk, which is also political, must continuously address major social changes and trans-formations in the economy, sciences, arts, and human relationships and customs. All of these larger forces influence how human beings – even young children – 'read' and deal with the realities of life. They determine the emergence, on both general and local level, of new methods of edu-cational content and practice, as well as new problems and soul-searching questions.

(Gandini, 1998, p. 60)

In 1992, Loris Malaguzzi received the Danish Lego award for his contri-bution to early childhood education. Additionally, in 1994, the Andersen Prize and one from the Mediterranean Association of International Schools were awarded to him posthumously.

At the 'Crossing Boundaries' conference held in Reggio Emilia in 2004, Peter Moss had this to say of Loris Malaguzzi: '. . . I see him as an inventor, a dissenter and an explorer, but above all as a utopian thinker and actor who could imagine new modes of human possibility and had an unquench-able hope for the future.'

Conclusion

The preschools of Reggio Emilia, and the Reggio Experience which has evolved from them, have inspired provision in institutions in Washington DC, Ohio, and California in the United States, in Stockholm, Sweden, in Thailand and Albania, and in other parts of the world. Yet the development of this philosophy is rooted in a particular time and place. The social and political forces which influenced the development of this Experience cannot be underestimated. In many ways, it could be said that the Reggio Experience emerged from the political maelstrom of the battle between Fascism and Socialism/Communism. In the Reggio context, and influenced by Socialist principles, the rights of children matter greatly and they are viewed, not as dependents, but as competent individuals in need of expe-riences of all kinds:

In such a school, where the child is fiercely defended from any imposi-tion of pre-established or biased models, that child has the opportunity to have his right to choose for himself restored. The school, inserted in the territory and in a relationship of co-responsibility and of discussion between the people and the institutions, has the privilege of finding, in this profound humanity, the basis of a culture and a professionality which regenerate themselves as they keep up with social changes and with the children's needs and values. Thus, the formality and rigidity of all ideologies are overcome.

(Barazzoni, 2000, p. 28)

Furthermore, it is interesting to note that the inspiration for this development came not from educators but from parents – men and women who wanted a secular education for their children. It could also be said that this development provided women with an opportunity to take control and be leaders at a time and in a country where it was not a widespread phenomenon. The fact that women in particular could take on such a task and engage in a struggle with the municipal authorities for so many years is testament to how strongly they felt about the cause of early-years education.

Reggio Emilia and its preschools influenced the course of pre-primary education in Italy. The monopoly of the Catholic Church on such education was broken from the moment the Municipality took control of the preschools in 1963. As a result, Municipalities throughout Italy began to fund such services, to a greater or lesser extent.

The Reggio Experience, with its emphasis on parental and community involvement, its provision of a physical environment rich in stimulation for young children, its enhancement of children's creativity, its building of relationships among staff, parents and the wider community, emerges from its sense of social responsibility towards all its children and their families. The legacy of the Reggio Emilia preschools and the Reggio Experience may lie in the fact that many of these tenets are now to be found in early-years settings in other parts of the world.

Perhaps the last word should be left to Loris Malaguzzi (Gandini, 1998, p. 51), who was, and still is, so strongly identified with the Reggio Emilia preschools and the Reggio Experience of early-years education and who pioneered, defended and supported them for so many years:

A simple, liberating thought came to our aid, namely that things about children and for children are only learned from children.

Part 2

Critical Exposition of the Reggio Emilia Experience

Learning and teaching should not stand on opposite banks and just watch the water flow by; instead they should embark together on a journey down the river.
(Malaguzzi, 1998)

Chapter 2

Principles into Practice

Reggio epitomizes for me an education that is effective and humane; its students undergo a sustained apprenticeship in humanity, one that may last a lifetime.

(Gardner, 1998a, p. xviii)

Principles Underpinning the Reggio Emilia Experience for Children

This chapter looks at the experiences of the children in a Reggio Emilia preschool. The role of the teacher, *atelierista* and *pedagogista* will be explored, as well as the expectations of the children, staff and parents. Many of the quotations (shown in *italics*) come directly from staff working in the schools who facilitated the International Study Group visits in 2005 and 2006. The unique nature of the schools, the simplicity and beauty of the indoor and outdoor environments, and the trust placed in the child as an active protagonist in the learning experience, will be examined. Reggio teachers state that they do not follow a particular theorist or curriculum, but it is clear that they have studied the most influential theorists and educational thinkers, and have internalized the essence of their thinking. In this chapter the links to current and past educational thinkers will be considered. Loris Malaguzzi (1998, p. 58), a founder and pedagogical director of the preschools, refers to the aspirations of the founding parents of the Reggio Emilia preschools, that they had built 'a different kind of school' from the traditional type they had experienced themselves. He elaborated on this, stating that one of the core principles of the Reggio Emilia preschool experience is that children are citizens with fundamental rights. Therefore, these children are entitled to an education which allows them to 'develop their intelligence and to be made ready for the success that would not, and should not, escape them'. He reiterates very strongly the parents' initial aspirations, 'expressing a universal aspiration, a declaration against the betrayal of the children's potential, and a warning that children

33

first of all had to be taken seriously and believed in' (Malaguzzi, 1998, p. 58).

These fundamental principles underpin the work of the Municipal Preschools of Reggio Emilia. They are held inviolate and generate a spirit of collegiality, collaboration and devotion to the task among the teachers, *atelieristas, pedagogistas*, parents and children of the schools. Gardner (2004, p. 17) believes that the legacy of Malaguzzi remains today in:

> The capacious and inspiring conception of children as active, engaged, exploring young spirits, capable of remaining with questions and themes for many weeks, able to work alongside peers and adults, welcoming the opportunity to express themselves in many languages, to create new ones, and to apprehend and enter into those modes of expression that are fashioned by their agemates.

Carla Rinaldi (2005) of Reggio Emilia stresses the reciprocity of the relationship between the schools and the wider community, '*the community generates a school and is in turn re-generated by the school, receiving vital sap, meaning and future*'. This is a fundamental guiding principle of Reggio work, and everyone – staff, parents and children – works very hard at building reciprocal relationships. There are two key values to which they adhere:

Value 1: Trust in mankind being educable. Education in this respect is viewed as a shared process, a construction not only of a private nature with the child's family but also of community and society. Education involves a process of participation in the construction of knowledge. One of the most thought-provoking concepts is the understanding that a 'problem' provides a means of opening dialogue towards a shared understanding and a shared resolution, while a 'quick solution' often closes dialogue. Therefore, emphasis is placed on the *process* of working though a problem rather than arriving at a speedy solution. This is important to us as educators in the west where speedy answers are often seen as a sign of intelligence.

Value 2: Declaration of the child as a subject of rights. This child is the bearer of rights, a social subject. Hence, preschool services are a right of each child as a citizen. The Municipality has been able to guarantee a place to any child who wishes to attend an infant–toddler centre or preschool since 2004. The Reggio child *is a citizen*, not a child being prepared to be a citizen; however, Reggio school staff believe that being a citizen cannot be taught in a didactic way: it must be lived. In fact, Reggio practitioners live by the belief that there is too much preparation for the future in school, stating that we should concentrate on the present, which holds the seeds of the future in it. 'Childhood is a social construction; it is constructed within each culture, which makes it visible and recognises it through rights, first and foremost the right to participate in the construction of the culture and community it belongs to' (Rinaldi, 2005).

Aspiring to the Inspirational

This philosophy of working with the young child is eminently laudable but it is not new; these principles have been espoused by educational thinkers for centuries. Gardner (2004, p. 17) believes that recognizing the rights of children in this way involves accepting the responsibilities and obligations of humanity, which can be very threatening. It necessitates that 'you trust children, you trust teachers, you trust in the power of the imagination'. Why, one might ask, is not this the universal way of working with children in the twenty-first century? Gardner (2006, p. 134) considers it paradoxical that in the first five years of life children learn so many things, including speaking, storytelling, singing and pretend play, yet, 'then they go to school and suddenly, in the very place where we are supposed to know how to teach them, it's very hard and many of them don't do well'. Lazear (2004, p. 163) believes that 'part of the problem may be our own misconceptions about the process of changes itself. Change in any organization is usually slow, painful, and difficult, even in the fact of the best research that clearly indicates the new directions needed.'

What do the Reggio Emilia schools do so well that they can offer pause for thought, reflection and dialogue to all those involved in early-years education? It is clear that the schools are very well resourced, financed and staffed. However, it not just a matter of resources; to work in this way requires a fundamental mind-shift towards the power relationships between children, parents and teachers, which is evident in most school systems.

Reggio teachers do not make claims about the standard of excellence embodied in their way of working and dealing with children. They do not claim to be experts; rather, they see themselves on a journey of discovery with the child, believing that the child will show them the way. They welcome visitors to see what they do, but they emphasize that they do not think their approach is easily transportable to other cultures. In fact, they stress that all good educational approaches must be culturally embedded. This ties the schools to the social and cultural contexts in which they are located and shows us that, although we have a lot to learn from Reggio, we must ensure that our school system is embedded in our own culture rather than seeking to import or impose another approach. Balaguer (2004, p. 32) states very emphatically that, 'to copy Reggio is simply not possible, unless you want to fall into superficiality'. Wien (2008, p. 6) summarizes this rather succinctly, stating of her own work, 'We are working with the ideas and philosophies of Reggio Emilia as catalysts to rethinking our own practices.'

Rinaldi (2005) reminds us that every community must answer questions about the role of the school in that society for themselves. Schools are places where values and culture are built, not just transmitted; families must be involved in building the educational program and everyone must *live* it, together. Part of the work of school and society should be to transform differences into some *thing* or some *value* to be shared. This has become very important in Reggio Emilia now as this city has the highest rate of immigration in all of Italy. Italy has had a history of emigration and is now in the process of welcoming immigrants to its shores. Malaguzzi invited practitioners to 'leap over the wall of the obvious, of the banal and of the irremovable and to go beyond the boundaries that separate places, ideas or subject matters that break with conformity' (Rinaldi, 2005). He asks that educators of the young open themselves up 'to new and passionate scenarios'. Reggio practitioners agree that this is inspirational and aspirational, but they suggest that we must keep aspiring to the inspirational. This is the key to the Reggio Experience as there is an emphasis on constantly reaching for the stars, of not accepting the everyday or the banal. Katz and Cesarone (1994, p. 33) comment that Reggio Emilia represents a new Italy, where the 'core of Italian values, in combination with Reggio Emilia's particular history of collaboration and solidarity, was enhanced immeasurably by the person and the vision of Malaguzzi, who articulated a broader view of children's social, intellectual, and creative competencies than had previously been imagined'.

Jerome Bruner, an honorary citizen of Reggio Emilia since 1998, states, 'It is imagination which saves us all from the obvious and the banal, from the ordinary aspects of life. Imagination transforms facts into conjecture' (Bruner, 2004, p. 27). In response to a question from a study group participant who asked, 'What is the magical ingredient of Reggio?' Reggio teachers stated, 'We replace *we can't* with *what if?* . . . The emphasis is on problem-solving, persistence, openness, questioning and experimentation.' Nutbrown and Abbott (2001, p. 4) stress that, in Reggio Emilia schools, 'time to discuss children and their project is an integral element of the professional role and development of all who work with children'. Hetland et al. (2007) refer to the vital development of this 'inner voice of reflection', or thinking meta-cognitively, through open-ended rather than closed questions. Reggio teachers observe what the children are interested in and intrigued by, and they look to see how they can prolong this interest. As one teacher said, 'We see how children face things and use the material, and we ask how we can offer this back to them in a new way.' This is reiterated by Spaggiari (1997, p. 10) with reference to a Reggio project on numbers: 'Thinking about what is possible is in itself an act of inventing, discovering, and planning, and this is also true for children.'

This is in sharp contrast to what Ritchart (2002, p. 6) describes as 'teaching for complacency, for orderliness, for dependence, and for superficiality' which is quite common in so many schools. He concludes from his observations of teachers' practice that it is far more common to see schools trying to fill students up with knowledge rather than teaching them to think well. Gardner (2006, p. 134) refers to the need to teach for understanding, where children can apply knowledge gained in one context to another. He says, 'I define understanding as the capacity to take knowledge, skills, concepts, facts learned in one context . . . and use that knowledge in a new context, in a place where you haven't been forewarned to make use of that knowledge.' This is the way Reggio teachers work with children, they offer them multiple opportunities to hypothesize, to test the hypotheses and to apply this knowledge in new contexts.

Reggio practitioners do not follow any one educational theorist as they feel that this would limit the possibilities open to them and to the children. They refer to the need for constant dialogue between theory and practice. They familiarize themselves with the work of a wide range of theorists both past and present and see if Reggio practice, described as a holistic anthropological approach derived from observing the child, *fits* with a theory. In fact, they state quite clearly that they believe if early-years practitioners decide to use a 'method' they have missed the point. Loris Malaguzzi's vision and commitment to setting up the preschools is evident everywhere in the schools and in the town. The new International Center, which opened in February 2006, has been named in his honor. He felt that children have the right to come out of anonymity, therefore documentation of children's work is paramount. Although Malaguzzi refers to the profound influence Piaget had on his thinking, this concept of the child shares much with Montessori and Vygotsky. The latter's emphasis on social interaction and social learning and the former's understanding of the child as someone with enormous potential, which must be stimulated in a prepared environment, serve as models for a Reggio preschool.

The Concept of the Child in a Reggio School

Many definitions of the child, or childhood, center on what the child can or cannot do, how he or she thinks, develops or behaves. Some definitions are rights based, focusing on the child with rights and how these rights may be enshrined in good quality practice. This child is seen as a cognitive or social being, and the emphasis is often placed on ensuring the child has opportunities to develop his or her potential fully. It sometimes seems that the child is fragmented into separate parts in our thinking as we plan activities designed to aid cognitive, social, physical, language or creative development. We try to fuse these areas of development together, and endeavor to join up our thinking, with the all-encompassing and frequently misunderstood aspiration to help the child develop 'holistically'. In Reggio Emilia the holistic concept of the child is framed in Malaguzzi's terms as someone

> who right from the moment of birth, is so engaged in developing a relationship with the world and intent on experiencing the world that he develops a complex system of abilities, learning strategies, and ways of organizing relationships. A child who is fully able to create personal maps for his own social, cognitive, affective, and symbolic orientation.
>
> (Rinaldi, 1998b, p. 114)

This very powerful concept and definition of the child, manifest in Reggio schools, underscores the entire philosophy and approach to the work of all those involved in the child's school and community life. Children who are strong, confident and competent are, therefore, expected to 'have their own ideas, express opinions, make independent choices and play and work well with others' (Thornton and Brunton, 2007, p. 11). Freedom of choice and flexibility of time have been shown to lead to increased concentration, completion of work and greater ownership of that work 'even 2-month-olds appear to take positively to experiences of control' (Lillard, 2005, p. 85). Montessori believed that the child achieved an inner peace and self-discipline by freely choosing work where the 'hand is at work and the mind guiding it' (Montessori, 1991, p. 185). This discipline comes through liberty; it is freedom without licence as she believed that free choice was one of the highest of all the mental processes. The child perfects his or her own discipline, moving through stages until he or she achieves an inner moral code.

Children in a Reggio classroom are expected to work closely together and to learn from one another. Boyd-Cadwell (2003, p. 4) describes the child in a Reggio school as a protagonist, a collaborator and a communicator. It is worth noting that the child as protagonist is understood to 'have preparedness, potential, curiosity and interest' in constructing learning and 'negotiating with everything' the environment has to offer. This is not a passive learner who awaits the imparting of information from a teacher. The child as collaborator is based on the social constructivist model where all learning is integrated in its social context. To help the child to communicate effectively requires a belief in fostering 'symbolic representation, including words, movement, drawing, painting, building, sculpture, shadow play, collage, dramatic play, and creativity' (Edwards et al., 1993), which Malaguzzi has immortalized as *The Hundred Languages of Children*. This concept relates closely to Gardner's (1983, 1991, 1999a) theory of Multiple Intelligences that focuses on the multiplicity of ways of knowing in each individual, which necessitates a re-conceptualization of the ways in which children think and learn, and the opportunities we offer to children to represent these multiple intelligences. Bransford et al. (1999) states that different parts of the brain may be ready to learn at different times, which has huge implications for pedagogy. The importance of this is reiterated by Gardner when he states, 'Unlike the carefully interlocking parts of a watch, the structures of the mind – and of the brain – seem to be able to evolve in different directions and at different paces' (Gardner, 1991, p. 29).

What Does a Reggio Emilia Preschool Look Like?

Malaguzzi (1998, p. 63) conceived of a school for young children 'as an integral living organism, as a place of shared lives and relationships among many adults and very many children. We think of school as a sort of construction in motion, continuously adjusting itself.'

The emphasis on school as a dynamic organism, constantly renewing itself, is a challenging one. There is no certainty, absolute truth or dogma to be adhered to; rather, school is a place of discovery, exploration, research and building relationships. This concept of the child as researcher is very similar to Montessori's (1991, p. 156) when she stated, 'If we leave children free in this new kind of environment that we have provided, they give us quite an unexpected impression of their nature and abilities.' The curriculum is not prepared in advance; in fact, it emerges from the interests of the children. All early-years practitioners endeavor to provide an environment for children that is welcoming, rich, aesthetically pleasing and open to multiple learning possibilities. However, in Reggio Emilia this is done to an exceptionally high degree.

The environment as teacher is considered to be of vital importance, with a significant amount of time and resources being devoted to developing 'ways to increase children's educational, aesthetic and social opportunities' (Abramson et al., 1995, p. 198). Bruner (2003, p. 137) describes the Reggio school as a 'special kind of place, one in which young human beings are invited to grow in mind, in sensibility, and in belonging to a broader community'. He refers to three essential components of the space as:

Primo: 'Mine, thine, and ours': 'A preschool space needs to provide places for each individual who occupies it: *mine and thine'*.
Secundo: 'in and of the broader community': Schools must invite families, friends and well-wishers in as part of the broader community of learning.
Tertio: 'A learning community': The preschool is a learning space where 'mind and sensibility are shared'.

(Bruner, 2003, p. 137)

Montessori stated that a specially prepared environment that would call to the child was vital for the child's development. She believed, as Reggio educators do, that children, through their unconscious memory or Mnème, are transformed by everything they see, hear, touch or encounter in any way in their environment. 'Whatever is formed at that time in the child's Mnème has the power to become eternal' (Montessori, 1991, p. 108). The child is in control of this environment, which empowers him or her. Lillard (2005, p. 28) reminds us that children in Montessori classrooms 'work as motivated doers, learning through self-instigated actions on the environment', which resonates with Malaguzzi's (1998, p. 67) thoughts on the Reggio classroom environment where 'what children learn does not follow as an automatic result from what is taught. Rather, it is in large part due to the children's own doing as a consequence of their activities and our resources.' Kinney and Wharton (2008) stress the importance of allowing children to access the resources and facilities to do what comes very naturally to them; to construct and make meaning of their worlds. The environment in a Reggio Emilia classroom, developed with great attention to detail, facilitates the child's learning in a very positive way. Ceppi and Zini (2003, p. 10) refer to the attempts to achieve an 'overall softness' to the children's environment that they describe as

an ecosystem that is diversified, stimulating, and welcoming, where each inhabitant is part of a group but also has spaces for privacy and a pause from the general rhythms. There is respect for others, listening: a 'strategy of attention'. It is a serene, amiable, livable place.

The environment provides a multi-sensorial experience for the child, which is again very much to the fore of Montessori's approach and in keeping with Gardner's Multiple Intelligences theory, where 'standard univocal solutions cannot be conceived for everyone' (Ceppi and Zini, 2003, p. 160).

Each classroom is integrated with the rest of the school, and the school with the surrounding community. The Diana School, for example, is situated in the center of a park and blends in with its surroundings in a very natural way. The children there are surrounded by images from nature all day and the indoor environment contains lots of growing evergreen plants. Although all the Reggio school buildings are different, some are custom designed while others are renovated factories, warehouses or schools; the interiors are designed in a very similar manner. The buildings range from single-level to multiple-level buildings so that one could not say there is a 'typical' Reggio preschool building in terms of its construction. The schools are full of light and have very attractive open places and spaces. There is a distinct lack of clutter everywhere. Each school makes its own statement by ensuring that there is personal information about the school displayed at the entrance foyer or *piazza*. The documentation is usually at two levels, one for adults and one for children. The material is always very artistically and attractively arranged to be appealing and inviting. This was part of a project done some time ago when the schools wished to preserve their history and to make it visible.

Many of the schools are named after people who influenced the thinking of the community. One of the infant–toddler centers, the Cervi School, is named after Genoeffa Cervi, a mother of 16 whose seven sons were killed by the Fascists in 1943 during the Second World War. Genoeffa was very widely read although she had received very little formal education, and she was described by her friends as a shy, reserved person with a quiet inner strength. After her tragic loss, she was mother to her own daughters and her daughters-in-law. She founded a peace movement and she displayed a passionate interest in education. Other schools are named after important events, for example 25th April (Squole 25 Aprille) after the liberation of Italy after the Second World War, or 8th March (Squole 8 Marco) in honor of International Women's Day, because the schools were developed as a result of the insistence, dedication and hard work of the women of the area. Others are named after well-known artists like Pablo Picasso or characters like Swift's Gulliver. Schools have been named in honor of artists, scientists, writers or poets, for example, Paolo Freire and Michaelangelo. Reggio schools are very proud of their history, the history of their city and that of their country. It is considered to be very important that this history is remembered and celebrated. In some schools descendants of the person after whom the school has been named are invited to the school to talk to children, staff and parents to ensure that their memories are kept alive.

The classroom areas are very thoughtfully laid out. The physical environment abounds with 'Paintings, drawings, paper sculptures, constructions, transparent collages coloring the light, mobiles moving gently overhead' (Gandini, 1994, p. 49). We visited a school after school hours, where the classroom had been prepared for the following day. The coloring pens and other materials had been placed very carefully and invitingly on the tables and unfinished work awaited the children's return. There was ample evidence of children's unfinished work artistically displayed in a most aesthetically pleasing manner. The attention to detail is remarkable. Work tables are often adorned with greenery to help integrate the indoor/ outdoor environment. In one infant/toddler school that we visited the baby area was separated from the outdoors by a floor-to-ceiling glass window. Outside the window a large, mature tree grew and some very inviting mobiles were suspended from the tree to attract the attention of the babies. Some were made of colored materials while one was made of CDs which caught the sunlight beautifully. In fact, the study group participants were asked to describe the schools after a day of visitations and the words commonly used were '*light, space, cleanliness, peace, order, nature, commitment, freedom and time*'. Reggio staff state that the way in which a workspace is presented to the children is a statement of how they think of education, stating that '*the way we propose how a school should be is an ethical, politic, social and economic responsibility for the entire community*'.

Boyd-Cadwell (1997, p. 92) believes the environment is a 'valuable teacher if it is amiable, comfortable, pleasing, organized, clean, inviting, and engaging. This is true of all space, whether big or small, open or furnished, public or private. This is true of floor space, ceiling space, and wall space.' This is the type of environment all practitioners aspire to providing for young children – a prepared learning environment in Montessori's terms, where the empowered child has everything he or she needs arranged in a most appealing and aesthetic manner.

The work areas all have an overhead projector where children explore the concepts of light, reflection, transparency and opaqueness. Sometimes one finds dinosaurs or other animals on the overhead projector magnified onto a wall or screen. Children often use the projected figures as models to draw. Large sheets of drawing paper cover the wall and the figures are projected onto this. One may also find videos of children at work playing in the classrooms. Reggio children become very accustomed to having themselves and their work videotaped or audiotaped. They regularly see themselves on videos in their classroom and are actively encouraged to step back and think about the work they have done, to '*re-consider knowledge that has been encountered during the day*'. This focus on reflection or on re-cognition based on dialogue is a core part of the way in which teachers work with children. Dialogue is not just considered as 'talk' in Reggio but has been described by Rinaldi (2005) as having '*the courage to change the Logos – way of thinking*'; this negotiation of points of view between children and teachers '*offers to the children a person who is searching – not someone who knows everything*'. Dialogue between partners involves listening and being open to change. One must embrace another person's point of view and '*not tolerate silence, dogma or absolute truth*'. The core belief here is that of the child as researcher, who is competent at learning; in fact, the Reggio classroom encourages children and adults to learn how to learn, thereby becoming flexible and adaptable in their thinking. This ongoing classroom research is continuously documented in detail.

Classrooms open onto a central *piazza* and access to the surrounding community is assured through wall-size windows, courtyards and doors leading to the outside of each classroom. This is very symbolic of the partnership between the children, teachers, families and the entire community of Reggio Emilia. Classrooms, hallways and foyers feature an extensive use of mirrors, plants and displays of children's work. Gandini (1994) describes the Reggio school environment as a reflection of the children's personal and cultural histories. Children's work is displayed in a most attractive manner and many exhibits of children's work are on show throughout the world annually. This culture of exhibiting children's work began in the early days when Malaguzzi believed they had to prove to the community just what they could do in the schools.

Each school has a cook who prepares food for staff and children. The menu is varied and nutritionally balanced for the children. The dining area usually has tables spread with attractive tablecloths and real delph. Children help to set up the dining area and serve the food. The attention to detail is very impressive. The dining area often has pictures of food or of children preparing food. In one school we visited, a shelf in the dining area contained some lovely green plants and an apple, cut in sections, attractively arranged. Other shelves contain jars of pasta or wheat. The ambience, attention to detail, lack of haste and provision of soft mood music makes eating an enjoyable social occasion, which is very much a part of Italian culture. This is totally at variance with other schools we have visited where snack time is more of a fuel or pit-stop rather than an integral part of the school experience.

The Roles of the Teacher/*Pedagogista*/*Atelierista* in Reggio Schools

Each class has two teachers: university graduates in child development and pedagogy, each of whom has equal responsibility for the class. This ensures that in the morning one teacher is there early to welcome children to the school, which gives the second teacher an opportunity to talk to parents,

staff and children as part of the important work of building up relationships. In Reggio a teacher has many responsibilities, which may be summarized as:

1. Making visible the way in which he or she is a teacher.
2. Making visible the languages, intelligences and traits of the children.
3. Making visible the relationships in school.

These goals do not emphasize the transmission of information to children,
preparing children for formal school or preparing children for citizenship.
They focus on showing the children's work, which is done in partnership
with children, parents and teachers. The emphasis is on making all work,
all learning *visible* to children, parents, staff, visitors and the wider community. This involves being constantly open to listening to children, to inviting
children to question, to sharing thoughts, ideas, plans with children,
parents and colleagues. This involves an openness we are not familiar with
in our culture. Reggio teachers do not consider just 'my class', but rather
how all the work of the school inter-relates in helping children to achieve
their potential. Reggio teachers believe that the child learns best when he
or she gets close to reality, that all work must be reflected upon, and the
interrogation of this work leads to the formulation of theories and to
further research. One must always build on prior learning, and be open to
all possibilities and potentialities, by being able to see with new eyes every
time one approaches a subject. This requires enormous breadth of vision
and total commitment to giving each child and each piece of work time
and patience to develop fully. Reggio teachers do not speak of a Reggio
'methodology 'or Reggio 'approach', but rather of the Reggio 'Experience',
which may seem like an exercise in semantics, but it makes an important
distinction. It clearly shows the intention that the children, staff and parents
all 'experience' the child as a researcher who asks fundamental questions
about life and the environment he or she lives in, where teachers and
children are co-researchers in the community of learners. The child also
experiences learning as something active, ongoing and enjoyable. The child
sees the teacher as a fellow researcher, a thinker, and from this, children
learn what good thinking routines look like. Ritchart (2002, p. 161)
reminds us that 'in thoughtful classrooms, a disposition toward thinking is
always on display'.

Reggio philosophy is grounded in Kantian thinking that we do not learn
about the world because we observe it, but rather because we ask questions
of it. Teachers meet every week to update each other and to learn from
each other. The morning time, as children filter in to school from

7.30 a.m. to 9 a.m., gives teachers the opportunity to catch up on documentation and to discuss plans with each other. This visible collaboration serves as a model for the children. The role of the teacher, who is respectful of the child, is founded on a pedagogy of listening. Rinaldi (2007, p. 67) says this 'is a difficult path that requires efforts, energies, hard work and sometimes suffering, but it also offers wonder, amazement, joy, enthusiasm and passion'. This pedagogy of listening is put into practice by careful and detailed documentation of the children's learning, of which more will be said later.

Although classes are structured based on the age of the child in the same way that we are all familiar with, one of the greatest cultural differences in the Reggio approach is the 'mingling' that is encouraged between classes. Strozzi (2001, p. 72) cites an instance of two five-year-old children who 'migrate' to the three-year-olds' classroom to help the teacher to set out the materials for the activities of the day and 'they volunteer to be tutors for the younger children'. In other countries many teachers teach mixed age groups, due to an insufficient number of teachers for single classes, but this is seen as a burden, rather than an opportunity, and the 'classes' are frequently separated, within the classroom, to do individual work. Montessori favored mixed age groups so that the younger children would learn from the older children and the older children could cement their understanding of a topic by teaching it to the younger ones.

Reggio educators envisage their role as one in which they produce learning situations in which children learn by themselves with as little adult intervention as possible. The child must know that the adult is there, attentive and waiting to guide if necessary, but always cognisant of the child's need to be the author of his or her own learning. In fact, one of the most striking images of the Reggio teacher and Reggio child comes from Kennedy (1996), who conceptualizes both roles as mirror images of one another. The method of assessment employed in Reggio schools, through project work and collaboration, is reflective of this concept of teacher and child, and provides much food for thought. It transfers ownership of the learning process from the teacher to the student, without negating the enormous importance of the teacher in the classroom. New (1999a, p. 282) believes that children 'benefit from working hard at learning together'. This is an exciting and innovative approach to providing a child-centered, emergent curriculum that combines meaningful, authentic assessment and is based on collaboration between children, parents and teachers.

In addition to the teachers, each school has an '*atelierista*' (artist) who has a completely different educational background from that of the teacher, having attending an Academy or Institute of Art. He or she enriches the school by bringing a different perspective to the work. The *atelierista* must, however, be aware of the needs of children in the different developmental stages. This is a full-time position, 36 hours per week, in which the *atelierista* shares in the entire process of the children's learning, therefore the work of the school is enriched by constant dialogue between the teacher, *atelierista*, *pedagogista*, parents and children. In fact, Malaguzzi insisted on having an *atelier* and an *atelierista* in each school and he described the *atelier* as 'a subversive eruption' in the school. Gandini (2005, p. 7) describes the *atelier* as 'instrumental in the recovery of the image of the child' as 'inter-actionist and constructivist' and she stresses the integral role of the *atelier* in foregrounding the role of the arts in education, stating:

> . . . the role of the *atelier*, integrated and combined within the general framework of learning and teaching strategies, was conceptualized as a retort to the marginal and subsidiary role commonly assigned to expressive education. It also was intended as a reaction against the concept of the education of young children based mainly on words and simple-minded rituals.

The influence of the *atelierista* is very evident in the work of the children and in the way in which the materials and the environment are presented to the children. The school must be very organized if it is to be a good learning environment for its learning community, therefore the *atelier* is always very well resourced with a multiplicity of inviting materials. These are carefully chosen materials that have multiple or unlimited possibilities and await the child's imagination. One of the study week participants, an artist, referred to the 'restraint' in the materials, which are chosen so that they enrich but do not dominate the environment. She highlighted the difference between what she saw in Reggio and the schools where she works. She referred to the lack of pre-cut materials available to be colored in/glued/folded etc., in the schools, as the Reggio practice is to allow the children to interact with the materials as they wish. Strozzi (2006) refers to the need to 'value the children's desire to experiment by providing materials that pose questions and elicit answers, not materials that impose'.

The materials are usually light, bright, clear and often transparent. Children often work on projects which allow them to explore the properties of light on the different materials. Gualandri (2005) states that 'materials brought into the school are re-readable and re-interpretable. When they are placed on a light table they take on a whole new life, especially when projected on to a wall; light changes the quality and gives unexpected results.'

The *atelier* (studio/laboratory) offers an incredible amount of supplies for the children's use as the children explore many themes through projects. Working with artistic materials helps to foster emerging esthetic awareness in the children, and they are encouraged to value themselves as unique individuals, who are also contributing members of the class group (New, 1999a). Many of the materials used are recycled or found materials. In fact, Reggio Emilia now has a recycling center which receives material from businesses and factories for the children to use. A teacher or *atelierista* may use this 'Re-Mida' recycling center for all their resource materials. These are displayed in the classrooms in transparent boxes so that the child's whole attention is on the material and not the container. This again is reminiscent of Montessori's thinking as each of her pieces of didactic material is designed so that the child focuses on one quality only to aid learning and to avoid distraction. Children do lots of their work with clay, which is very plentiful in the region. Clay 'is valued for its transformational properties, ideal for moving ideas from one context to another' (Thornton and Brunton, 2005, p. 42), and this, together with wire, which is very manipulative, is used extensively by the children. The *atelier* also abounds with natural materials such as cones, shells, leaves and seeds, and a wide range of see-through or opaque buttons or beads.

Katz (1990) attests to the very careful planning necessary to achieve such remarkable environments, which are characterized by their esthetic qualities and the attention to detail. This is very much part of the value system of Reggio Emilia, and Costa and Kallick (2000, p. 87) remind us that 'establishing value is really what defines a classroom. We demonstrate what we care about by how we spend our time and attention.' Lella Gandini, United States Liaison for the Reggio Emilia Program in the United States, refers to the sense of welcome achieved by the Reggio environment. The attention to color, sense of transparency and the profusion of plant life, together with an absence of clutter, emphasizes the serene aspects of the space. In fact, the environment is conceptualized as a third teacher. The display of children's work is particularly striking. Reggio teachers do not underestimate the children's capacity for sustained effort when working, which Montessori noted from her extensive observations of children, nor is there an overemphasis on coverage of a topic, in the emergent curriculum. The materials found in the classroom reflect life in the community. Children use pottery they are familiar with and not plastic delph or cutlery, which is also an important feature of Montessori's philosophy. These are real-life experiences for the child, who learns to respect and to be careful with glass or pottery. The cupboards are filled with real foods and the children may view the cooks as they prepare meals using pots and utensils similar to those used at home. The similarity to Montessori's approach here is overwhelming, yet none of the teachers or contributors to the study week readily acknowledged this influence.

In Reggio schools, art is not viewed as a separate part of the curriculum but is fully integrated into every aspect of the child's experiences. 'Teachers consider the learning process to involve both creative exploration and problem-solving' (Edwards et al., 1998, p. 15), and the freedom and encouragement to be expressive helps children become capable of rational and imaginative thought. The children's activities and constructions are valued and may be expressed in myriad ways; in fact, Malaguzzi (1993d) refers to the 'Hundred Languages of Children' as the wide variety of symbolic and graphic modes of representation of the children's work. Gardner (1999b, p. 91) refers to multiple intelligences to express this concept, stating that the 'use of multiple representations or intelligences, furnishes a powerful set of entry points to the community's cherished truths, sense of beauty and ethical standards'.

The Reggio environment endeavors to provide opportunities for children to use their multiplicity of expressive languages at all times guided and helped by the *atelierista* and teacher.

The schools all benefit hugely from the contribution of the *pedagogista* (curriculum specialist) who is shared between a number of schools in a district to work, in collaboration with the teachers and *atelieristas*, on the development of the curriculum. Each *pedagogista* works with several schools in a district, therefore he or she is uniquely placed to gain an overall perspective on the work of groups of schools. The *pedagogista* may have many different areas of expertise, but many have degrees in psychology. The interrelationship between these three key roles of teacher is a fundamental part of the organization and functioning of the schools; it is in essence what makes a Reggio school so unique.

The collaboration between different schools is also very important, as exemplified when several preschools and primary schools in the area collaborated on a project, 'Light in the City', in the new Ray of Light Atelier, which is based in the International Center Malaguzzi. In the Ray of Light Atelier, where all the materials were made by the fathers of children in the schools, we were able to work with a group of fellow study group participants, exploring how rainbows are made. We conducted our experiments in the same way the children do, by trial and error, discussion, generation of hypotheses, and asking myriad questions. The focus was not on how the end product, the rainbow, looked, but rather on the lengthy discussion of the *process* of our learning that took place after the period of experimentation. This *atelier* is very different from other children's museums in that there is no information available on *how to do* things; rather the resources and equipment are made available for exploration in a most inviting manner. It mirrors the *atelier* found in all schools as a place of discovery. The central role of the adult in a Reggio school was defined by one *pedagogista* as 'to activate, especially indirectly, the meaning-making competencies of all children as a basis of all learning'. The provision of a well-resourced environment is key to this learning.

Project Work – *Progettazione* – in a Reggio Emilia School

Reggio Emilia project work is unusual and distinguished in several ways, not the least of which is the role played by the teacher. Rinaldi (1998b, p. 118) refers to project work in this way,

> . . . the potential of children is stunted when the endpoint of their learning is formulated in advance. Instead, at the initiation of a project, the teachers could get together and proceed in terms of *progettazione*, that is, discuss fully all the possible ways that the project could be antici-pated to evolve, considering the likely ideas, hypotheses, and choices of children and the directions that they may take. By so doing, they prepare themselves for all the subsequent stages of the project while leaving ample space for changes, for the unexpected, and for moments of stasis and digressions.

Reggio teachers see their role as that of both learner and teacher, partners in the children's process of learning, and this concept of partnership empowers children and builds self-esteem. Teachers work as a collaborative group, sharing with each other during lengthy and extensive planning sessions (Neugebauer, 1994). Lewin-Benham (2006, p. 26) points out that the organizational system in Reggio schools 'evolved as a system to enhance teachers' full potential, as well as the children's'. This understanding, that opportunities for ongoing professional development must be an integral part of the teacher's experience, enhances the status of the teacher in the learning community.

Interestingly, Rinaldi (1998b) conceptualizes the role of the teacher in the same way as Montessori did, when the latter stressed that the teacher must trust in the child as constructor of his or her own learning and give him or her the space in which to work freely, stating 'as soon as concen-tration has begun, act as if the child does not exist' (Montessori, 1991, p. 255). Although Montessori's words have been misinterpreted at times to mean that the teacher's role is not important, nothing could be further from the truth. In fact, Montessori considered the teacher, or directress, as a key part of the child's learning environment. She stressed the need for the teacher to be so aware of the child's development that she would know when to withdraw and not interfere or impede the learning process. Rinaldi (1998b, pp. 118–19), states very clearly just how pivotal a role the teacher plays, by saying

> . . . the challenge for the teacher is to be present without being intrusive, in order to best sustain cognitive and social dynamics while they are in progress. At times, the adult must foster productive conflict by challenging the responses of one or several children, at other times the adult must step in to revive a situation where children are losing interest because the cognitive map that is being constructed is either beyond or beneath the child's present capabilities. The teacher always remains an attentive observer, and beyond that, a researcher.

Thus the key role of the teacher is to know the children so well that he or she knows when to intervene but not to interfere in the work. In Vygotskyian terms, a good teacher (or competent peer) knows when help is required to help the child develop his or her potential and move to the next Zone of Proximal Development, or ZPD (Vygotsky, 1978). Hendrick (1997) looks at this point and compares Reggio teachers with American teachers. She points out that American teachers, and many others no doubt, are very hesitant to intervene in a child's work. They provide the materials, and unless the child is in any danger, they prefer to leave it to the child to discover how to maximize their use. Reggio teachers guide the children more directly, which Hendrick (1997, p. 46) admits that she found troubling until she understood the reasoning: 'they [the teachers] maintain that lending adult assistance when needed, whether it be bending a recalcitrant piece of wire or hammering in a reluctant nail, empowers youngsters to move ahead with their creations in a satisfying way'. The difference is subtle but important in that Reggio teachers will help the children manipulate the materials but will not tell them what to do with them; the children make these decisions on their own, which may be summarized as, 'I have come to think about this that there is a vast difference between showing a child how to use a brace and bit to make a hole and telling him where to put the hole or what to do with it once drilled' (Hendrick, 1997, p. 46).

Guidici (2005) identifies some of the questions Reggio educators consider with regard to group project work. They ponder the questions of how much individual learning can be reinforced or dampened in a group situation, whether there is such a thing as group learning, and whether it is possible for a group to construct its own style of learning. These questions are of interest because, although there is a vast literature on individual and/or group learning, there is little available on individual learning in a group, particularly in relation to how young children learn. The topics grow out of the children's interests, and multiple experiences with media are used to aid the children's understandings of concepts. The word 'project' is too limited to fully conceptualize the work done in Reggio schools. Their projects are long-term, in-depth studies of some aspects of life, environment, science or culture in which the children have expressed an interest. The themes considered may start from a chance event, a problem posed by one of the children, or a planned event. Children work mainly in small groups which helps to foster dialogue, collaborative problem-solving and a social context for the work being undertaken (Malaguzzi, 1993d). Parents interact frequently with teachers and are involved with curriculum development activities. Reggio teachers place a high value on their ability to help children enjoy, explore and respond to the unexpected. This involves a total commitment to the role of teachers as co-explorers rather than experts in the classroom. Katz (1998, p. 33) shows the commitment to experimentation evident in the work of Reggio teachers, stating, 'willingness to explore a topic that might not work very well is part of their commitment to experimentation, and to exploring together with the children what kinds of experiences and ideas might emerge from an experiment'.

Project work allows space for the children to pursue projects which are difficult and complex and which need to be pursued over an extensive period of time. This involves a great deal of planning and organization. Anyone who has worked with young children will appreciate the enormous amount of planning each outing takes. In Reggio Emilia schools, children may need to make several outings to different environments as they explore a topic. It is not enough that the children would visit a site and then graphically illustrate what they have seen. An extensive project in a Reggio Emilia school involves generating hypotheses, testing them out, reflecting on them, re-visiting and documenting the learning at all stages. Katz (1998) speaks of a project on supermarkets undertaken by the children in a Reggio school, which involved numerous visits to the supermarket both when it was open and when it was closed. This allowed the children to explore the space with and without shoppers. They had opportunities to look at the merchandise, run up and down the aisles, discuss the layout of the shop and interview the manager about his role. The children also shopped at the supermarket by preparing a list and managing the money. They prepared a list of things to improve the shopping experience to present to the manager.

This unique approach to project work distinguishes the Reggio Emilia schools. They do not confine themselves to a pre-determined amount of time; rather, they prefer to allow the children to dictate the time-frame for the work. Each child is expected to engage in long-term project work, as well as the everyday work of the school during his or her stay there. Montessori (1988, p. 13) believed this level of social interaction and social development was indicative of the older child, stating 'social integration has occurred when the individual identifies himself with the group to which he belongs. When this has happened, the individual thinks more about the success of his group than of his own personal success' (Montessori, 1988, p. 213). However, Reggio schools have demonstrated that younger children are more than capable of this level of social development. Reggio Emilia educators and researchers at Project Spectrum at Harvard Graduate School of Education collaborated for many years, exchanging ideas about children's work, their social development, collaboration and their multiple representations of understanding.

Project Spectrum at Harvard and Reggio Emilia – Using a Multiple Intelligences Approach

Observers of young children throughout the centuries have chronicled their observations and developed theories of learning based on these observations. Rousseau, Froebel, Piaget, Dewey and Montessori, among others, allowed their observations to lead them into theorizing on children's developmental needs (Ridgway, 2002). Darwin (1871), in his groundbreaking work, formed the opinion that mental aptitude appears to be inherited along with one's physical characteristics. Galton (1869), Darwin's cousin, argued that intelligence is inherited and that natural ability is subject to the law of deviation from the average, following the bell curve (Gardner et al., 1996). At the time when Galton was using sensorially based psycho-physical tests to explore individual intelligence, Alfred Binet was investigating judgment and reasoning skills as indicators of intelligence, particularly in the light of the growing need for mass education and assessment. It is not surprising that the idea of scientifically measuring intelligence became popular with both psychologists and educators. This understanding of intelligence dominated western psychological circles, perhaps due to the relative ease of administration of the tests to the growing numbers of schoolchildren.

Gardner's Multiple Intelligences Theory (MI Theory) challenges the concept of intelligence that is fixed and unitary. It is based on neuro-biological, neuro-psychological, psychological, historical and evolutionary evidence and specific psychological tasks (Gardner, 1983, 1991, 1999a; Armstrong, 1994). Gardner developed this theory from a psychological premise that the standard notion of intelligence, as a single capacity, was in error. He was not at that time working in the area of educational reform, but having been educated as a psychologist in the wake of the behaviorist era, he felt that the study of child development was receiving a breath of fresh air with the work of Piaget. Gardner (1983) defined intelligence as the capacity for solving problems and fashioning products deemed valuable in society. However, he *refined* this definition in the light of his subsequent work and experience, by emphasizing the potential that may be developed or lost, when he stated intelligence to be 'a biopsychological potential to process information that can be activated in a cultural setting to solve problems or create products that are of value in a culture' (Gardner, 1999a, pp. 33–4).

This revised definition places the focus more clearly on intelligences as potentials, a very clear move away from the idea of a measurable unitary intelligence. Gardner outlined eight ways of thinking and knowing, thereby naming eight intelligences, because he was interested in accounting for the variety of adult roles or 'endstates' which exist across cultures. This entailed a fundamental mind-shift from the practice of explaining scores received on IQ tests (Gardner, 1993). He envisages the intelligences as having emerged over the millennia as a response to the environments in which humans have lived, constituting, as it were, 'a cognitive record of the evolutionary past' (Gardner et al., 1996, p. 3). It appears that we, as humans, develop *what* we need *when* we need it, thereby placing different demands on our society and our system of formal education. This emphasis on the development of our potential intelligences makes it clear that the value placed on any intelligence will vary, depending on the needs of the society one lives in. Certainly, many of the activities we deem to be intelligent in the western world would have little value in a tribal society in the rainforest, with the reverse also being true. Campbell and Campbell (1999, p. 7) look at the manner in which a narrow definition of intelligence limits the ways in which we view children's potential and reiterate that 'understanding intelligence is a prerequisite to significant improvement in pedagogy'.

Gardner purposefully chose to use the word 'intelligence' rather than 'talent' to emphasize the existence of a plurality of intelligences, in contrast to the existing concept of intelligence as a single entity. But he also wished to challenge existing ideas by seeking to place equal value on each of these intelligences, or languages in Reggio terms, contrary to the general practice of valuing linguistic or logical intelligences only. Gardner cites Piaget's

comprehensive model of logical–mathematical intelligence, Erikson for
personal intelligences, and Chomsky or Vygotsky for developmental models
of linguistic intelligence. This concept is not unrelated to Montessori's
(1992) premise of 'sensitive periods' for learning, and both have enormous
implications for early-years practitioners in the differentiated classroom, as
is to be found in Reggio Emilia. Fleetham (2006) refers to this as a person-
alized approach to learning.

The Eight Intelligences

Gardner (1983, 1991, 1999a) outlines the different capacities of the eight
intelligences as described below; he has contextualized these by citing
examples of 'endstates' or occupations which would embody the relevant
intelligences in action, thereby moving his theory into actual living
examples.

Linguistic Intelligence

This intelligence indicates the capacity to use words effectively both orally
and in written form and to express and appreciate complex meanings. It
also includes the ability to manipulate the structure, phonology, semantics
and pragmatic dimensions of language. Those who exhibit high linguistic
intelligence include poets, playwrights, journalists and those who engage
in rhetoric, or have competence in metalanguage. This was the most highly
prized skill one could develop and was traditionally viewed as *the* indicator
of intelligence. Consequently, pedagogical practices centered almost exclu-
sively on this approach to the detriment of children who cannot process
information in this manner.

Logical–Mathematical Intelligence

This intelligence includes capacity with numbers, logical patterns and
relationships. 'It enables us to perceive relationships and connections, to
use abstract symbolic thought' (Campbell, 2008, p. 3). Persons who exhibit
high logical mathematical intelligence use processes such as categorization,
classification, calculation and hypothesis testing, and include mathemati-
cians, accountants, statisticians, philosophers and scientists. Together with
linguistic ability, mathematical ability was also highly prized, and constantly
assessed in school settings traditionally.

Spatial Intelligence

Spatially intelligent people have the ability to perceive the visual spatial world accurately. 'It is the ability to think in three dimensions. Core capacities of this intelligence include mental imagery, spatial reasoning, image manipulation, graphic and artistic skills, and an active imagination' (Campbell, 2008, p. 3). This intelligence is in evidence in architects, artists, inventors and designers, as one needs to be sensitive to color, line, shape, form and space, and to be able to orient oneself in a spatial matrix. Ability in this intelligence area 'makes it possible for people to perceive visual or spatial information, to transform this information, and to recreate visual images from memory' (Hyland, 2000, p. 7).

Bodily–Kinaesthetic Intelligence

This shows expertise in using one's body to express ideas and feelings. The physical skills necessary for bodily–kinaesthetic intelligence include co-ordination, dexterity, flexibility, as well as proprioceptive, tactile and haptic capacities. 'This intelligences also involves a sense of timing, and the perfection of skills through mind–body union' (Campbell, 2008, p. 3). Those who exhibit strength in this intelligence may be notable for the use of their hands to produce or transform things as a sculptor, mechanic or surgeon would.

Musical Intelligence

The development of this intelligence area involves the capacity to *perceive* musical forms as a music aficionado, *discriminate* as a music critic, *transform* as a composer and *express* as a performer. Musical intelligence allows people to 'create, communicate, and understand meanings made out of sound' (Hyland, 2000, p. 7). Musically intelligent people have high sensitivity to the rhythm, pitch or melody and timbre of a musical piece. People who exhibit musical intelligence usually need music to make their lives full, even if this entails listening to music rather than playing an instrument or being part of a musical group. This is a very important distinction as the majority of people who find their lives enriched by music do so as listeners rather than performers. Campbell (2008, p. 3) states that 'interestingly there is often an affective connection between music and the emotions, and mathematical and musical intelligences may share common thinking processes'.

Intrapersonal Intelligence

This intelligence includes having an accurate picture of one's strengths and limitations and an awareness of one's inner moods, intentions, motivations and desires. It means that one has a high degree of self-knowledge and the ability to act adaptively on the basis of that knowledge. This intelligence is very relevant to most occupations. Traditionally, I believe this intelligence was linked to introversion in an over-simplistic and narrow manner, without acknowledging that introverts draw strength from within, rather than from other people necessarily, but this does not mean they cannot function very well as team members. In fact, one needs the reflective nature of the introvert to balance any team, as they can provide a stabilizing force.

Interpersonal Intelligence

This is the second of the personal intelligences and includes the ability to perceive and make distinctions in the moods, intentions, motivations and feelings of other people, which is, of course, a very necessary quality in teachers. Again, this has been linked to extroversion in an overly simplistic way, with both of the personal intelligences being seen as personality types only, without the status of an intelligence.

Naturalist Intelligence

In 1995 Gardner, invoking new data that fit the criteria, recognized an eighth, *naturalist* intelligence which is demonstrated by the ability to function well in the natural environment and 'the recognition and categorization of natural objects' (Gardner, 1998b, p. 20). It allows people to 'distinguish among, classify, be sensitive to, and use features of the environment (farmers, gardeners, botanists, florists, geologists, archaeologists)' (Hyland, 2000, p. 7). Those with high naturalist intelligence develop the skills of observing, collecting and categorizing, which 'may also be applied in the "human environment"' (Gardner, 1998b, p. 20) as children become very aware of what is currently popular among their peer group. This could apply to clothes, cars or multi-media.

Armstrong (2003, p. 7) stresses that the development of literacy, which is a focus of much of our work with young children, means using all our intelligences together, as it 'emerged out of our oral language capacities, our logical capabilities, our physical movements, our image-making abilities, our musical proclivities, our emotional life, our attempts to decipher and control nature, and our impulse to connect meaningfully with others'.

Hyland (2000, p. 7) reminds us that while each area is identified as a discrete intelligence, 'each also interacts with others in complex ways to produce the richness of human behaviour and achievement . . . Ordinary human functioning requires such interaction.' In Reggio schools, the multiple intelligences of the children are honored and supported in a very meaningful way. The multiplicity of intelligences is given expression in a multiplicity of expressive languages which serve to allow the child, as researcher and scientist, to develop to his or her full potential.

Krechevsky (1998, p. 1) outlines the history of Project Spectrum, the early-years project at Harvard Graduate School of Education, which began as the project team set about devising a set of curricular and assessment materials to tap a wide range of cognitive and stylistic strengths, bearing in mind the narrow focus of traditional testing methods. Project Spectrum was a ten-year research and development project, a collaborative work between the Universities of Harvard and Tufts, both of which are in Cambridge, Massachusetts. Spectrum uses a Multiple Intelligences approach and deals with the preschool child. The project had two original aims: 'to try to broaden conceptions of intellectual potential in young children, and to provide practical techniques for assessing as many of these areas of potential as possible' (Feldman, 1998, p. 14). The goal was to develop a new means of assessing the cognitive abilities of preschool children. The Spectrum Project (Krechevsky, 1998) is based on the theory of Multiple Intelligences (Gardner, 1983) and the non-universal theory (Feldman, 1980/1994). The non-universal theory (Feldman, 1980/1994) is founded on Piaget's developmental concept, which Feldman (1998, p. 10) states 'is basically a framework for expanding the field of developmental psychology to better encompass cognitive effort that does not occur spontaneously, but requires individual effort and external support'. Its central assumption holds that many of the activities pursued by children and adults are developmental but not necessarily universal. One of the most interesting aspects of non-universal theory for the preschool child is its emphasis on the understanding of transitions, the ways in which children progress from one developmental level to the next as they acquire expertise in any field of study or endeavor. This, of course, has profound implications for the education of young children, which must focus on establishing an environment in which children may explore, discover new concepts and achieve mastery of a topic.

One of the key issues in the Spectrum approach is in its view of the teacher as learner, viewing both in an inextricably intertwined manner.

Spectrum values the interactions and conversations between teachers and children as an invaluable part of the child's learning, a way of leading a child to his or her Zone of Proximal Development (Vygotsky, 1978). The Spectrum assessment schedule surveys seven different domains of knowledge: movement, language, mathematics, science, social development, visual arts and music, as well as a list of various working styles that describe a child's approach to a particular task. Spectrum activities allow children to explore multiple domains and work on a wide range of educational goals (Ridgway, 2002). Spectrum researchers endeavored to develop an alternative form of assessment which would be compatible with the view that children should grow at their own pace, in an environment that is broad and pressure free. The inextricable link between assessment, curriculum and pedagogy is at the core of Spectrum's philosophy, together with an emphasis on allowing children's voices to be heard and on making their learning visible; hence the links between their work and that of Reggio Emilia is readily apparent.

Documentation of Learning – Making Learning Visible

There is a great emphasis on the documentation of children's work in the Reggio approach. Documentation of children's learning is an effort to share that learning between all the partners in the education system. This serves as an individual and collective memory of the children's activities and provides a means of reflection, which leads to new experiences. The work is then shared with parents and other interested parties and provides a means for continued growth and development (Vecchi, 1993). Children's work is displayed prominently in Reggio schools, showing the history and development of the work and not just the current project being considered. Dahlberg et al. (1999, 2006, p. 148), who collaborated with Reggio educators over many years, state that the process of documentation 'involves the use of that material as a means to reflect upon the pedagogical work and to do so in a very rigorous, methodical and democratic way'.

Edwards et al. (1998) refer to the needs of children, which may be addressed through documentation. The Reggio teacher needs to hold together the ideas of individuals and the group. Reggio teachers respect the children's spontaneity and see themselves as actively co-operating in the children's creative activities. They communicate their regard for the children's activity by documenting the process of learning and creating, and by displaying the photographs taken and the examples of the children's work. The children's work retains its individuality while making a powerful esthetic statement. Boyd-Cadwell (2003, p. 97) refers to her work in the

United States with groups of teachers who have been inspired by the Reggio philosophy on documenting learning by stating,

> I realize that seeing, noticing, observing, being fully present, paying attention and creating, collecting, and sharing documents (lists, notes, photographs, writing, videos, notebooks, files, delegated tasks, shared processes) is now the central way in which we work. With this shared practice as our frame of reference, we are like anthropologists interpreting recorded observations, photographs, and collected artifacts.

This emphasis on making learning visible has opened up the minds of practitioners to be creative in their thinking and to move forward from an over-reliance on traditional media and forms of representing children's thoughts and work. The excitement that this innovative approach has generated among practitioners has been captured by Boyd-Cadwell (2003, p. 97) when she says, 'We are amazed and excited every day.' This is what working with young children should always be like for all of us.

Kinney and Wharton (2008, p. 1) record their work in documenting their practice following a visit to Reggio Emilia, stating '[visiting] Reggio Emilia made a significant impact on us and caused us to reflect more deeply on how we could be more effective in hearing, seeing and feeling what children were communicating to us'. In other words, documentation opens our eyes and ears to seeing what the children are learning. Documentation also allows the child to return to his or her own work from time to time and to view the process and progress of the endeavor, which empowers the child and gives him or her a sense of ownership of the work and a major part in the assessment process. The documentation includes the children's interpretations of their experiences and their explorations. This helps the young child to begin a process of developing the lifelong skill of self-reflection and constructive critique of his or her own work. This was borne out in research done with children of five and six years of age, who constructed their own reflective portfolios (Ridgway, 2002).

In this process the terms 'documentation', 'assessment' and 'feedback' are used inter-changeably. Documentation involves active listening, dialogue and the development of a relationship between the child and the environment. Documentation in Reggio Emilia is part of the process of giving the child a sense of place in his or her own community; a visible acknowledgement of the child's voice. Margini (2005) attests to the curiosity of Reggio teachers concerning '(through) what processes does a child manifest his/her intelligence and how is this different to the adult's'. Knowledge is constructed in so many different ways and stages through the process of social interaction. She emphasizes the belief that 'We need other people to construct our knowledge. This process and these interactions generate and re-generate knowledge of ourselves and, what has been activated in our cognitive and personal learning, to arrive at this knowledge' (Margini, 2005).

The three strands of good documentation of the child's learning are observation, interpretation and documentation. '*To observe is to interpret. To observe it is necessary to predispose the environment for it*' (Margini, 2005). Rinaldi (2000b) refers to the three strands as a spiral of documentation, similar to Kolb's (1984) experiential learning cycle, while reminding us that documentation is a way of guaranteeing reflective practice, which involves valuing another's point of view (Rinaldi, 2002).

This observation cannot be separated out from the work of the child, there is a reciprocal demographic involved; the observation is not just done by the teacher and the work done by the child. Each teacher feels that learning occurs for the teacher as he or she observes. The question Reggio teachers keep to the forefront of their work is, '*On the basis of what elements can I say that the child has had a good experience?*' During the observation of children at work, teachers must remain open to '*welcome theories/ hypotheses/ideas of children that come from experiences they have had*' (Margini, 2005).

Observation in Reggio schools is a creative act which requires interpretation. On the basis of their work and observations, teachers compile extensive and detailed documentation. The children also document their own work. This documentation is described by Reggio teachers as the gathering of materials to allow for the collegial experience of sharing with colleagues. This is a very new concept for us. Documentation is not just about making short notes about a child's progress but is an integral part of the learning experience. It is open and visible to all. It makes it possible to plan further work and to re-experience past work; it provides what Reggio teachers call '*archives of experience*'. Each school seeks to cultivate its own identity through documentation; it serves to make its own cultural identity readable.

Documentation gives the practitioner information in many different ways. Kinney and Wharton (2008, p. 2) remind us once again that this is crucial if we are to respond appropriately to the child's needs. It helps us to 'hear' children more clearly and to respond in a manner which is transparent to our colleagues, therefore, 'we must acknowledge and confront power relations between children and adults'. The children document their work using multiple media approaches and they constantly discuss their thoughts, work and ideas with their teachers. Language becomes an integral part of the classroom with continuous encouragement for self-expression and communication. Language is attached to an abstract idea and transforms the knowledge gained into a key, which the children can use for further exploration in their world. Vygotsky (1986, p. 113) states, 'Writing, in its turn, enhances the intellectuality of the child's actions. It brings awareness to speech.' Vygotsky (1986) and Piaget (1963) both remind us of the reciprocal reinforcing links between thought and language. Reggio teachers are cognizant of these important links and work to ensure the children become confident and skilful communicators.

Teachers make notes every day on the experiences of the day. These notes are often accompanied by video or audio recordings. They are made available to parents as they collect their children from school. As the notes help to generate collegial discussion, the plans for project work take place. Gualandri (2005) states that as children work in groups on projects, they learn to '*look at what they are working on through each other's eyes*'. Barchi (2005) elaborates on this idea when she says that as children work together they build up relationships with each other and with the materials with which they work. It '*makes it possible for children to be the protagonists of their own learning, through sharing ideas, imitation, listening and giving value*'. Documentation of the work makes visible the values of the group and '*makes permanent the assessment carried out by children and adults*' (Barchi, 2005).

Filippini (2006) refers to their documentation as a *second skin*, stating, '*documentation helps give us the conceptual tools to consider, What is a child?*'

In practical terms, Kinney and Wharton (2008, p. 6) acknowledge 'that this means the child is actively involved in making decisions about which learning processes he/she engages with. On the basis of this, the educators and the child (children) through a collaborative process negotiate the context for learning together.'

Mardell (2001, pp. 278–9), one of the researchers on the collaborative work between Project Spectrum and Reggio Emilia, offers a cautionary note, stating that although educators have been moved by the work of children in Reggio schools and the rich documentation of learning, many have questioned the amount of adult help which is given: 'We have been told that it is impossible for young children to produce such outstanding work without undue adult interference, and that only by neglecting other more important responsibilities could teachers have the time to create such thoughtful pieces of documentation.'

Mardell, however, considers this to be an over-simplification based on dichotomous thinking. As a kindergarten teacher he has had experience of dealing with the issues of concern to all early-years educators. As a doctoral student and researcher at Harvard, he has valued the collaboration with Reggio Emilia and the opportunities given to explore the cultural differences between the responses to the issues in the United States and Italy.

He has responded to the difficulties expressed in understanding the power and benefits of rich documentation of learning by focusing on three areas:

1. *Cultural Knots*: The decisions taken by teachers regarding how to teach and document learning are guided by their educational worldviews, i.e. their working theories on teaching and learning are rooted in their own cultural experiences. He expresses the opinion that these world-views can limit us to seeing possibilities. In fact, many practices are rooted in tradition rather than informed understanding of what children and teachers really need to develop.
2. *Reggio as a Mirror*: The opportunities presented by cross-cultural collaborations offer a microscopic view of the assumptions, beliefs and values that shape educational decisions. By having to explicate our pedagogical principles we can reflect on them and re-shape them. What do we mean by the terms 'child-centered' or 'holistic development'? How do we think of the children and teacher and their role in the class?
3. *False Dichotomies*: The absence in Reggio schools of many of the dichotomies present in our thinking gives us pause for thought. These include teaching/learning, theory/practice, adult-directed/child-centered curriculum, or individual/group learning, which help to simplify the complex nature of teaching and learning. It is part of our human nature to try to assimilate information and accommodate it in the light of our worldviews; however, 'there are times when something is not one thing or the other, but both. This recognition can prove important when grappling with ideas about learning in groups and documentation' (p. 283).

(Mardell, 2001, pp. 278–83)

Rinaldi (2005) summarizes the Reggio understanding of the importance of constant rich documentation by saying,

Documentation alters the dynamic within group learning from individual learning in a group to group learning. A group characterised by an increased awareness of the interdependence of learning, a greater sensitivity to the learning experience of the other, and richer possibilities for choosing ideas. A model from which to draw inspiration and differentiate energy.

This encapsulates the understanding that all children, parents, teachers and other community members participate in different ways in Reggio project work, operating as an individual and as a group member, each bringing something different to the enterprise (Cagliari et al., 2004). Documentation of learning involving the provision of ongoing, rich feedback between children and teachers is a core part of the Reggio philosophy of working with children. It enriches the child's and the teacher's experience and allows the child to take responsibility for his or her work and to become reflective, respectful and thoughtful about that work from a very young age.

Conclusion

Malaguzzi (2005) refers to the development of children being dependent on the centrality of the inter-relationship between children, teachers, families, the physical environment and the working environment, with each participating and collaborating to enrich the children's experiences. In fact, Malaguzzi (2005, p. 29) speaks of the traditional isolation of teachers in the classroom, 'as a sort of longstanding existential imprisonment, an obstacle to the professional growth and knowledge' and of schools from the broader community, and advocates much greater collaboration. This underscores his commitment to the professional development of Reggio teachers by emphasizing the need for classrooms with two teachers, and schools that have the expertise of an *atelierista* and a *pedagogista*. The staffing levels and resources available in Reggio schools immediately mark them as different. The attention to detail in providing a learning environment for children is remarkable, and clearly shows a very high level of motivation and commitment among staff. However, it is the commitment to collaboration and partnership between children, parents and teachers that ensures that children have exceptionally rich experiences in the schools.

Hoerr (2000, p. 1) refers to the inter-connectedness of today's society, which demands that we display excellent team work and collaborative skills. This emphasizes the development of our two personal intelligences to a very high level, and it is clear that the work of the Reggio Emilia schools, focusing as it does on the inter-connectedness of children/parents/ teachers/community, is a very appropriate and apt way to work with, and empower, young children. Strozzi (2006) encapsulates it thus, '*School is not a place for anonymous users, everyone is part of a relationship.*'

Presenters and Contributors to the International Study Weeks of 2005 and 2006

Barchi, Paula (2005)
Filippini, Tiziana (2006)
Gualandri, Emanuela (2005)
Guidici, Claudia (2005)
Margini, Deanna (2005)
Rinaldi, Carla (2005)
Strozzi, Paola (2006)

Chapter 3

Partnership with Parents and Families

Introduction

The municipal infant and toddler centers (*nidi*) and preschools of Reggio Emilia provide an extraordinary example of what can be achieved when early-years services work in partnership with parents. Malaguzzi, along with the others involved in setting up and organizing the preschools, was concerned with creating a context or type of organization that would give practical expression to the theoretical ideas that they had gleaned through talking with and reading the work of the different thinkers and writers, and which they had reflected on and discussed in order to establish fundamental principles or values to underpin their work. They were also concerned with putting the principles of democracy and citizen participation into practice. In this context, children, teachers and parents are all seen as active participants in a collaborative educational endeavor.

Malaguzzi and the others involved in setting up and operating the preschools read and consulted widely. Carlina Rinaldi, president of the Reggio Children organization and formerly *pedagogista* with the Reggio preschools, has written and lectured extensively on the Reggio Experience (e.g. Rinaldi, 1998a; 1999; 2007; Rinaldi and Moss, 2004). She gives us many insights into how they were able to draw on the thoughts and ideas of well-known thinkers from the fields of education and human development to provide a theoretical foundation for their practice, and to give practical expression to their principles. The previous chapter addressed the pedagogical implications of this, and the chapter which follows looks in detail at these theoretical foundations.

This chapter will focus on the way in which the Reggio educators work in partnership with parents and families.

An Ecological Perspective

Malaguzzi himself, in the article entitled 'A Bill of Three Rights', set out his views on the rights of children, of teachers and of parents, all of them seen as active participants in an educational partnership. Regarding the rights of parents, he says that:

> Parents have the right to participate freely and actively in the elaboration of the founding principles and in their children's experiences of growth, care and learning while entrusted to the public institutions . . . there should be a presence and a role for parents such as the one valued by our institution's long tradition and experience.
>
> (Malaguzzi, 1993a, p. 9)

He goes on to speak about how the network of communication between parents and teachers can lead to 'a more true and reciprocal knowledge about the child and learning'. In his view, the role of parents is not confined to sharing knowledge about their own children. They are also involved in developing pedagogy. Together, teachers and parents research the 'ways, the contents and the values of a more effective education'.

The way in which the Reggio Emilia educators relate to parents, families and the community is very much in tune with the ideas of Urie Bronfen-brenner, whose bio-ecological view of human development has informed much of the work of early childhood programs in recent years. Bronfen-brenner's view, as expressed in his influential work *The Ecology of Human Development* (1979), was that development cannot be isolated from the context in which it occurs, the environment, which he visualized as 'a set of nested structures, each inside the next, like a set of Russian dolls' (Bron-fenbrenner, 1979, p. 3). The child is at the center of this nested series of environments. The *microsystem* level contains the home, the immediate neighborhood and the other places where the child spends time: with rel-atives, carers, in nursery, preschool or school. Parents are the child's first educator, and the learning that takes place in the very early years lays the foundation for all future learning. It is in the context of home and family that babies and young children first learn to communicate, to love, to trust, to explore their own capabilities and the world around them. Later, the care of parents is supplemented, perhaps by the extended family and neighbors, perhaps by paid care-givers, and later again by teachers. Children develop attachments to those who look after them, and they need this secure base so that they are confident and able to venture into the wider world of neigh-borhood, preschool and school. The concept of attachment is of particular importance to those who work in the Reggio preschools and infant–toddler centers. As we will see, special attention is paid to helping children to make the transition from home and to form attachments within the group and with their teachers. The adults concerned are also encouraged to develop a group identity and a sense of identification with the infant–toddler center (*nido*) or preschool.

The next layer in Bronfenbrenner's model is the *mesosystem*. This consists of the relationships between the elements of the microsystem which affect the child's experience in each. So, for example, a harmonious relationship between the child's parents and their extended family living nearby means that the child gets to know and appreciate a greater number of adults and older children than would happen if the family lived in isolation. Relationships between home and school fall into this category too, and the child benefits when both work in harmony. This concern with relationships is central to the Reggio Emilia approach. Good communication is vital; Rinaldi speaks of the child's almost physiological need 'to live in a network of communication to relate to and benefit from' (Rinaldi, 2007, p. 40). Continuity between the different elements of the microsystem also reduces the stress of transition; either the 'horizontal' transition between the different settings in which the child experiences at a given time in his or her life, or the 'vertical' transitions that happen when a child moves on to the next stage, when he or she leaves the nursery and begins primary school for example (Kagan, 1992; Regional Education Laboratories, 1995).

At the next level is the *exosystem*, where wider influences begin to be felt, such as the availability of support networks for families, and here one can place the municipal structures that support and fund the Reggio preschools and infant–toddler centers. Reggio is a prosperous city, and the funding decisions taken over the years by the municipality have contributed to the excellence of its early-years services. Bronfenbrenner's final level, the *macrosystem*, includes the prevailing ideologies, social policies and funding arrangements which determine the availability and nature of services and supports for families. As discussed in Chapter 1, it is the prevailing views on childhood, education and the family as well as those on democracy, citizenship and civil society that have shaped the Reggio municipal early-years services. This ecological approach may be seen as inspiring attempts to adopt an integrated approach to early-years services, and it perfectly describes the systems that underlie the Reggio Emilia nurseries and preschools.

A Pedagogy of Relationships

One of the most striking characteristics of the Reggio Emilia infant–toddler centers (*nidi*) and pre-primary schools is their almost organic connection with the community, and especially with the families of the children who attend them. In part this is a reflection of the historical and social context in which these nurseries and preschools were founded and developed; in part it is a deliberate choice by the founders of the municipality and the schools themselves. As described in Chapter 1, these preschools came about in the aftermath of the Second World War as a result of the desire of the parents for 'a different kind of school' (Malaguzzi, 1998). The Reggio approach to early-years education and care emphasizes the social and cultural values of solidarity, democracy and participation (Rinaldi and Moss, 2004). It prioritizes the development of high quality and enduring social relationships among both children and adults, and has even been described as a pedagogy of relationships (Malaguzzi, 1993a). Malaguzzi stated his belief that

> No other school distorts and abuses its nature like schools for early child-hood – when they fail to connect to families, to customs, to culture, to local problems and are preventing from conversing freely and demo-cratically with the place that generates them.
>
> (Malaguzzi, quoted in Catarsi, 2004, p. 8)

In the late 1960s and early 1970s there was extensive discussion in Italy at national and local level on the role of the state in the provision of early-years care and education. This debate included seminars and meetings held in Reggio Emilia, at which Malaguzzi and his colleagues shared their views and experiences. The widespread discussion leading up to the passing of the laws on the provision of publicly funded preschools (in 1968) and infant–toddler centers (in 1971 and 1999) helped to shape the belief that child care is a public service to which all children are entitled and that 'quality childcare and early education, as defined in Italian social policy and discourse, is a service for children *and their families*' (New, Mallory and Mantovani, 2000, p. 601, original emphasis). Rebecca New, reporting on a collaborative research project with five Italian communities including Reggio Emilia, identifies three features that characterize early childhood programs in these settings and which are drawn from larger Italian cultural values. These are:

- the significance attributed to children's social relationships;
- the congruence between developmental goals for children and the communal/civic expectations of the adults; and
- the diversity of interpretations associated with the promotion of these social relations.

(New, 1999b)

L'inserimento: The Child's First Transition

In Italy generally and especially in Reggio Emilia, particular attention is paid to the process of *l'inserimento* – the child's first transition to out-of-home care, or as Malaguzzi himself describes it, 'the child's transition from a focused attachment on parents and home to shared attachment that includes the adults and environment of the infant–toddler centre' (Malaguzzi, 1998, p. 62). Thus, unlike the approach which is more common elsewhere and particularly in English-speaking countries, where the emphasis is on settling in the child to the new setting and getting the child to accept separation from parents as quickly as possible, the emphasis in Reggio is on forming new relationships and new attachments as well as making the transition as painless as possible for all concerned. New (1999b) describes how, in Reggio Emilia, unlike most of the other Italian cities in her study, this process of *l'inserimento* is seen as extending far beyond the initial days or weeks that the child attends. There are numerous opportunities for parents and children to meet before the first 'official' starting day. During the first week, parents and children both attend, and parents work closely with the teachers to help the child to explore and feel comfortable in this new environment. Parents gradually move to adjacent rooms, taking part in other activities and checking occasionally that the children are content. These parents will continue to meet as a group all through the time that their children attend the center, and will get to know each other's children well over the years.

Carlina Rinaldi (2007, pp. 42–3) describes a range of possibilities for interacting and communication with the families of children who attend the infant–toddler center. These begin long before the first day that the child attends. The initial meetings, at home or in the *nido,* allow the child, the family and the educators to get to know one another. There are individual and group meetings, a few months before and again a few days before the child starts, to agree strategies for *l'inserimento,* the child's first days in the setting and to make sure that any questions that parents may have are answered.

This is the beginning of an ongoing relationship with parents, which finds formal expression in the many occasions at which parents and educators meet. Apart from the everyday interaction that takes place as parents bring and collect the children, there is a series of events which bring parents and educators together (Rinaldi, 2007, pp. 42–3):

- In the early days, parents stay to settle in the child – a process planned and agreed to meet the needs of the child, parents and staff.
- Class meetings at which teaching methods and projects are presented to parents.
- Group meetings to discuss and explore a particular topic – (Rinaldi gives as an example the father's role with an infant) – organized at the request of staff or parents.
- Individual interviews (parent–teacher meetings or conferences) to discuss matters relating to an individual child.
- Open meetings with invited speakers.
- Meetings organized by the parents, to which the teacher is also invited.
- Working meetings – when parents, family and friends come together to work on a practical project for the *nido*.
- Workshops and cookery evenings.
- Parties and other social occasions, including a party when grandparents are invited to come and experience the *nido*.
- Day trips and longer outings where children, parents and staff spend time together.
- Visits to children's own homes.

The centrality of relationships is acknowledged by the time that is devoted to ensuring that parents, children and teachers establish a relationship of mutual trust and understanding. The attention paid to the process of *inserimento* not only promotes continuity and security for the child but helps the teachers to get to know the children better with the aid of insights from their parents. It also lays the foundation for ongoing dialogue and partnership. The children act as a catalyst for relationships between the adults in the child's life – the child's own parents, those of the other children in the group, and the teachers and auxiliary staff in the early childhood setting. These relationships are reinforced over time – the children have the same teachers throughout the three years they spend in the preschool and there are many opportunities for the parents of the children in the group to meet and to get to know one another. Malaguzzi saw this practice of keeping the group together as allowing the construction of a history of relationship and a shared culture, which in turn creates a sense of community, recognizes children as part of families and ensures their well-being

(Edwards, 1995). This sense of belonging may explain why so many parents continue to be involved with and support the preschools long after their own children have gone on to primary school.

Partecipazione: More than 'Participation'

Partecipazione (participation by parents and families) is now a recognized element of early-years education all over Italy, and along with *gestione sociale* (social management), it is enshrined in the laws governing preschools. It is one of the defining characteristics of the Reggio preschools. Carlina Rinaldi explains this *partecipazione* as 'the sharing and co-responsibility of families in the "construction" and "management" of the *nido*' (Rinaldi, 2007, p. 40). 'Construction' here refers to the co-construction through dialogue and communication by parents and educators of the way that the *nido* is structured, in terms of the physical space and the organization of the *nido* but also the ways of being and doing things with the children. The Italian concept of *partecipazione* thus appears to carry a weight of meaning that is not adequately expressed by the English word 'participation' which can be understood in a more limited way. For instance, it might be understood to mean parents taking part in activities designed and organized by the school rather than a more equal relationship between home and school.

Partecipazione is much more closely related to the concept of partnership with parents, which has been widely acknowledged as an essential element of quality early-years services and of successful schooling later on. See, for example, Epstein (1995, 2001), Henderson and Berla (1994), Henderson and Mapp (2002), Mendoza et al. (2003), Pugh and de'Ath (1989), Wolfendale (2004). It includes all those elements listed by Epstein (1995, 2001) in her work on home–school partnerships: parenting, communicating, volunteering, learning at home, decision-making and collaboration with the community. Parents contribute in all these ways in Reggio Emilia; they also receive support in their parenting role through the infant–toddler centers and preschools. Parents understand that participation includes the way in which they interact with their children at home, and they speak of constructing their role as parents through reflection and dialogue with the teachers (Fontanesi et al., 1998).

A striking element of the way in which *partecipazione* is put into practice in Reggio is the way that parents are involved in debates around pedagogy, and the inclusion of their voices, along with those of the children, in many of the writings produced by Reggio children. A second striking feature is the way in which *partecipazione* is seen as a way of bringing about social change. Rather than attempting to shape children to fit an existing society, Malaguzzi and the others involved in founding the Reggio preschools and infant–toddler centers saw the possibility of changing society to meet the needs of children and families through the active involvement of parents and the wider community.

While Reggio is not by any means unique in Italy in attributing considerable importance to relationships with parents and involving them in the management of early-years services, it is noticeable how teachers, parents and policymakers there all acknowledge its central role. According to Paola Cagliari, *pedagogista* with the Reggio Emilia municipality, the Reggio nurseries and preschools are by definition a participation-based project, which recognizes that 'everyone – children, teachers and parents – is an active subject in the educational relationship, each contributing complementary and essential knowledge' (Cagliari et al., 2004, p. 28). This sense of being part of an educational project that is not set in stone, but that continues to grow and evolve for the mutual benefit of all, is also expressed in a quote from one of the parents:

> For me it is looking for growth through times of shared reflection, through opportunities for exchange, comparing points of view, taking our thoughts further, so that I am closer to my child as a parent, so that we grow together as people.
>
> (Excerpt from the minutes of the City and Childhood Council of the Anna Frank nursery school, quoted in Cagliari, 2004, pp. 29–9)

Antonella Gaspari, *atelierista* at the Anna Frank Municipal Preschool, describes Reggio as

> . . . an educational project that has as its base and as its principal objectives relationships, communication and solidarity, characterized by dialogue and exchange, where the presence of the families is as essential as the children's and staff's role as protagonists, where the necessary co-responsibility of the educational process is created. School must be a place of participation and exchange, and education an ongoing process of dialogue and listening among children, teachers, and parents.
>
> (Quoted in Ghiardi, 2002, p. 33)

Carlina Rinaldi, who was the first pedagogical co-ordinator for the Reggio Emilia municipal infant–toddler centers and preschools and who worked alongside Malaguzzi for many years, agrees. She states that 'the school in itself is a "participatory" place, a place of participation by the children, the teachers and the families in an educational project that is based on and hinges on values which have to find expression in daily action'. She goes on to say that 'dialogue with families, participation by the town, has always characterized the identity of the experience – participation in the sense of being part of a project, being a protagonist together with other protagonists' (Rinaldi, 2007, p. 155).

At the 1984 conference of the Gruppo Nazionale Nidi, Rinaldi herself discussed the topic of family participation in the *nidi*. While Rinaldi in this talk was specifically addressing the question of participation in the *nidi*, much of what she says is applicable to the preschools also. The conference took place at a time when the *nidi* were still at an early stage of development in many parts of Italy. As Rinaldi explains, Malaguzzi and the conference organizers were anxious to make it clear that

> . . . family participation was not a choice but part of the identity of the *nido*, the children's right beside being the parents' right. Defence of and expansion of services could only come about with family understanding, solidarity and support, achieved by parents coming to the *nido* not to be instructed and educated on parenthood but to bring their parental knowledge. They would then see the *nido* as a place where value was attributed to them and they could attribute value to childhood as a social and cultural heritage.
>
> (Rinaldi, 2007, p. 26)

Rinaldi does not claim that this ongoing process of dialogue and participation is always easy or that the various participants are always in agreement. The long process of negotiation and dialogue was in itself a learning experience for all concerned. It helped parents, teachers, administrators, politicians and others to realize that 'participation is not only a fundamental strategy of politics; it is also a way of being, of thinking of oneself in relation to others and the world. It is therefore a fundamental educational value and form of educational activity that the child can appreciate from a very young age' (Rinaldi, 2007, pp. 155–6). Rebecca New and her colleagues, in their study of home–school relationships in five Italian cities, claim that the Reggio experience appears to have had a direct influence on the interpretation and implementation of Italian national laws governing early-years education and care (New et al., 2000).

As with all other aspects of the Reggio Experience, the concept of participation was and continues to be the subject of reflection and dialogue. Those involved in Reggio continually revisit their ideas, and resist attempts to oversimplify or codify them. Rinaldi underlines the centrality of the *nido* in fostering the interaction and the relationship between child, teacher and parents, not through 'illusory simplifications of educational continuity but by highlighting instead the dialogic nature and permanent dialectic duality of the relationship' (Rinaldi, 2007, p. 27). Thus, dialogue and social relationships are central to the organization and operation of the *nidi* just as they are to the preschools. Differences are acknowledged but are seen as challenges and opportunities for growth rather than primarily as problems. The relationship between educators and parents is a dynamic one, which changes because of the different needs and characteristics of each individual and family and which also changes over time.

Discussing communication with parents and families, Rinaldi tells us that it requires 'new contents, new tools and new methods' (Rinaldi, 2007, pp. 38–9). Rather than viewing the young child as limited and focusing on what the child cannot (yet) do, the contents should include the 'constant discovery of the child's extraordinary abilities'. Together, parents and teachers can help one another to understand the child better and identify the actual and possible contributions that the child can make to the educational project. The tools should include what Rinaldi calls 'images and traces': photos, slides, videos, pictures, marks and other work produced by the child, displays of the children's work, panels about projects, and so on. All of these can supplement and even on occasion replace verbal language. They also form part of the constant documentation of children's learning that is an integral part of the Reggio approach. Rinaldi also mentions the usefulness of standard forms, particularly for the younger children – for example, daily diaries or reports detailing the child's daily routine, whether the child has slept and so on – which allow parents to raise any other concerns they may have.

Finally in this regard, Rinaldi (2007) identifies the need to move beyond the traditional class meeting, where parents gather at a fixed time to listen to the class teacher, and to discover new methods and ways of bringing parents, children and staff together. She talks of needing a 'spectrum of opportunities' for people to meet, taking into account the difficulties that parents might have in attending at fixed times, or the practical difficulties that arise when they have younger children to look after. Rinaldi also mentions the possibilities opened up by the introduction of new media, without, however, specifying how these might be used. One can envisage possible ways of reaching today's computer-literate parents using email, texting, social networking sites, blogs and so on to keep them informed about happenings in the preschool, to follow projects as they develop and to allow them to leave comments and suggestions. A possible drawback is the danger of further disadvantaging those who do not have access to such media. One must also remember the important part played by gestures, smiles, looks and tone of voice in communication. The personal encounters that are at the heart of building meaningful relationships, and which are such a noticeable feature of early-years services in Reggio Emilia, may be supplemented but will never be completely replaced by new methods of communication.

Gestione Sociale: Social Management

In the Reggio preschools and infant–toddler centers, participation is embodied both in the everyday experience and in the formal management structures that support them. Community-based or 'social' management – *gestione sociale* – is central to the educational experience, and its goals are a fundamental part of the underlying Reggio philosophy of democracy and citizen participation.

In order to understand how this came about, one must look again at the context in which these infant–toddler centers and pre-primary schools were set up. As described in Chapter 1, the first of these preschools were built by the parents themselves, using their own hands and the rubble from buildings destroyed during the Second World War. The educational initiatives at that time begun by women's groups, unions, ex-resistance fighters and co-operatives included people from all across the social spectrum and emphasized the values of co-operation and involvement (Spaggiari, 1998). The national laws passed in 1970 governing infant–toddler centers led to community-based management and participation becoming formally enshrined in law, with the national government providing funding, the regional government taking charge of overall planning, and the municipal governments responsible for community-based management. The municipality provides the pedagogical direction and supervision. City-School Committees were set up to run the preschools, looking after administration and the setting up of new services. These later became known as Advisory Councils, with the participation of families and staff as their primary focus.

Parents and families are formally involved at two levels. First, each of the 32 schools and centers has a Community Advisory Council, including representatives of parents, teachers, educational co-ordinators, cooks, auxiliary staff and community members. Second, there is an Advisory Council Co-ordinating Board which has representatives from all the Community Advisory Councils, along with representatives from the pedagogical team and the municipal administration (Spaggiari, 1998, p. 101). However, the role of the parents in the Reggio Emilia municipal preschools goes beyond participating in management. Their participation from the beginning meant not simply the involvement of families in the life of the school but 'a value, an identifying feature of the entire experience, a way of viewing those involved in the educational process and the role of the school' (Cagliari et al., 2004).

From his experiences during the war and afterwards, Malaguzzi became acutely aware of the relationship between schools and society. He saw early childhood schools as 'agents in a great civil strategy which aims to win back society for children' (Catarsi, 2004). Rather than seeing the schools as places where children are socialized into an existing society, they become a driving force for social change. The city itself becomes transformed to meet the needs of its children. Participation in the life of the schools also empowers parents and citizens as they become aware of how they can play an active role in transforming society.

> Schools cannot be conceived of as bodies separated from a context, but as tools which are profoundly integrated with the families and their local area . . . a school which sees itself as a living part of the social fabric, and of the urban and environmental condition of the children, which is careful to see their potential . . . to steep itself in their formative processes together with the other subjects involved.
>
> (Luciano, citizen, quoted in Cagliari et al., 2004, p. 29)

New and her colleagues found, over and over again, in the course of the research mentioned above (New, 1999b; New et al., 2000), that both parents and teachers acknowledged the role of early childhood programs in helping young children to 'be together' with others. The high priority placed on children's social development reflects the Italian belief in the importance of close relationships, not just with members of the immediate family but with other citizens of their community. This is given even greater importance as families in Italy are smaller than was the case in the past and a greater proportion of the care of young children takes place outside the family setting. The Reggio Emilia preschools and infant–toddler centers pay particular attention to fostering links with the families and the communities they serve. New attributes the continued and active participation of parents in the Reggio Emilia school management councils long after their children have left the preschools to the attention paid to promoting this concept of participation. She also credits this with providing the basis for the community and financial support for early childhood programs.

The Children and the City

According to Jerome Bruner, 'You cannot understand the Reggio schools if you don't understand the city that made them' (Reggio Children, 2005, p. 2). The relationship between the preschools and the city is an interesting one. As well as the formal structures that exist, there is a sense in Reggio that the city belongs to all its citizens, including its youngest ones. The children themselves are aware of their relationship to the place in which they live and the people who live there. In Reggio, the environment is seen as 'the third teacher', after the parents and the preschool teachers themselves (Gandini, 1998). This applies not just to the immediate classroom environment but the city and its surroundings in which they live. The children frequently go out into the city as a group, explore and document it, and their contribution to the life of the city is valued. *Reggio Tutta* (Reggio Children, 2000), a guide to the city by the children of the municipal preschools, shows how they see the city not just as a collection of buildings but as a series of places that are meaningful for them. The images they portray are related to the experiences they have had there: the stone lions that they have climbed on, the markets that sell doughnuts and pasta. They see the city as a place for encounters, for meeting people, for forming relationships, for sheltering and nurturing families. Rebecca New notes how the ritual evening stroll, *la passagiata,* through the historic center of town, is a way of cementing this shared life as a community, and whole families, children included, take part in it (New et al., 2000). This close relationship between the children and the city is at once a reflection and a consequence of the emotional and structural ties that the Reggio preschools have with the municipality, which has grown out of their history and is integral to their culture.

The sense of community is also reflected in the architecture of the city and of the schools themselves – the shared life that is symbolized and embodied in the *piazza,* the public space which belongs at once to each individual and to the community as a whole. Each preschool also has a central *piazza* where children and adults from the different classes, as well as parents and visitors, can meet and mingle. This concept of the *piazza* goes beyond that of a physical space – it becomes a metaphor for the meeting of minds and the sharing of ideas and experiences.

The spirit of social solidarity that exists in Reggio Emilia means that participation goes beyond the immediate families of the children. The level of participation by the citizens is reflected in the management of the preschools at local and city level, but the support given by the municipality is not all one way. Rather it is a mutually beneficial relationship. Apart from their role in supporting parents and families and providing high quality early-years experience for children, the preschools bring many visitors to the city every year from all around the world. As the number of teachers and researchers who were interested in visiting the Reggio municipal early childhood services increased, the Municipality of Reggio Emilia, along with other interested parties, set up Reggio Children, a mixed public–private company, in 1994, to manage these pedagogical and cultural exchanges. Reggio Children collaborates with groups from all around the world to organize study visits, conferences, seminars and exchanges. The Loris Malaguzzi International Center which opened in 2007 will act as a focus for all of these, hosting exhibitions and much more, as well as being a center for research. It will also, and perhaps most significantly, be a place where children and young people can learn through play, and the children of Reggio have themselves had an input into its design.

The relationship that the preschools have established with the wider community means that citizens and businesses contribute in many different ways, including practical ones, to the life of the schools. Field trips are a regular feature of the preschools, bringing children into contact with the daily life of the city. Communal responsibility is also seen in Reggio's innovative recycling project, REMIDA, which collects unsold, rejected or discarded material such as paper, cardboard, ceramic, paints, cord, leather, rubber, wood and so on from business and enterprises and makes them available not only to the infant–toddler centers and preschools for use in their projects but to other educational and cultural organizations.

Inclusion and Integration

The dynamic relationship that exists with parents and families and the city at large is fundamental to the way in which the Reggio educators face new challenges. They look back on the history of the schools, on past debates and controversies, and see that they have achieved an understanding with people from different ideological backgrounds through this process of debate and dialogue. They see this as the way forward in establishing relationships with families from the many different nationalities who have now come to live in Reggio Emilia. Reggio has the highest proportion of foreign residents of any Italian city. In 2006, 11.4 percent of the population were from outside the European Union and 32 percent of the children of preschool age in the municipality were immigrants (Council of Europe, 2008). Integrating these newcomers of many different nationalities, religions and ethnic groups has not been without its difficulties; nor has this influx of newcomers been universally welcomed. The aim of the Reggio Municipality, however, is 'the consolidation of a pluralist society', and it has drawn up a policy on integration and interculturalism that includes the key words 'dialogue', 'inclusion', 'citizenship' and 'participatory planning':

> As (a) pluralistic and collaborative city Reggio has drafted a Policy focused on integration, inclusion and co-habitation. The aim of this plan is to support and regulate social transformations, favoring the active participation of immigrants and minorities and the dialogue of the citizens of foreign origins with local agencies and associations.
>
> (Council of Europe, 2008)

Reggio is one of ten European cities taking part in the Intercultural Cities program, a joint initiative of the Council of Europe and the European Commission. Many of the city's institutions and schools have taken on a role in this program. Given the large number of preschool children from immigrant families, it is likely that the preschools and infant–toddler centers will have a major role to play in this process of integration, inclusion and cohabitation. The potential benefits go beyond the immediate; in the past, many parents have gone from involvement in the *nidi* and preschools to wider civic involvement, and no doubt this will be the case again for some of the newcomer families through their participation in early-years services.

Children with Special Rights

Language is a powerful tool which affects the way we think about things, and nowhere is this more evident than in Reggio Emilia. Along with the discourse of citizenship, participation and inclusion, is the view that children too are citizens who have rights. While elsewhere the phrase 'children with special needs' is used, the Reggio educators prefer to speak of 'children with special rights'. The focus is not on the child as needy but rather on the child having rights to whatever will enable him or her to participate as fully as possible. Children with physical or emotional needs are given priority for admission to the *nidi* and preschools.

Support for the inclusion of children with special needs is given by a psychologist-*pedagogista*, who co-ordinates between the preschool or *nido* and those in the health or social services who deliver medical or therapeutic services to the child. An extra teacher is allocated to the class where the child is placed. This teacher works as a supplementary teacher for the whole group, rather than concentrating solely on the child who needs extra support. Ivana Soncini, psychologist-*pedagogista* with the municipal early childhood services of Reggio Emilia, describes her role in a wide-ranging interview with Cathleen Smith (Smith, 1998). She places particular emphasis on building a positive relationship with parents, and on the process of *l'inserimento* – the transition from home to the *nido* or preschool described earlier. For children with special rights, this process begins even earlier than usual. Soncini gives the example of a child with autism, where the parent and child visited the center for an entire year before the child formally began to attend. The early-years team tries to learn as much as possible about the child's habits, needs, likes and dislikes from the parents, and this extended dialogue also helps to set the pattern for future inter-actions. Together, they try to develop shared ideas about how best to enable the child to use his or her capabilities, to form relationships with peers and teachers, and to participate as fully as possible in the life of the group. The emphasis is on inclusion, while acknowledging and giving the extra help and support that the child needs. When the child has settled in, the parents are encouraged to help with classroom projects, so that they can feel that they are contributing to the well-being not only of their own child but of the class as a whole.

Documentation: 'Making Learning Visible' to Parents

The use of documentation to record, reflect on and plan for children's learning has been discussed extensively in Chapter 2. In this section, we focus on the way in which documentation is used in Reggio to share children's learning experiences with their parents and to involve them in their children's learning. Documenting, reflecting on, presenting and sharing every aspect of the children's work is a central part of the work of the Reggio teachers, but this is done in collaboration with the children and their parents. Topics for projects may emerge from the children's interests, from observ-ation of the children's spontaneous play, or from developmental or socio-cultural concerns on the part of parents or teachers, but how they are pursued is negotiated between children and teachers. During the process of compiling, assembling and reflecting on the documentation, parents are encouraged to add their comments and suggestions. As with other aspects of Reggio, there is a recognition that each has something valuable to contribute. Conscious as the Reggio preschools are of their own history, documentation and displays are retained from year to year and an archive is built up so that the children and their parents are aware of the history of their school and of the children who have attended it before them:

Even the classroom environment serves to connect children and families, past and present. Documentation panels purposefully promote the importance of children learning together, rather than highlighting the individual child. Photographic displays also consistently include examples and images of former children and their families, thereby contributing to the sense of continuity and connection between one cohort of children and those coming before and after.

(New, 1999b)

The dialogue that takes place with parents on educational matters is an essential element of the partnership that is a fundamental element of the Reggio approach. Many visitors to the Reggio preschools and infant–toddler centers have been struck by the fact that the people who escort them on their visits and who speak so knowledgeably and with such commitment about the schools and the pedagogical approach are parents rather than professional educators. At the heart of this dialogue with parents is the shared documentation of the children's experiences and thoughts. Rather than being presented with a finished product, parents are made aware of and are involved in the ongoing processes. Malaguzzi tells us that the Reggio educators wanted to find ways of communicating with parents, keeping them informed about the work of the school, in a way that would enable them to appreciate the work being done by the children:

> We wanted to show parents how the children thought and expressed themselves, what they produced and invented with their hands and their intelligence, how they played and joked with one another, how they discussed hypotheses, how their logic functioned. We wanted the parents to see that their children had richer resources and more skills than generally realized. We wanted the parents to understand how much value we placed in their children.
>
> (Malaguzzi, 1998, p. 74)

This meant that the Reggio teachers had to refine and develop their skills of observation and documentation in order to be able to share the children's daily experiences with parents and with the wider community. As parents come into the preschool, they can see the work in progress, can make suggestions or offer help. The displays, which utilize the 'hundred languages of children', offer endless possibilities for communication and dialogue. This familiarity and ease with different ways of documenting and communicating becomes even more important as the number of children from immigrant families attending the preschools and infant–toddler centers increases.

Malaguzzi tells us that this steady flow of information serves three purposes. First, it means that the teachers are constantly reviewing and questioning their work. Second, it

> ... introduces parents to a quality of knowing that tangibly changes their expectations. They re-examine their assumptions about their parenting roles and their views about the experiences their children are living and take a new and more positive approach towards the whole school experience.
>
> (Malaguzzi, 1998, p. 70).

Finally, it means that the children not only contemplate the meaning of what they have achieved themselves but that they see their parents and teachers collaborating, discussing and working together. Katz and Chard (1996) suggest that it is the sharing of children's experiences within this environment with their parents that helps to engender the enthusiastic and active support by parents which is such a notable feature of the Reggio Emilia schools and which in turn enhances the quality of the children's experience.

Putting 'Reggio' into Practice

As we have seen, the Reggio Emilia preschools and infant–toddler centers are deeply rooted in their own culture, environment and history. The close relationship that the Reggio preschools and infant–toddler centers have with the families of the children who attend them is located within a very specific social and cultural context, and this makes it impossible to 'transplant' intact to settings elsewhere which may have a very different history, purpose and ethos. The Reggio educators also resist the idea of a 'Reggio model' that can be codified, saying that it is continually developing and that people need to work out a system that relates to their own situation, history and needs. Gunilla Dahlberg and Peter Moss, both of whom have been engaging with the Reggio early-years services for a long time, say that while Reggio is not a model, a program, a 'best practice' or benchmark, we need more Reggios in the sense of other communities that are prepared to embark on local cultural projects of childhood (Dahlberg and Moss, 2007, pp. 20–1).

As we have seen, *partecipazione* in all its forms is an essential element of the Reggio Emilia approach. The partnership between home and preschool or infant–toddler center is, we would argue, one of the reasons why the excellence of the Reggio Emilia early-years services is acknowledged worldwide. While we have argued that the relationship between the municipal infant–toddler centers and preschools and the parents and community of Reggio Emilia is intrinsically related to their social and cultural setting and history, it is also the result of much work and purposeful attention to the concept of *partecipazione.*

As we have said, the Italian term *partecipazione* used in Reggio seems to carry more weight than its English equivalent. It means more than 'involvement' if we understand this to mean taking part in events or activities organized by the school, worthwhile though this may be. *Partecipazione* in practice in Reggio seems to mean something much closer to what we call partnership, which in Gillian Pugh's words is a 'working relationship that is characterized by a shared sense of purpose, mutual respect and the willingness to negotiate . . . (with) a sharing of information, responsibility, skills, decision-making and accountability' (Pugh and de'Ath, 1989, p. 6). It certainly fits well with the NAEYC's recommendation that 'In reciprocal relationships between practitioners and families, there is mutual respect, cooperation, shared responsibility, and negotiation of conflicts toward achievement of shared goals' (NAEYC, 2009, p. 23).

As the Reggio educators would recommend, we turn now to the idea of partnership itself, to reflect on why it is so significant in the context of early-years services, and to ponder on what we might learn from the Reggio experience in this regard, in the hope of identifying ways of promoting partnership with parents in our own contexts.

This concept of partnership, as Pugh and de'Ath (1989, p. 59) point out, differs radically from programs which set out to change some aspect of parents' behavior with the implicit assumption that the professional knows best. While Reggio parents acknowledge the support that they receive in their parenting role, they see it as happening in the context of shared dialogue and mutual respect (Fontanesi et al., 1998).

Partnership between parents and early-years educators has become generally accepted as a fundamental principle of high quality early-years provision. For example, it is a fundamental principle underlying *Síolta, the National Quality Framework for Early Childhood Education in Ireland* (2005), the Scottish *Curriculum for Excellence* (Learning and Teaching Scotland, 2004) and the *Birth to Three Matters* framework in England (Abbott and Langston, 2006). Communication and co-operation with parents is also a feature of the NAEYC guidelines on developmentally appropriate practice (NAEYC, 2009) as well as being a stated principle of numerous early intervention and parent support programs (Flett, 2007). The quote below from the *Síolta* website sums up the generally accepted view on partnership with parents:

Quality early childhood care and education must value and support the role of parents. Open, honest and respectful partnership with parents is essential in promoting the best interests of the child. Mutual partnership contributes to establishing harmony and continuity between the diverse environments the child experiences in the early years. The development of connections and interactions between the early childhood setting, parents, the extended family and the wider community also adds to the enrichment of early childhood experiences by reflecting the environment in which the child lives and grows.

(*Síolta*, 2005)

The first reason for this consensus is the recognition that parents are their children's first educators. It is through the loving relationships, the conversations, activities and routines that take place within the family that children first begin to learn about the world and their place in it. In these early months and years, children also begin to develop attitudes and dispositions towards learning. Ideally, as they develop their language and motor skills, they are also encouraged to develop their innate qualities of curiosity, creativity, attention and persistence, all of which will help them to learn and to grow as people.

The second reason is that there is a considerable body of research to show that children whose parents are involved with their education do better in the long run and that early-years programs that work in partnership with parents are more effective. For an overview of the relevant research, see Henderson and Mapp (2002). See also Booth and Dunn (1996), Epstein (2001), Kelleghan et al. (1993), Mendoza et al. (2003). The relationship between home and school that is established in the early years often sets the tone for later years. There is some evidence to show that parents who are involved in the early years are more likely to continue to be involved in their children's education as their children grow older (Epstein, 2001). Throughout childhood, parents continue to support their children's learning through the real-life activities they share with them, as well as by supporting the work of school. In turn, early-years services can support parents in their parenting role.

However, it is necessary to explore what we mean by 'partnership with parents'. The underlying conceptual model is important, as are the implicit assumptions about the respective roles of school and home, parents and teachers. Early-years services such as the Reggio infant–toddler centers and preschools serve two main purposes: they offer educational experiences to young children and they also offer support to parents, both in their parenting roles and through allowing them to take on paid employment.

Preschools are the most commonly available form of family support, whether or not this is their stated or primary purpose. Marion Flett (2007, p. 45) classifies parent support programs into three types:

1. The 'deficit' model which implies that parents' parenting skills and/or knowledge are deficient and that they need to be shown how to become better parents.
2. The 'involvement' model which recognizes parents as the primary educators and suggests that their children will benefit from their greater knowledge of child development and activities if they participate in programs.
3. The 'empowerment' model which acknowledges the strengths and knowledge that parents already have and enables them to build on it and to share it with the professionals.

It is this last, the 'empowerment' model, which the Reggio educators espouse, and it finds its expression in and through the elements of participation and social management that we have discussed. There is no doubt that true partnership and empowerment requires not only much thought, goodwill and planning, but also structures to enable and support it. It is often seen as an ideal rather than a reality:

> The concept of 'partnership' represents an ideal or model for parent–professional relationships, based on the assumptions that parents and programs can gather and pool their strengths and resources to make decisions and take action toward the shared goal of creating optimal situations for children.
>
> (Mendoza et al., 2003, p. 70)

Partnership is thus much more than an attempt to harness parents to serve the aims of the school or to give them a token voice in matters relating to their children's care and education. It requires a respectful and ongoing dialogue, and it requires time and space for debate. Parents and educators will not always be in agreement, but if they are in agreement that both have the best interests of the children at heart, then they are more likely to reach a solution. Partnership then can empower and benefit parents and early-years educators. Perhaps most importantly, it can also be of great benefit to children.

Through partnership, parents feel welcome in the early-years setting. They find it easier to talk to and negotiate with their children's early-years educators because they meet them often and get to know them as people.

They can share their knowledge of their children's likes and dislikes, interests and strengths, with the teachers, and they can feel that their family's values and beliefs are respected and taken into account as far as possible. They get to know more about their children's experiences in the preschool or early-years center so that they can talk to their children about it. They can also offer suggestions as to how the children's experiences might be enhanced, and they can also support and extend the children's learning at home. Finally, they can have increased confidence in their own parenting skills when the teachers and carers recognize the wealth of knowledge that parents have about their own children.

Partnership with parents also benefits early-years educators. It means that they can learn more about the children, their likes, dislikes, interests and capabilities. They can then use this information to make learning more enjoyable and rewarding. They can benefit from parents' skills and expertise and the contributions that they can make to the service. Early-years educators often have a wealth of specialized knowledge about how children learn and develop, which they can share with parents. Partnership with parents helps them to provide a more emotionally secure environment for the children. It enables educators to help children develop a sense of identity and belonging in the setting by building on their family values and beliefs, and by reflecting aspects of their home in the school setting. Finally, it helps them to provide appropriate support for children's special educational needs because they know more about them through their parents.

The greatest benefits of partnership are experienced by children. Ongoing communication between parents/families and early-years educators helps children to feel more secure and to feel that their needs will be met. Learning is more meaningful and enjoyable when children can relate it to their life at home and outside of school. For children whose home language is not that of the majority, hearing and seeing their home language being used in the early-years setting reinforces their sense of identity and belonging. For children with additional needs, or 'children with special rights', the term preferred by the Reggio educators, the involvement of parents is even more critically important. For children who may be dealing with many different professionals, it is the parents who provide continuity. It is also the parents who work together with the professionals to meet the child's needs, whatever these may be. In many cases, it is only after a long struggle by parents that the child's needs are recognized and met. Finally, partnership helps to make transitions easier for children as they move from one setting to another, as we have seen in the way that Reggio deals with *l'inserimento*, the first transition from home to nursery or preschool.

Partnership therefore involves parents, families and early-years educators working together for the benefit of children, each recognizing, respecting and valuing the contribution that the other makes to promoting the well-being, happiness, learning and development of the child. However, the exact role that each partner plays will depend on several factors. Some relate to parent and family circumstances – such as the parents' working hours, whether they have younger or older children and their other responsibilities. Participation – we will use the term in its Italian sense here, meaning involvement in the widest sense – is made easier if family circumstances are taken into account and if there is a wide range of opportunities to participate so that each person can opt for those that best suit him or her. For example, the timing of events, whether they require a daily or weekly commitment and whether there are care arrangements in place for younger children, can all affect a parent's ability to take part. Evening meetings may suit some parents, while others may find it easier to attend during the day. There also needs to be an understanding by employers of parents' needs for time off or flexible work practices to allow them to participate.

Parents' decisions to be actively involved are influenced by the way in which they are invited and by the way they are welcomed into the setting. Reggio's openness to visitors, the architecture of the buildings, the fact that the staff work as a team rather than in isolation, and the regular and obvious presence of parents, all contribute to the likelihood that parents will feel comfortable coming into the preschool or early-years center.

Conclusion

Looking at the Reggio Emilia experience of working in partnership with parents and families, therefore, we can draw some conclusions as to why it appears to be so successful a feature of their practice. An important factor in parents' decisions about involvement is their view of what is appropriate and of what their role should be. Bronfenbrenner says that 'roles have a magic-like power to alter how a person is treated, how she acts, what she does, and thereby even what she thinks and feels' (Bronfenbrenner, 1979, p. 6). Hoover-Dempsey and Sandler (1997) agree that parents' construction of the parental role affects their decision to become involved, i.e. what activities relating to their children's education do they see as important, necessary and permissible to engage in? This role construction will be shaped by the expectations of the groups to which they belong – the family, the school or the workplace. Where all of these groups are consistent in their expectations, the pressure to become involved will be strong.

Participation in early-years services is therefore not merely a decision by the individual but is shaped by the values and mores of the wider community. Through the level of public engagement with debate, the high visibility of its preschool provision and its whole ethos, the importance of *partecipazione* seems to be generally accepted by the citizens of Reggio, and it is therefore not surprising that parents see it as part of their role. Another factor is whether they perceive that the child and the school want them to be involved, as expressed in specific invitations, demands and opportunities for involvement. The Reggio preschools make sure that parents know that their involvement is expected and welcomed at every possible opportunity.

Finally, the decision to become involved is influenced by parents' own sense of self-efficacy, i.e. whether they feel that their activities will positively affect children's learning and development. Here, the Reggio preschools take a proactive approach, running workshops and talks for parents, sometimes on topics chosen by the parents themselves, to help them to learn more about how they can help their children to learn. Their contributions and ideas for the children's ongoing projects and activities are also welcomed. The involvement of parents in management at school and municipal level means that they can have a direct influence on decisions affecting not only their own children but all the children of the municipality. Parents can act as advocates not only for their own child but for the benefit of all the children, and they frequently go on to become active in other spheres.

There is no doubt that in Reggio, parents know that they are expected to be involved, that they are recognized as an important part of their children's lives and that they have a part to play in the preschool as well as in supporting their children's learning at home. This is conveyed to them from their very first contact with the preschool or infant–toddler center, and it continues through the many formal and informal occasions that are organized by parents and educators throughout the year. While many settings elsewhere recognize the importance of partnership with parents, in Reggio it is an integral part of the approach and the ethos. Parents are important to the Reggio educators, and they make sure that the parents are constantly reminded of this.

Chapter 4

Curriculum: Ideology and Pedagogy in Reggio Emilia

Introduction

The opportunities provided by any educational system emanate from the curriculum that is followed. Rugg (1936), one of the founding fathers of what is today called the field of curriculum, once referred to the word as something ugly, awkward and academic. Indeed, it still continues to be a term about which much confusion, uncertainty and obfuscation abound.

The nature of education in any society is contingent upon the salience of ideologies and their ability to attract public and professional support. Nevertheless, since educational ideologies are interrelated with others (e.g. political, social, cultural, technological), the relative prominence of any particular ideology is not necessarily a reflection of its inherent attractiveness, nor of the activities of its proponents (Kelly, 1995). Indeed, the rivalry and struggle for dominance among the ideologies can be viewed as political, since it influences the distribution, exercise and justification of power in education which 'is itself a major agency for controlling social groups' (Taylor and Richards, 1985, p. 36). Viewed from this perspective, curricula, rather than being inert syllabi or compilations of information, can be seen to have considerable cultural and political significance.

In recent decades, the preschools in Reggio Emilia have received acclaim and accolade from a world-wide audience of practitioners and academics. This has occurred against a backdrop of debate regarding the role of early childhood education in society, with the pendulum oscillating from demands for increased literacy and numeracy development, accountability and outcomes, at one end of the continuum, to calls for more child-centered, progressive and reflective practice at the other.

This chapter begins by looking at some of the main ideological perspectives that underpin the different models of early-years curricula. By isolating their key ideas and features, we hope to contextualize and evaluate the practice in Reggio Emilia preschools. Furthermore, cognizant of the fact that curriculum implementation is contingent upon training, motivation and understanding of practitioners, the final section of this chapter looks at the theory of reflective practice and its application in Reggio Emilia preschools.

As discussed in Chapter 1, in the case of Reggio Emilia the political history of the region strongly influenced what was to eventually become known as the Reggio Experience. 'Elements of past and present history and culture, such as strong regional traditions of participatory democracy; that is, citizen alliances for solidarity and co-operation . . . are fundamental to what educators in Reggio Emilia feel about their educational vision and mission' (Edwards, 1998, in Edwards et al., 1998, p. 8).

Forman and Fyfe (1998, p. 240) state that in Reggio Emilia schools 'the curriculum is not child-centred or teacher directed. The curriculum is child originated and teacher framed.' Full appreciation of this statement necessitates an exploration of competing educational ideologies and their epistemological implications.

What is the Curriculum?

Curriculum is often described in an idealistic sense, as if there were a perfect model of a curriculum against which all individual curricula pale into insignificance. Such a notion has about as much conceptual clarity as the lyrics of the Procol Harum song 'A Whiter Shade of Pale' (1967). A variant of this is the view that the curriculum is merely a syllabus, a book of instructions for teachers' use. Within such simplistic understandings, comments like 'Would you please pass me the curriculum?' fit well, since they equate the curriculum with a written prescription of what should happen in schools.

Though to many politicians, practitioners and pupils, curricula have 'an aura of permanence and inevitability' (Taylor and Richards, 1985, p. 16), the curriculum is not a concept but is, rather, a socio-cultural construction which must be viewed as arising out of a particular set of historical circumstances and as reflecting a particular social milieu. Hence, no curriculum has an *a priori* existence and 'if we scratch the surface of educational practice . . . we find not universal laws but beliefs and values' (Grundy, 1987, p. 7). The ideological perspective is thus useful in attempting to characterize the nature of current discussion in education, since educational ideologies are representative of the various clusters of values, beliefs, sentiments and understandings which endeavor to explicate the purpose of education and its relationship to society (Taylor, 1982).

Kelly (1989, p. 21) asserted that 'the school curriculum has been described as a battleground of competing ideologies'. Notwithstanding the difficulties inherent in attempting to categorize the various ideological stances, it is possible to see them as broadly falling into four main categories:

1. Category 1 could be seen to embrace the conservative model, classical humanism, religious orthodoxy and rational humanism, all of which (to varying degrees and with different agenda) view the curriculum as content and the role of education as one of transmission.
2. Category 2 could be said to include utilitarianism and instrumentalism, being concerned primarily with the vocational and economic functions of schooling.
3. The Romantic ideology, progressivism and cognitive pluralism could form Category 3, all stressing the complexity of, and necessity for, viewing and supporting education as a form of personal and social development.
4. Category 4, in essence a development of Category 3, could be comprised of the democratic ideology, reconstructionism and critical theory.

Category 1

The traditional 'classical' curriculum was based on the implicit assumption that education is linked to the symbolic control of society' (Ross, 2000, p. 101). Skilbeck (1976) states that classical humanist curricula today belong to the oldest and traditionally the most esteemed of all the curriculum ideologies. Curricula designed on this model revolve around subjects or disciplines through which the cultural content valued is formally transmitted and then assessed. Assessment is norm-referenced and externally imposed. This form of curriculum has very strong classification and equally high levels of framing (Bernstein, 1971). Strong classification means that the boundaries between the subjects are watertight and that the content of each one is well insulated from the others. Subjects are also arranged in an accepted hierarchy of value and importance. Strong framing means that both the content and the pace of learning are determined. The content-based curriculum is characterized by a 'belief in a refined cultural heritage and, until the mid-twentieth century, was seen as being reserved for the education of a relatively elite custodian class' (Ross, 2000, p. 102). Thus, the neo-classical, rationalist model of curriculum focuses on the transmission of what is deemed to be the most important and highly valued knowledge of western civilization. Smith and Lovat (1990, pp. 3–4) suggest that, from this perspective, 'curriculum should consist of permanent studies –

grammar, reading, rhetoric, logic, mathematics and the greatest books of the Western world'. Nothing, including human values, is a matter of opinion but rather one of fundamental truth (Kelly, 1995).

Kelly (1995) has argued that this is a very subtle, insidious method of social domination, a policy of controlling if not appeasing the masses, akin to the *panis circique* of imperial Rome, since the ideology to be promulgated through the education system will be that of the dominant group within society, the group which controls the system and especially the school curriculum. Thus, 'how a society selects, classifies, distributes, transmits and evaluates the educational knowledge it considers to be public, reflects both the distribution of power and the principles of social control' (Bernstein, 1972, p. 47). This institutionalization of values, it is argued, 'leads to . . . social polarization and psychological impotence' (Illich, 1971, p. 9). Furthermore, it glorifies knowledge that is highly abstract and esoteric in nature, a perspective that has resulted in hierarchies of knowledge where practical and artistic pursuits are relegated to the bottom-most echelons. It copper-fastens the dichotomy between body and mind, denouncing the former while ennobling the latter, thereby effectively making the development of any coherent theory of one's affective being virtually impossible. 'The unity of the human being is entirely lost in this account' (Walsh, 1969, p. 32). Thus, for many, '. . . Socialisation into knowledge is Socialisation into order, the existing order, into the experience that the world's educational knowledge is impermeable. Do we have another vision of alienation?' (Bernstein, 1971, pp. 240–1).

In other words, the emphasis is on states of knowledge rather than on ways of knowing; on acceptance rather than on speculation; on convergent rather than on divergent or innovative thought (Kelly, 1995). Moreover, the specific focus of this model is on universals and sameness (which underscore conformity and acceptance) which inevitably leads to a lack of appreciation of individuality and a move towards homogenization. This is a difficult pursuit when one takes cognizance of the socio-cultural complexity of life, and it supports Ross's contention that 'until quite recently, it has been axiomatic that such a cultural tradition was properly to be reserved for the relatively small elite who would require it' (Ross, 2000, p. 102).

Category 2

Product ideologies embrace what Habermas (1972, p. 211) calls the technical interest and fall within the remit of the empirical-analytic sciences and their 'hypothetico-deductive connections of propositions, which permit the deduction of law-like hypotheses with empirical content' (p. 308). He contends that the inherent attraction of this model is the amenability to minute analysis and dissection of what is viewed as knowledge. Such scientific scrutiny provides explanations from which it is possible to pinpoint regularities upon which rules can be formulated, thus facilitating control of the environment. Transferred, therefore, to an educational context, this model, through experimentation and scientific rigor, would isolate the salient features of the educative process and package them hierarchically for promulgation. Theory has, thus, a prescriptive, not a propositional relationship to practice. Put succinctly, the technical interest is a fundamental desire to control and shape the environment through rule-following action based on empirically grounded laws (Grundy, 1987).

It could be claimed that this model of curriculum design is informed by a technical cognitive interest which seeks to control pupil learning so that, at the end of the teaching process, the product will conform to the *eidos* expressed in the original objectives. This notion of teaching embodies an action similar to Aristotle's *poietike*, which is a form of action dependent upon the use of skill (or the disposition he calls *techne*) to produce a product which satisfies the craftsman's original conception (Grundy, 1987). Thus, one's flexibility in the dialogical/educational encounter is always circumscribed by the original *eidos* of what is to be created or produced, and the practitioner's efficacy is also determined by the extent to which the 'product' conforms with the *a priori* specifications.

One of the earliest proponents of this model in education was Bobbitt (1918) who argued that 'an age of science is demanding exactness and particularity [in education]' (Bobbitt, 1918, cited in Davies, 1976, p. 47, bracket added). Another pioneer of the movement was Charters (1924) who again introduced 'a scientific, behavioural, job-analysis flavour . . . (the) general purpose being to introduce into educational practice the kind of precise, scientific methods that had begun to yield dividends in other spheres of human activity and especially in industry' (Kelly, 1989, p. 51).

However, probably the best exponent of this design model, a man who systematized it into a coherent rationale, was Tyler (1949). The Tyler rationale, as it has become known, centers on four main cyclical stages which he believes are imperative in the development of any curriculum. (It is interesting to note the metaphors of construction and building in the Introduction to his work (1949, p. 1), which are indicative of the technical, product-centered approach to curriculum.) The first involves the specification and clarification of goals, i.e. what it is hoped the curriculum will achieve. These specific goals are intended to pinpoint both the type of behavior to be developed in the pupil and the area of content into which he or she is to be introduced. Closely formulated statements of intent of this nature are termed 'objectives' (as distinct from aims which are more general and non-specific – see Mager, 1962; Taba, 1962; Bloom et. al, 1956; Wheeler, 1967; Popham, 1977, for arguments regarding even more complex levels of specificity). In the light of such objectives, the learning experiences to be offered to the students are selected at stage two, and are organized (at stage three) to reinforce each other, thereby producing a cumulative effect. The final stage is that of evaluation, which investigates the extent to which the objectives have been realized in practice, in effect a quality control mechanism as was evidenced in a widespread interest in testing which dominated educational development in the United States in the 1930s. However, as has been noted by Moss (2006a, p. 108), this perspective has widespread support even today:

> A dominating discourse, inscribed with the disciplinary perspective of developmental psychology, tells us what the child should be; and an array of concepts and practices – quality, excellence, outcomes, developmentally appropriate practice to mention but a few – creates a dense network of norms and the means to ensure conformity to these norms. In this way, schools become, first and foremost, places of technical practice and normalisation.

The curricula which stem from the ideological stances of Categories 1 and 2 support the belief that education's role is to transmit and perpetuate cultural knowledge and values and/or achieve national, social, economic and political goals. In both, the practitioner assumes the role of a technician who delivers a pre-set curriculum to a passive, homogenized student body, where little, if any, consideration is given to social differences such as class, race and gender. Practitioner and pupil are disempowered – pupils seen as either receptacles to be filled with knowledge or 'materials' to be worked on; and educators who 'have no power to decide broad curriculum goals and (whose) values have no place in the curriculum' (McDonald-Ross, 1975, p. 357).

This is a foil against which the progressive, child-centered/emancipatory ideology which underpins practice in Reggio Emilia schools can be contextualized. Unlike the content and product approaches to education which prescribe the content and/or the objectives, Reggio schools do not have any formal pre-packaged 'curriculum'. They are 'against all pedagogy whose purpose is in some way to predict the result, which is a sort of predictor that pre-determines the result, and that becomes a sort of prison for the child and for the teacher, and for the human being' (Rinaldi, 2007, p. 181, quoting Malaguzzi).

Category 3

At an academic level, at least, the late twentieth century evidenced a move away from the prescription and dogmatism of content and product ideologies. It is a movement which is somewhat reminiscent of Heraclitus and Socrates, a shift away from the certainties of positivism, rationalism and universalism towards an acceptance of a more tentative, less authoritarian view of knowledge – a transformative rather than a cumulative view. Thus, 'the western/industrial world view based on certainty, predictability, control and instrumental rationality has become fractured and incoherent' (Slaughter, 1989, p. 255). The child-centered/progressive view of curriculum is underpinned by the assertion that knowledge is resultant from the creative, adaptive powers of the individual mind as it organizes experiences to form ever more complex, personal systems of understandings, intentions and recollections. Knowledge is seen as emanating from a socio-cultural matrix, wherein the individual perceives logical connections between data, categorizes experiences and infers increasingly sophisticated chains of meaning. Knowledge as reified is anathema to this orientation since it is regarded as subject to individual interpretation and is, thus, in many ways unique to every human being who, as a meaning-maker, is able to build data 'into his own scheme of things and relate it uniquely to what he already holds as experience' (Postman and Weingartner, 1969, pp. 94–5).

The child-centered view of education was a revolt against the traditional view which focused on the purveying of certain kinds of abstract knowledge and the development of rationality. Although some earlier educationalists and theorists, in an embryonic manner, were moving in this direction, it was Rousseau in the eighteenth century who first demarcated this watershed with clarity and precision. This was further developed by his successors, notably Froebel and Montessori, all of whom argued vehemently that the focus for educational planning should be the child and his or her development, and not primarily a consideration of the knowledge to be passed on or the economic or utilitarian goals to be achieved.

Earlier attempts to pinpoint precisely what this entailed were criticized on the grounds that it was all things to all people, *laissez-faire* in nature, and idealistic rather than realistic. However, there have been two major twentieth-century developments which have endowed child-centeredness with a more substantive theoretical basis. The first is the new epistemological reorientation; the second is constructivist psychology, substantiated in more recent times by medical research.

Kelly (1995) locates the emergence of the first development (i.e. this new paradigm – the epistemological revolution) in three specific historical movements. The first, existentialism, emerged in the nineteenth century in opposition to German idealism, especially that propounded by Hegel. These existential philosophers shared 'the desire to re-establish the claims of the particular against the universal, the individual against the varied kinds of collective, whether class, state or even humanity as a whole, into which rationalism and essentialism would dissolve him or her'(Kelly, 1995, p. 64).

From this perspective it is asserted, therefore, that it behoves every individual to assert his or her own existence as an individual since, according to Sartre, existence precedes essence; the individual first exists as an individual and what he or she becomes is his or her own responsibility and choice. The second historical factor to which Kelly alludes was a 'Revolution in Philosophy' (p. 65) which endeavored to establish a radical alternative to traditional, essentialist, rationalist and positivist approaches and their concomitant *a priori* metaphysically-acquired knowledge base. This new wave of conceptual clarity has led to a recognition of the fact that value assertions are fundamentally and logically distinct from scientific assertions, so that the task of moral philosophy becomes the analysis of the language of morals and of the concepts which moral language encapsulates, rather than the search for 'irrefutable moral prescriptions' (p. 66).

The third major catalyst in the evolving intellectual climate of this century was 'the particular version of empiricism which was developed by John Dewey and which he termed "pragmatism"' (Kelly, 1995). Dewey was the child of a new age of evolution, science and psychology. He was born in 1859, when Froebel's kindergarten was being transplanted in America amidst the furore caused by the publication of Darwin's *The Origin of Species*. Darwin's work (propounding a theory of evolution, growth and transformation) and Froebel's philosophy (proclaiming the sanctity and individuality of each child) profoundly influenced him. The third influence on Dewey was the University of Johns Hopkins in Baltimore. Unlike other American colleges, it had adopted an investigatory approach to learning. Finally, Dewey's educational philosophy was a response to changing social conditions in his country. Increasing industrialization and the mass influx of European immigrants together transformed rural societies into rootless urban populations which lacked the security of rural life. However, this new society was democratic, and Dewey stressed the need to adapt educational practices to suit this 'mode of associated living of conjoint communicated experience' (Dewey, 1966, p. 87). Consequently, he studied traditional methodology and assessed its validity.

What resulted was a scathing attack on traditional practice which he felt was a means of forcing children passively to accept a set of simple skills and static knowledge. Such education, with its fixed desks, book-work, subjects and immobility, was simply made for listening. According to Dewey, the traditional school was authoritarian and took little notice of advances in scientific knowledge. It failed to take cognizance of the fact that 'a society which is mobile, which is full of channels for the distribution of a change occurring anywhere, must see to it that its members are educated to personal initiative and adaptability' (Dewey, 1966, p. 88). Conventional practice not only prevented the growth of individual initiative, but its restrictive organization 'in which the conditions of the social spirit are eminently wanting' (p. 28) also stifled social education and democracy.

Dewey believed that the school curriculum in its content, organization and method should strive to meet the needs of both the individual and society. Central to his new approach was the realization that the curriculum should be child-centered. The methodological epicenter should be transferred from the subject matter to the child. Dewey draws a parallel between this change and the Copernican revolution which placed the sun at the center of the universe. The child became the sun, with education evolving around his or her own self-activity.

As an alternative to what has been termed 'the banking concept' (Freire, 1970), i.e. the idea of knowledge being passively lodged in the child, Dewey developed a theory of knowledge which he called 'instrumentalism'. Simply stated, this implies that ideas and knowledge are instruments in the process of inquiry and may be transformed in the process. Thus, knowledge is evolutionary and open to challenge and change, rather than being fixed and immutable. Allied to this is the concept of growth. The traditional viewpoint centered on the child's immaturity as justification for immersing him or her in knowledge. Dewey, on the other hand, saw immaturity as an opportunity to learn from experience. He argued that growth does not have an end but is an end in itself. Thus, education is not a matter of age, since 'living creatures live as truly and positively at one stage as at another' (Dewey, 1966, p. 51). Education then became an enterprise which supplies the conditions so as to ensure growth, irrespective of age. 'Education is a constant reorganizing or reconstructing of experience' (p. 76).

Supported by the evolutionary theory, Dewey stated that humans have acquired their superior intelligence through practical experience. He believed that such experience resulted from their efforts to overcome difficulties in the fight for survival. Consequently, he decided to transfer this pattern to the classroom environment, confronting the child with disturbing situations to foster thought and inquiry. To do so, Dewey maintained that the best methodology would be a simplified version of the scientific method, which has come to be known as 'The Problem-Solving Approach'.

Dewey's school sought to narrow the gap between the school and the home; to base all instruction in the 'Three Rs' within the background of everyday experience; to take cognizance of individual needs and aptitudes; and finally to introduce interesting subject-matter which would be of value to the child. Like Froebel, he recognized the role of the teacher as guide and stressed the unity of knowledge, stating that 'the child's life is an integral . . . He passes quickly and readily from one topic to another, as from one spot to another' (Dewey, 1966, p. 151). Children were allowed to work actively in groups, while attempting to solve a particular problem. Such inquiry often provided motivation for reading or computation – subject barriers were dissolved. This problem-solving method has developed into the more familiar 'Project Method', mainly through the writings of Dewey's associate, W.H. Kilpatrick. The project-based aspect of Reggio Emilia pedagogy, therefore, found a receptive audience in the United States.

In retrospect, Dewey can be credited with having brought the cumulative theories of his predecessors (especially those of Comenius, Pestalozzi and Froebel) into the twentieth century. It is from this summative body of knowledge that progressive, child-centered, integrated, environmentally orientated curricula have emanated. In accordance with the child's inherent proclivity to interact with and examine his or her environment, these prescribe a heuristic approach to learning, yet one that is tempered with the teacher's insight and sagacity.

Moreover, of seminal importance in the evolution of this model has been the development and refinement of the study of child development which, more than anything else, has further reinforced the critical importance of a child-centered perspective, revealing and clarifying not only how children best learn but, more importantly, how their minds develop. This work has led to the emergence not merely of a new theory of learning but, much more crucially, to a new concept of learning, one in which it is regarded in terms of the development of understanding rather than the mere acquisition of knowledge (Kelly, 1995).

Piaget (1952, 1954, 1962a, b), Vygotsky (1962, 1967, 1978) and Bruner (1968, 1972a) were the key influences in the development of this understanding – all arguing that knowledge is actively constructed through interaction between nature and culture. The role of the practitioner is to facilitate learning, by guiding and supporting the child as a co-learner. Neuroscientific research further underscores the interaction between nature and environment in the development of the brain.

Recent technological advances (e.g. Positron Emission Tomography (PET) scans and functional Magnetic Resonance Imaging (fMRI)) have dramatically changed the manner in which child development is viewed. Neuroscience has revealed that, by increasing the complexity of language and experience, the brain is changed physiologically (Jacobs et al., 1993).

This brain research is now giving an interesting new dimension to learning, by changing the focus from heredity *versus* environment to heredity *plus* environment (Kagan, 1994). This has been encapsulated by the term 'emergentism', which signifies the dynamic interplay between nature and nurture (Elman et al., 1998). Until recently, so little was known about the brain that it was sidestepped by most theorists when trying to explain intelligence. It is now acknowledged that the basic genetic composition of the brain underpins all learning and much emotional behavior. When these inherited patterns interact with the child's environment, 'plasticity' guarantees an unlimited number of interesting variations. The final pattern is determined by the way each individual uses that unique brain.

The recent developments in brain research indicate that the first years of life are critical to the brain's development. This has been succinctly encapsulated by Chugani, a neurobiologist, who states that the experiences of the first year 'can completely change the way a person turns out' (Chugani, cited in Kotulak, 1996, p. 46) and is reiterated by Kotulak (1996, p. 7) who notes that 'a kind of irreversibility sets in . . . by age four you have essentially designed a brain that is not going to change very much more'. Hence, although significant learning and development does occur after age four, much of the brain's infrastructure is now in place.

Greenough et al. (1987) contend that some systems in the brain, which they call 'experience expectant', are specifically designed to be easily activated by the type of environmental information that a member of a species may ordinarily be expected to encounter. Most human infants, for example, have sufficient visual, auditory and tactile experiences to activate circuits for seeing, hearing and touching. Although these brain cells require adequate age-appropriate stimulation, even a brief period of normal input causes connections to be formed.

Interestingly, some aspects of more complex skills like language also seem to be built into this 'experience expectant' system; the brain 'expects' to be stimulated by a set of sounds and basic grammatical rules, so these abilities are learned readily by children who have even minimal language experiences in early years. However, it is important to note that the developmental potential of experience-expectant neurons can be thwarted by inadequate stimulation during critical periods of development (see, for example, Rymer, 1993).

The open circuitry that accounts for many human learning abilities develops from connections that Greenough calls 'experience dependent'. These systems are unique to each individual's experience. For example, learning about one's physical environment, mastering a particular vocabulary, or trying to comprehend algebra means the brain must receive enough usable stimulation to carve out its own unique systems of connections between cells (Healy, 1990). The very flexibility of 'experience contingent' systems makes neural plasticity a double-edged sword. On the one hand, brains are adaptable, and immense potential for growth and development exists, yet, on the other hand, inadequate stimulation may result in atrophy.

The brain grows best when it is challenged, so an 'enriched' environment is important (Jensen, 1998, 2006). This concept of enrichment, however, differs from historical images of 'talent' or 'giftedness' and refers to 'a positive biological response to a contrasting environment in which measurable, synergistic, and global changes have occurred within the brain' (Jensen, 2006, p. 158). The correlates of such an environment include: engagement in coherent, meaningful tasks; an attentional mindset; learner-controlled feedback; repetition of tasks and opportunities for massed practice; low to moderate stress.

Challenge is important. However, the curriculum for young children needs to be considered in terms of brain-appropriate challenge. Shore (2002) suggests that children of their own volition, through particular proclivities at various stages, indicate their brains' readiness for stimulation in specific areas. Hence, 'sensitive caregiver *responsiveness* is the key' (p. 146).

Therefore, in child-centered, progressive environments, curriculum design is organic, holistic and web-like and is responsive to individual children's needs and interests. Rinaldi (1993, p. 102) encapsulates this process:

> The teachers lay out general educational objectives, but do not formulate the specific goals for each project or each activity in advance. They formulate instead hypotheses of what could happen on the basis of their knowledge of the children and of previous experience. Along with these hypotheses, they formulate objectives that are flexible and adopted to the needs and interests of the children.

In this process, both practitioner and child are empowered: the child's needs and interests determining the content and direction of learning; and the practitioner, through interaction and reflection, selecting content that 'must always be justified in terms of moral criteria relating to the "good", not simply justified cognitively' (Grundy, 1987, p. 76). In other words, *a priori* knowledge is seen as an insufficient base for curriculum planning. Instead, education is seen as a process, where the fundamental values are found in the nature of human development and its potentialities (Kelly, 1995; Blenkin and Kelly, 1988).

Category 4

> In their work, the teachers of Reggio have struggled to raise the emancipatory potential of democracy, by giving each child possibilities to function as an active citizen and to have the possibility of a good life in a democratic community.
>
> (Dahlberg and Moss, 2007, p. 10)

Critical theorists such as Apple (1979, 1980, 1982a, b) and others [see also Bernstein, 1971, 1977a, b; Young, 1971; Giroux, 1981; Freire, 1972b; Gramsci, 1971; Bowles and Gintis, 1976, 1977; Bourdieu and Passeron, 1977, 1979] have approached the curriculum from a critical perspective, arguing that the school (through the curriculum) has been utilized as an agent for the creation and recreation or reproduction of the ideological hegemony of the dominant classes and class segments of society, turning the dominant culture into a commodity or 'cultural capital' (Bourdieu et al., 1979) for domination in the curriculum, thus ensuring the perpetuation of the *status quo.*

The main proponents of these emancipatory ideologies argue that education should be harnessed to provide pupils and practitioners with the cognitive and affective skills necessary to view their problems in a reflexive perspective, thus enabling them to gain some control over their lives – in other words, the necessity 'to formulate a critical pedagogy committed to the imperatives of empowering students and transforming the larger social order in the interests of a more just and equitable democracy' (McLaren, 1989, p. xi).

According to Habermas, the approach of the critically oriented sciences incorporates the emancipatory cognitive interest, emancipation being identified with a state of autonomy and responsibility (*Mündigeit*). Although emancipation, contingent upon the act of self-reflection, is an individual matter, it also moves beyond this to a societal level since emancipation is also linked inextricably with concepts of justice and equality. Thus, a fundamental interest in emancipation and empowerment has as its corollary autonomous action arising out of authentic, critical insights into the social construction of human society (Grundy, 1987, p. 19).

Practitioners who operate within this emancipatory paradigm believe that they can work with children, families and communities to create environments that are enabling, democratic and just (Jungck and Marshall, 1992, p. 100). They are concerned with oppression, inequality, discrimination and marginalization and the socio-political and economic structures that impede the development of a wiser and more just society (Carr and Kemmis, 1986). Thus, they need to constantly question the content and methodology of their practice and the underlying values to see if any bias exists. However, critical practice moves beyond this and engages children's knowledge and voices in the collaborative explorations of what is just and unjust. Underpinning this practice is a view of children's learning being culturally constructed rather than developmentally determined. Therefore, the child's gender, ethnicity, class, language and the discourses they have access to, are all significant in their understanding of the world.

Practice in Reggio Emilia centers has evolved and developed through their interpretation of child-centered/progressive and emancipatory ideologies. The Piagetian, and especially the Vygotskian, focus on 'maturing' children actively constructing their own knowledge in an enabling, supportive environment (social constructivism), seems to co-exist with an appreciation of more culturally situated, powerful children, who have the agency to challenge and transform through discourse with adults (social constructionism)

Pedagogy and Practice in Reggio Emilia

Education in Reggio schools moves seamlessly from ideology through pedagogy. Rinaldi (2007, p. 206) notes that 'instead of formal teaching of a predetermined curriculum (writing, reading, counting, etc.) to be evaluated using some testing procedure, both teachers and children document their own daily activities and learning in symbolic systems with which they are comfortable'. The 'contextual' curriculum is determined by 'the dialogue among children, teachers and the environment surrounding them. But the emphasis on context also values participatory strategies and the possibility that not only families but the community to which the children belong could participate in curriculum' (p. 205).

Any attempt to explicate the nature of the interaction implicit in the above quotation necessitates the exploration of the key components of social constructivism and social constructionism and the progressive/emancipatory ideologies of Categories 3 and 4. These include, in particular, an appreciation of the potential of the child; an understanding of education as a process which takes as its starting point the child; an awareness that knowledge is not static but emanates from a socio-cultural matrix through a reciprocal teaching encounter; a belief that the purpose of education is towards understanding which empowers and can lead the transforming of the larger social order in the interests of a more just and equitable democracy; and a realization that autonomy and responsibility go hand in hand.

The Reggio Child

The starting point of all practice in Reggio Emilia schools is the child, and the image of the child is that of the child having rights rather than simply needs (Malaguzzi, 1993a, 1998; Rinaldi, 1993). According to Malaguzzi's Charter of Rights for Children (1993a, in Malaguzzi, 1996, p. 214):

> Children have the right to be recognised as subjects of individual, legal, civil, and social rights; as both source and constructors of their own experience, and thus, active participants in the organisation of their identities, abilities and autonomy, through relationships and interaction . . .

Hence, children should also 'have opportunities to develop their intelligence and to be made ready for the success that would not, and should not, escape them' (Malaguzzi, 1998, p. 58). The child in Reggio is seen as a unique individual, rich in resources, strong and competent, who can make his or her own meanings and influence the world. Relationships between this child and adults involve the exercise of power in and through discourse by each side. This is the social constructionist perspective (Mac-Naughton, 2003, p. 73). However, these children are also viewed as having '. . . potential, plasticity, openness, the desire to grow, curiosity, a sense of wonder, and the desire to relate to other people and to communicate' (Rinaldi, in Edwards et al., 1998, p. 114). This latter perspective is more social constructivist in nature – evocative of Froebel's contention that a child's nature is an expression of divine activity which propels him or her to strive after perfection and completeness.

From either perspective, the child is the starting point and focus of all educational planning. At first glance, this statement may appear to contradict Malaguzzi's comment regarding the absence of planning (1998, p. 89). Rinaldi offers clarification when she states that although teachers abandon 'rigid programmes and plans and excessively planned objectives . . .' (1994a), they find 'the way using a compass rather than taking a train with its fixed routes and schedules' (Rinaldi, in Edwards et al., 1998, p. 119).

Progettazione, Process and Co-construction of Knowledge

Social constructivism underpins practice in Reggio Emilia classrooms. The term 'social constructivism' is used to explain the epistemological and philosophical notion that mental activity emerges from the dynamic, transactional and negotiated relationships between individuals and the socio-cultural context (Wertsch, 1991). New (1998, p. 264) states that:

> Reggio Emilia classroom teachers, *pedagogisti*, and Loris Malaguzzi himself have focused on the processes and potentials of children's learning, the symbolic meanings assigned to that knowledge, and the ways in which adults might use such knowledge in children's best interests.

Practice in Reggio has been deeply influenced by Vygotskian theory which underscored the primary significance of the social dimension of knowledge construction which he described as a genetic law of relations among people underlying all higher functions and their relationships (Vygotsky, 1962/1986, 1978).

Indeed, Malaguzzi (1998, p. 83) stated that Vygotsky 'reminds us how thought and language are operative together to form ideas and to make a plan for action', while Staley (1998, p. 21) notes that in Reggio schools 'only as children articulate to others that which they believe to be true do they come face-to-face with errors in their thinking'.

Through individual, large and small group activities, questioning and discussion, teachers and children learn together to 'co-construct knowledge' (Malaguzzi 1993b; Rinaldi 1998a). As discussed in Chapter 3, this educational process is further enriched by collaboration with families and the broader community.

Exploration of the compass metaphor brings one clearly into the realm of 'process' and *progettazione*. *Progettazione* is a word that conveys a complex network of hypotheses, observations, predictions, interpretations, planning and exploration. It refers to the process of adult thought, reflection and dialogue that precedes the development of a project as teachers try to anticipate all the possible ways the activity could develop based on the likely ideas and choices of the children. It further refers to the process of following the activity in extended investigations, accommodating changes and unanticipated directions. (Fraser and Gestwicki, 2002, p. 303).

Although children in Reggio schools engage in free play, group games, singing, cooking, rest, story-telling, drama and mealtime together, much of the contextual curriculum revolves around projects that involve children as navigators on a journey from hypotheses through discoveries using language and number. Children are afforded the opportunity to explore, observe, discuss, question, represent, and then proceed to revisit their initial observations and hypotheses in order to further refine and clarify their understandings (Forman and Fyfe, 1998).

When Malaguzzi was questioned about the sources of inspiration for the philosophy of the centers in Reggio Emilia, he listed some 25 names, among them John Dewey (Edwards et al., 1998). The legacy of Dewey's philosophy, as discussed above, is clearly visible in the process of *progettazione* and is evocative of Spodek and Saracho's claim that in innovative approaches we must 'understand that [often] we stand on the shoulders of giants' (2003, p. 4, bracket added)

Furthermore, the key features of *progettazione* would appear to be totally consistent with neuroscientific findings regarding brain enrichment. Jensen (2006, p. 72) contends that 'random, useless tasks will create little or no change in the brain', as children get bored or irritated. 'They have to buy into the task.' Once children's innate curiosity is harnessed, so is their concentration which is vital as 'the more a student's mind wanders, the less the rate of change'. Equally important is the nature and timing of social exchanges and feedback between learner and collaborator. 'If the feedback is too general, too fast, or too irritating, the learner will become distressed and success will drop. Ideally, subjects should be able to adjust the level and type of feedback' (p. 73). The child's level of empowerment and his or her perception of the degree of choice or control he or she is afforded is equally significant, 'otherwise, the stress from that loss of control may neutralize the positive effects from the learning' (p. 72). Children also need opportunities to strengthen or reinforce the new connections in the brain that result from new learning. Ideally, this would involve 30–90 minutes daily, three to five times a week. 'This length of practice is critical or the brain won't change much' (p. 73). Indeed, Malaguzzi confirmed this when he noted that:

> Ours is a genetic–constructivist and creative perspective. We believe that the brain is not imprisoned by genes, that thought can be modified in as much as it interacts with the environment, and that intelligence is the result of the synergistic co-operation of the various parts of the brain.
> (Malaguzzi, 1996, pp. 29–30)

The onus is upon the practitioner to gain an in-depth knowledge of each individual child so as to maximize that child's understanding and powers of critical reflection upon which moral and value judgments are predicated.

In this way, education strives to bring to fruition the developmental potential of every child to 'function as a human being, that is, as a creature with the greatest possible control over his or her own destiny and thus with the widest practicable range of options and possibilities open to him or her' (Blenkin and Kelly, 1996, p. 10). Thus,

> A process model [of curriculum development] rests on teacher judgement [i.e. knowing when and how to intervene to maximize understanding], rather than teacher direction [in the form of prescription]. It is far more demanding on teachers and thus far more difficult to implement in practice, but it offers a higher degree of personal and professional development.
>
> (Stenhouse, 1975, p. 95, brackets added)

The term 'mediating variable' has been used for understanding how students learn (e.g. Doyle, 1978; Lowyck, 1986; McDonald, 1988; Peterson, 1988). This stresses the role of the learner in 'determining *what* is processed, *how* it is processed, and, therefore, *what* is learned' (Doyle, 1978, p. 171). Built on the concept of a reciprocal teaching encounter, it highlights how the teacher must constantly adjust to the student's changing needs, interests and understandings – a task which necessitates a flexible concept of curriculum. Therefore, while consistent with Piagetian theory, this is not as circumscribed by orthodox views of stage determinism and thus presents a more highly developed constructivist view of knowledge (Resnick, 1989).

Vygotsky speaks about the 'meditational means' which are the shapers of the particular type of sense one makes of the world. He argues that intellectual development cannot adequately be understood in epistemological terms which specify the nature of the knowledge to be acquired nor solely in psychological terms which focus on some supposed inner and spontaneous developmental process. 'Rather, he understood intellectual development in terms of the intellectual tools, like language, that we accumulate as we grow up in a society and that mediate the kind of understanding we can form or construct' (Egan, 1998, p. 5).

This was what Bruner had in mind when he spoke of the 'educational process . . . providing aids and dialogues for translating experience into more powerful systems of notation and ordering' (Bruner, 1966, 1968, p. 21).

Though Dewey saw education as a continuous process rather than goal-directed activity, he also realized the necessity for Rinaldi's 'compass'. Indeed, he argued that teachers and children must establish aims, albeit flexibly, so that they recognize that engagement in the activity will give them greater understandings and insights than they had when embarking on the journey. Activity which originates with the child, to be scaffolded and guided by the teachers, leads to interest, engagement and ultimately understanding. 'If we can discover a child's urgent needs and powers, supply an environment of materials, appliances, and resources – physical, social and intellectual – to direct their adequate operation, we shall not have to think about interest. It will take care of itself' (Dewey, 1913, pp. 95–6).

Malaguzzi (1998, p. 83) echoes this belief, stating that the 'aim of teaching is to provide conditions for learning'. As discussed in Chapter 2, the teachers take each child as their beacon but offer ideas, opinions and support while suggesting potential avenues for development.

This reframing of interests into activities and experiences is not capricious. Activities and experiences must have substance, significance and depth; they must be suited to a wide range of developmental levels; they must build on the children's existing knowledge through disciplined thought and emotional and imaginative engagement; and they must be presented in concrete and challenging ways, and lead to the discovery of the connection of things.

Nevertheless, while the basic orientation of practice in Reggio Emilia centers appears to be social constructivist, their focus on meaning-making and understanding (Habermas, 1972, p. 310) moves them in the direction of social constructionism. This type of understanding 'is grounded in the fundamental need of the human species to live in, and as part of, the world, not to be – as it were – in competition with the environment for survival' (Grundy, 1987, p. 13). This interest in understanding, tolerance, co-habitation and co-operation moves one broadly into the moral sphere. The development of knowledge through understanding and meaning-making falls within the remit of the historical–hermeneutic sciences (i.e. the interpretative agendas of sociology and some branches of psychology and historical and literary interpretation). It is argued that hermeneutical understanding is a pre-eminent form of knowledge upon which action can proceed. Rather than merely claiming that knowledge and application of sets of rules is a sufficient basis for action (as asserted by both the rationalist and positivist ideologies), this perspective stresses the importance of reflection on and scrutiny of both the meaning of the rules and the situation in which they are to be applied prior to acting on them (see, for example, Gadamer, 1977; Ricoeur, 1979).

Once knowledge is redefined as a process of making meaning of the world, then education changes from mere transmission to what Eisner

(1993) describes as 'invention'. In similar vein, Buber (1980) refers to the 'critical reflective encounter' while, for Freire (1972), knowledge involves a constant unity between action and reflection upon reality. Thus, knowing and understanding become a process through which the educator invites the learner to recognize and then critically unveil reality, this *dénouement* contained in the dialectic movement from action to reflection and from reflection upon action to new action.

Knowledge which is concerned with understanding is not to be judged according to the success of the operations arising as a consequence of that knowledge, but rather according to whether the interpreted meaning facilitated the process of discerning how to act rationally and morally (Grundy, 1987). Such knowledge is neither objective nor is it acquired objectively. Rather, it is a subjective knowledge, acquired and developed through interaction with the environment, whether human or organic. In other words, this is an 'interest in understanding the environment through interaction based upon a consensual interpretation of meaning' – a process through which student and teacher interact with a view to making meaning of the world (Grundy, 1987, p. 14).

The type of interaction inherent in this process is akin to what Aristotle called *phronesis* – phronesis being the disposition from which emanated practical judgement and knowledge 'which is "owned" by the actor' (Grundy, 1987, p. 61). It is difficult to capture the essential nuances of this Greek word, but, according to Gadamer (1979), it is essentially a combination of knowledge, judgment and taste – the guiding *eidos* being the 'good': 'It constitutes a special way of knowing. It belongs in the area of reflective judgement . . . Both taste and judgement are evaluations of the object in relation to the whole to see if it fits with everything else, whether, then, it is "fitting"' (p. 36).

According to Rinaldi (2007, p. 125), this requires a 'powerful' teacher, the only kind of teacher suitable for our equally 'powerful' child. School thus becomes a place of research where the children, along with the teachers, are the primary researchers. With respect to the essentials of the reciprocal teaching encounter, Rinaldi lists observation and documentation (see Chapter 2). However, she also emphasizes the importance of recognition (*ri-cognizione*). This does not simply mean 'gathering' thoughts but the enrichment of one's own knowledge through the knowledge of others.

The Role of Conflict

However, for social exchanges to result in collaborative cognition, socio-cognitive conflict and a resultant desire for its equilibration are considered necessary within the Reggio Emilia model. Piaget, Vygotsky and Dewey all shared this stance. Rogoff (1990, p. 186) states that socio-cognitive conflict is part of children co-constructing an appreciation of 'the meanings and rules of serious life'. Vygotsky also stressed the adaptive function of this collaborative cognition – where exchanges of differing views lead to 'a higher plane of thinking' (Berk and Winsler, 1995, p. 12).

Thus, when children collaborate with others, especially with more knowledgeable or skilled partners, they can achieve a higher level of cognitive functioning. Vygotsky terms the range of ability between what children can achieve on their own and what they can achieve when assisted by others as the Zone of Proximal Development. Malaguzzi (1998, p. 84) maintains that where there is a very small gap between what the child and adult see and where the child shows an 'expectation and readiness to make the jump (then) the adult can and must loan to the child his judgement and knowledge. But it is a loan with a condition, namely, that the child will repay.'

Practitioners in Reggio schools accept that the co-construction of knowledge may involve discord, debate and conflict – these are celebrated and valued. Malaguzzi noted that 'even when cognitive conflicts do not produce immediate cognitive growth, they can be advantageous because by producing cognitive dissonance, they can in time produce progress' (1993b, p. 12).

Rinaldi, similarly, saw conflicts and the recognition of difference as critical and not only part of the process of socialization and cognitive development but also as 'an essential element of democracy – [and] the driving forces for growth' (1998a, p. 118). The notion of conflict is totally consistent with the Reggio idea of knowledge which Malaguzzi likens to a 'tangle of spaghetti' (1998). Hence, 'learning does not proceed in a linear way, but rather is constructed through contemporaneous advances, standstills, and "retreats" that take many directions' (Rinaldi, 2007, pp. 131–2). In this way, learning is seen as a spiralling process in which thoughts and opinions are expressed, reflected upon, revisited and re-expressed as all parties consolidate their feelings and understandings.

The Reflective Practitioner in Reggio Emilia

The problems and deficiencies of teacher education are frequently aired (see Hargreaves and Fullan, 1992; Furlong and Maynard, 1995; Hargreaves, 2002; Deegan, 2008). They range from a criticism of the lack of reflective thinking in teacher education to a call for an exclusive, or almost exclusive, concentration on the basic skills of teaching, most of it taking place in schools. Much of the criticism is connected with aspects of teacher education: the tension between theory and practice, the 'washing out' of the effects of teacher education in the teaching situation, and the low ratings given by teachers to most aspects of their education, with the exception of practice teaching.

A recurring argument in recent years is that professional education should take place much more in a reflective–practicum situation and concentrate more on developing the problem-solving abilities of students. Howey and Strom (1987) stress that the changing and complex nature of the societal, community and social setting in which teachers must be competent to operate, makes particular demands on their knowledge and powers of adaptability. Since the shape of the future is unknown, student teachers, it is argued, must be given the mental tools needed to meet professional tasks in ways that are adaptive, questioning, critical, inventive, creative and self-reviewing. They contend that 'without knowledge, derived from and open to rational enquiry, teaching (no matter how 'good' the intention) becomes whimsical, non-rational and irresponsible' (p. 8). They are critical of the pedestrian, technical conception of teaching that is prevalent in some of the literature and discussions on teaching. Reflective decision-making ability, they claim, is an essential prerequisite to professionalism and should be at the core of teacher education and, indeed, of all professional preparation.

Pre-service and In-service Education in Italy

Since 1998, teachers in Reggio Emilia are required to undergo a four-year concurrent university degree. This course is run simultaneously for both pre-primary and primary teachers who share the first two years of study. Years three and four are specialized. The curriculum includes psychology, social anthropology, pedagogy, teaching methodology, hygiene–medical and skills related to school integration of students with disability, drawing and other figurative arts, music and sound communication, language and literature, maths and informatics, and physical, natural and environmental sciences. Teaching practice is included from year one.

In 2004, Directive no. 47 established the priorities of in-service training for teachers which include university specialization courses, professional training initiatives promoted by accredited bodies and updating of information technology. Teachers can take five days annual leave for participation in such courses.

Every year, the Ministry for Education in Italy issues the directive to define the priority objectives for the annual plan of teacher in-service training. Organization of the courses can vary but must follow three categories: in-classroom lectures, study cases, simulations and various types of exercises; action research; e-learning (www.eurydice.org).

Teachers in Reggio Emilia schools each do about 190 hours of work outside the classroom annually. This includes 107 hours of in-service training, 43 hours of meetings with parents and committees, and about 40 hours for other seminars, workshops, school celebrations, and so on (Filippini, 1998, p. 130).

The Role of the Teacher in Reggio Emilia

Teachers in Reggio Emilia have been described in many ways, including protagonists (Rinaldi, 1993), provocateurs (New, 1991), partners, nurturers, guides (Edwards, 1998), and classroom ethnographers (New, 1994a). They also assume the roles of collaborator and co-learner with children and their families (Rankin, 1993; Edwards, 1998; Gandini, 1997a). Gandini noted that 'teachers consider themselves to be partners in this process of learning' (1997a, p. 19). Thus, teachers are not seen, nor do they see themselves, as omniscient pedagogues or experts whose task it is to dispense knowledge. Rather, the role of the teacher becomes one that can be shared by all members of the group. Malaguzzi (1998, p. 68) uses the metaphor of a ping-pong match to describe the relationship – both players, adult and child, needing to shift and adjust in order to allow for and advance optimal growth and learning. Edwards and Raikes (2002) liken this to expanding a relationship dance where the educator gradually can encourage the child to experiment with more complex moves, tempos and partners. According to Edwards (1998), this relationship must be a supportive, caring, accepting and nurturing one where the teacher is physically available and accessible.

Facilitating children's learning in the light of their questions, proclivities and current understandings also means that the teacher assumes the role of researcher (Edwards et al., 1993; Malaguzzi, 1993d). Rinaldi (2006, p. 102) claims that pedagogy implies choices and that 'choosing means having the courage of our doubts, of our uncertainties, it means participating in something we take responsibility for'.

A pedagogy of listening, observing, suggesting, questioning, challenging and guiding is one of the hallmarks of the classroom environment in Reggio (Edwards, 1998; Forman and Fyfe, 1998). Allied to this is the process of documenting the process of learning. This focuses intently on the thoughts, questions, reflections and ideas of the children – giving insights into their understanding and emotion. Gandini (1997a) states that this is a critical part of the learning and qualitative assessment process, facilitating the development and planning of the curriculum and conversation with parents and *pedagogisti*. As discussed in Chapter 2, authentic assessment and documentation allow for children's learning and development to be captured in multiple forms (the '100 Languages of Children': Edwards, Gandini and Forman, 1998a). It is the teacher's role to make visible the process of learning and interpret the ways in which the children construct knowledge.

Moss (2006b, p. 2) contends that 'The process of evaluation then becomes ethical rather than technical, inherently subjective and provisional, a collective question that is both essential and unanswerable. Pedagogical documentation provides a tool for evaluation as democratic meaning making.'

Interestingly, Rinaldi (2007) discusses how the process of documentation and the ensuing collaboration by all parties also reveals the teacher's limitations. 'So, it's more and more visible – your limits and your vision about the child . . . You don't show the child, but the relationship and the quality of your relationship, and the quality of your looking at him or her. That is why it's so dramatic because the king is naked!' (p. 196).

Thus, the context in which pedagogical documentation is carried out is crucial. 'If it's an individualistic and competitive context or if it's a context that places value on dialogue, negotiation and interdependency' (Dahlberg, in Rinaldi, 2007, p. 196).

In Reggio Emilia, dialogue, negotiation and interdependency converge through the process of reflective practice – a process in which they have engaged for over four decades and which 'forecast the premises now put forward by contemporary writers on teacher development and reflective practice' (New, 1998, p. 276).

Reflective Practice

The central premise of the paradigm of reflective practice is that meaning is constructed and it relies heavily on the work of the German philosophers Habermas (1971, 1972, 1979) and Gadamer (1977, 1979). It thus acknowledges the fact that students at pre-service level, like any other subgroup of society, are not homogenous but, rather, bring with them their multifaceted life experiences (racial, ethnic, gendered, etc.) which, in turn, influence their experiences of teacher education programs. Therefore, irrespective of the commonality of specified formal pre-service curricula, they are experienced differently at an individual level (Gomez, 1992). Much of the emerging popularity of the concept of the 'reflective practitioner' in modern education is as a result of Schön's seminal works (1983, 1987, 1990a, b, 1995). Arguing that professional schools are dominated by an over-reliance on convergent thought in an effort to provide neat, prescriptive answers to often extremely complicated situations, he states:

> How comes it that in the second half of the twentieth century we find ourselves in our universities, embedded not only in men's minds but in the institutions themselves, a dominant view of professional knowledge as the application of scientific theory and technique to the instrumental problems of practice?
>
> (1995, p. 30)

Professional action, as he sees it, is more akin to 'professional artistry' which is the type of competence practitioners display in unique, uncertain and conflicting situations of practice. This is grounded in, and draws heavily from, the 'repertoire of examples, images, understandings and actions [of] the whole of his experience in so far as it is accessible to him for understanding and action' (p. 38). The professional's relation to activity is, therefore, always transactional; in other words, the situation is shaped by the practitioner but he or she is also transformed by his or her encounter with the situation. Schön delineates two forms of reflection – 'reflection in action' and 'reflection on action'.

'Reflection in action' refers to those moments when a practitioner responds to a problematic situation, drawing intuitively on his or her relevant prior knowledge, tacit understandings and personal theories of teaching and learning. As the term suggests, this type of reflection happens 'in action' or concurrent with the evolving situation.

'Reflection on action' refers to the retrospective evaluation and review by the practitioner of the teaching encounter. This can be undertaken individually or collaboratively. In Reggio Emilia schools, the latter is prevalent. Often these teaching encounters will have challenged aspects of the practitioner's conceptual framework and created a level of cognitive dissonance which allows for new or expanded understandings to form.

According to Barrow (1990), Schön's thesis has been misinterpreted and used to justify the rejection of traditional theory by practitioners, which is an erroneous claim since in order to reach conclusions other than 'This works', a conceptual framework is required within which such cogitation can be undertaken.

Similarly Giroux (1981) stated that student teachers must draw upon as many forms of knowledge as possible to begin their journey of understanding. If teachers are expected to move beyond a reliance upon the acquisition and refinement of traditional practice into a mode of work which allows for the exercising of autonomous judgment, then certain prerequisites/co-requisites are vital. These have been identified by Carr and Kemmis (1986) as those relating to knowledge, control and action. 'First the attitudes and practices of teachers must become more firmly grounded in educational theory and research. Secondly, the professional autonomy of teachers must be extended . . . Thirdly, the professional responsibilities of the teacher must be extended' (p. 9).

The promotion of democratic citizenship in Reggio Emilia preschools by involving parents and community in choices and decisions regarding policies, curriculum and management is impressive. However, the development of such a learning community is contingent upon practitioners creating professional identities that are receptive to challenge, questioning and the existence of multiple perspectives. In this, the process of reflection is vital.

Reflective discussions range from conversations with children, co-teachers, *atelierista*, *pedagogista*, the whole school staff, to parents and experts in the community. Additionally, practitioners engage in workshops designed for particular types of teachers and large assemblies of teachers from the municipality. According to Edwards (1998, pp. 189–90), teachers and staff offer one another emotional support, encouragement and advice as part of this process. However, she further highlights the mutual criticism and self-examination which attend the atmosphere of open and frank communication. '. . . they (teachers) readily accept disagreement and expect extended discussion and constructive criticism; this is seen as the best way to advance'.

Implicit in the above model of 'interactive collegial relationship' (Rinaldi, 1994a) is trust: teachers who trust themselves and have the confidence to admit their uncertainty; teachers who trust each other, children, support staff and parents; and teachers who are trusted by all participating parties. Rinaldi (2006, p. 105) has said that Malaguzzi 'never concealed his great aspirations, hopes and expectations of teachers . . . (since) . . . trusting in children meant and means trusting in teachers'.

Therefore, at the core of the Reggio Emilia approach is an appreciation of the fact that practitioners learn not only by reflecting in isolation on their practice but also through relationships and conversations with trusted others. These others 'look for the knowledge that teachers are already using and reflect it back to them, making teachers' own stories, rather than established authority, the starting point for learning' (Jones, 1993, pp. xviii–xix). Through this process, theory and practice co-exist, and teachers become critically conscious of the complexity of teaching and learning – their own and the children's. In this respect, Rinaldi (2007, p. 93) argues that 'education is a difficult job because it means, above all, reflecting on and talking about ourselves, our taboos, silences, hypocrisies, fears, about our real feelings and emotions regarding children – our children – and ourselves'. The real challenge here is bringing to light through awareness and reflection personal, frequently hidden biases.

Recognition of difference is the first step for critical educators who strive to create environments that will facilitate children's critical reflection in their world and their ability to act to transform injustices in it. Educators must then use dialogue with children to develop their capacity to reflect critically. Browne (2004, p. 50), however, argues that 'Critical analysis of both the theories underpinning the "Reggio Approach" and the day-to-day practice in the infant and toddler centres and preschools certainly suggests that in some instances a disjunction exists between the theory and the practice.' In particular, she refers to the unquestioned, uncontested acceptance by practitioners of traditional gender discourses and gender power relations. Therefore,

> . . . despite the rhetoric about Reggio pedagogical methods attaching importance to the role played by 'interactional qualities' in helping children to develop their self-identity (Rinaldi, 2001, p. 40) it would appear that the adults in preschools are not concerned about helping the children to think critically about the dominant discourses that are shaping their understanding of gender.
>
> (p. 53)

Exercising professional autonomy requires a high degree of self-awareness, since we are all the product of our own culture and upbringing. In Reggio, though the teachers 'have struggled to raise the emancipatory potential of democracy' (Dahlberg and Moss, 2007, p. 10), it is obvious that this process is, and needs to be, ongoing.

Conclusion

> Relationship is the primary connecting dimension of our system, however, understood not merely as a warm, protective envelope, but rather as a dynamic conjunction of forces and elements interacting toward a common purpose.
>
> (Malaguzzi, 1998, p. 68)

Above all, Reggio Emilia schools are viewed as public spaces and sites for ethical and political practice 'where relationships combine a profound respect for otherness and difference with a deep sense of responsibility for the other, places of profound interdependency' (Dahlberg and Moss, 2007, p. 10). The notion of education as relationship brings into sharp focus particular forms of democratic participation and community.

Edwards (1995) explores community from a variety of perspectives: the moral community (as put forward by Piagetian educators, DeVries and Zan, 1994); the community of enquiry (as outlined by Kennedy, 1994), and the community of learners (discussed by Vygotskian cognitive–anthropologist, Rogoff, 1994). The Moral Community theory is based on the cognitive–structural theories of moral development and education of Kohlberg (1976) and Piaget (1932). By focusing on the social life of the classroom and optimizing interaction among and between the teacher and children, the teacher establishes a socio-moral atmosphere 'where social relationships are characterised by relative equality and by the reciprocity conducive to decentering and perspective-taking' (Edwards, 1995, p. 5). While acknowledging that 'these notions are surely similar to Malaguzzi's views', she further pinpoints the limitations of a constructivist model of learning – its focus on the promotion of the morally autonomous individual, and its notion of community as only encompassing children and practitioners.

The Community of Inquiry, suggested by Kennedy (1994), is 'conceptualized as participatory, transactional and transformative – based on interaction, dialogue and collaboration among meaning-makers' (Edwards, 1995, p. 6) and Kennedy's writings show 'the high level philosophic discussions that can take place among teachers and very young children . . . (within) a supportive classroom context'. However, though the community of inquiry shares the social–constructivist orientation of the Reggio Emilia model, it 'is not sufficient by itself to create such a transformed community; inquiry is only one dimension of the larger work of community-building which must take place across all domains of school life' (p. 6).

Rogoff's contribution regarding the community of learners suggests that children's construction of knowledge takes place through their apprenticeship to the rites, rituals and routines, as well as the possibilities inherent within a classroom, a family or a society (Rogoff, 1990). Through a process of guided participation, adults provide guidance, support, challenge, direction and impetus. However, 'as participants move from being newcomers to being experienced members of the community, they take a more and more active role in managing their learning and co-ordinating with others' (Edwards, 1995, p. 8).

Knowledge acquisition and knowledge itself are both distributed/ stretched across culturally-provided tools and discursive practices (Rogoff, 1990, 1998a; Hatch and Gardner, 1993). In the distributed view, learning is seen as transacted, or 'jointly composed' (Salomon, 1993, p. 112) where solo and distributed cognitions interact, affecting each other, developing each other and changing over time. Learning is described as being 'appropriated' in authentic cultural contexts which define these as communities of practice where 'the focus is on understanding processes of participation in shared activity' (Rogoff et al., 1993, p. 533).

However, this view of learning begs the question: what type of participation do contemporary democratic societies need and want for their citizens?

Historically, the Reggio Emilia approach is situated in and emerges from 'a time when after the anti-Fascist resistance and the war, the harshest spirit of Marxist tradition encountered and came into collision with the humanist, critical and open left-wing, the left-wing of dialogue' (Mantovani, 2006, p. 114). Malaguzzi claimed that this propelled them to give 'a human, dignified, civil meaning to existence, to be able to make choices with clarity of mind and purpose, and to yearn for the future of mankind' (Malaguzzi, 1998, p. 57). The earlier chapters of this book have shared practical examples of the strong civic community of Reggio Emilia in operation with multiple layers of horizontal participation, co-operation and reciprocity. Putnam's (1993) research further underscores 'the deep reserves of "social capital" in this part of Italy, produced by, and productive of, trust, mutuality, co-operation and other social values' (Moss, 2007, p. 133).

Moss (2006b) argues that the field of early childhood is increasingly dominated by the Anglo-American discourse of instrumental rationality and technical practice. This discourse, embedded in the ideologies of Categories 1 and 2, is located in a neo-liberal political and economic context and 'is highly instrumental and calculative in rationality [viewing] early childhood education and care as a technology for social stability and economic success. Early childhood institutions are understood, first and foremost, as places of technical practice' (pp. 1–2, brackets added).

In Reggio Emilia, ethics are viewed primarily as relational and linked to responsibility and inter-dependence. There is a move away from the narrative of modernity and its preoccupation with objectivity, mastery and universality. 'As such, Reggio Emilia serves as one of the islands of dissensus (*sic*) that can disturb the complacent flow of the dominant discourse' (pp. 1–2).

It is clear that in Reggio Emilia, politics and ethics have interacted synergistically to create an approach to education which moves beyond the ideologies of transmission and production. Nevertheless, 'many educators are perplexed by the lack of empirically-derived data with which to validate Reggio Emilia's practices' (New, 1998, p. 278). Though the qualitative nature of reflection and documentation, as the primary means of research and evaluation, is consistent with the progressive and emancipatory ideologies which are espoused, some academics and policy-makers continue to ask for studies 'that would measure lasting child-related outcomes and evaluate program quality based on external criteria' (Edwards, 2002). Edwards suggests a variety of qualitative and quantitative methods which could be used to supply 'a new kind and level of information' to validate the effectiveness of the approach and analyse its strengths and weaknesses. In similar vein, Katz (1999) questions the widespread, unquestioned, uncritical acceptance of Reggio Emilia practices in the United States. The Reggio community would take serious issue with the validity and usefulness of such research. However, notwithstanding the above criticism, it is evident that Reggio Emilia ideology and pedagogy offers 'a kaleidoscope which mirrors and in which we can be mirrored' (Rinaldi, 2006, p. 105).

Chapter 5

A Discursive Analysis of Reggio Emilia

Introduction

Citation indexes, exhibitions of the 'Hundred Languages of Children', study tours to Reggio Emilia's educational institutions, conference brochures, journal articles, book chapters, books, electronic lists, audio-visual resources, and blogs testify to the popularity of the Reggio approach in education and to the enthusiasm, even fanaticism, with which it is embraced internationally. 'Reggio Children', a limited company, was founded in the early 1990s to disseminate Reggio ideas and practices through study tours, exchange initiatives, development courses for children's centers, educational institutions, teachers and parents (Municipality of Reggio Emilia, 2000). Reggio Emilia is certainly on the map!

'Midst the multitude of books about education issued these days, few stand out. This book that you hold in your hands does.' These are the first two sentences of Howard Gardner's Foreword to what is probably the best known among the above resources on the Reggio Emilia approach: *The Hundred Languages of Children: The Reggio Emilia Approach – Advanced Reflections* (Edwards et al., 1998). This particular resource is widely cited and we have drawn extensively on it already in this volume. Referring to the various Reggio exhibitions that have been mounted and the films and videos that have been made, Gardner advises readers of the benefits of visiting Reggio Emilia: 'There is no substitute for a visit to Reggio Emilia, and without a doubt, the publication of this book will increase traffic to the lush and civilized Emilia Romagna area' (Gardner, 1998a, p. xvi). The promotional language promising pleasure, beauty and 'high culture', arguably more in the style of a holiday travel book than a professional book on education, is inseparable from the messages about pedagogy that this Reggio text is communicating.

Earlier chapters of this book have presented and analysed the origin, principles and methods associated with the 'Reggio Experience'. This chapter seeks to understand how the so-called 'unique approach to early childhood education' (Gardner, 1998a, p. xv) is represented in the considerable literature that has been published and circulated so widely across nations and continents. The chapter explores the practices and perspectives in relation to children and childhood that are valorized, rendered significant, and favored. But crucially it examines the rhetorical mechanisms that are used in the Reggio literature to produce the 'preferred' meanings that readers are expected to construe for themselves as they read the prose, view the pictures, videos, slides, and of course interpret their experience of visiting Reggio centers. Such analytic work is useful in helping us understand something of the Reggio 'movement', particularly its capacity to recruit so many subscribers, followers and loyal disciples all over the world.

This chapter sets out to answer two overarching questions:

1. What are the powerful and dominant discourses of the Reggio movement?
2. What symbolic resources and rhetorical devices are used to establish the legitimacy of those discourses?

These questions can be broken down into the following, more specific questions:

- How is learning talked and written about?
- How is childhood framed?
- How are educators perceived and their roles defined?
- What assumptions are made about appropriate childhood experiences?
- What might be both liberating and constraining about the Reggio practices that are endorsed?

It is important for us to explain the orientation we are adopting and the assumptions underlying our analytic approach here. We are influenced by several post-structuralist writers (Foucault, 1991; Locke, 2004; MacLure, 2003; Gee, 1999) who have furnished researchers with conceptual tools for analysing practices, policies, perspectives, theories, and, in this case, linguistic representations of Reggio's principles and practices. A key assumption for us is that meanings are constructed, as opposed to given, and so we are interested in making visible how meanings in the published material on Reggio are produced. Such an approach makes it easier to examine and challenge those constructions and so resist the intended meanings any text is inviting one to accept. We are recognizing that language is not transparent and that it doesn't describe an objective reality 'out there'. Language is never neutral or innocent, rather we subscribe to the view that in describing the world, language simultaneously creates it. In this sense we are claiming that Reggio texts talk, write and draw Reggio into life, into being.

This means that, in addressing the above issues and questions, we are interested in all of the following: what is not said as well as what is said, the constraints on what is sayable; the cultural scripts or discourses drawn upon; the legacies or histories of discourses that are deployed; the ways in which ideas are recruited, used, endorsed, rejected, reconstituted; the kind of claiming evident in relation to ideas and perspectives; and the kinds of experiences it is legitimate for Reggio children to have.

Discourses are ways of behaving, believing, being and acting on the world. They are naturalized or taken-for-granted ways of being in the case of people who are on the inside of a discourse, who view the world through their own discursive lens. Frequently, those inside a practice regard their own position and practices as matters of common sense rather than a particular version of reality (Locke, 2004). The loosely post-structuralist perspective that we are deploying in this chapter does not see the individual child, teacher, carer, parent, author i.e. actor, as acting in a totally autonomous way that is unconstrained by cultural scripts of how to be a practitioner, learner, boy, girl and so on. What are those cultural scripts or discourses? Probing this question helps us to highlight the constructedness of the Reggio philosophy, to hold it up for scrutiny and critique. It is important that we point out, though, that we do not see the strategy of naturalization or taken-for-grantedness, along with the representational devices used to accomplish this naturalization and common sense taken-for-grantedness, as in some way dishonest. Like other discourse analysts (e.g. Nespor and Barber, 1991) we recognize that we deploy rhetorical devices ourselves in this writing. We do not challenge the use of rhetorical strategies – we appreciate that there 'is no non-rhetorical vantage point from which to survey a text' (Latour, 1988, p. 168). Rather, we are trying to understand how such strategies achieve their effects in the Reggio representations.

Furthermore, the point of our analysis in this chapter is not to say that Reggio ideas are 'good' or 'bad', nor is it to get at some true meaning underlying Reggio texts, since texts can never be reduced to a single meaning. However, we do aim to unsettle, disrupt and review meanings, especially the preferred or intended ones (MacLure, 2003). In this way new questions and meanings may be generated, and from the point of view of the overall aim of the book, new understandings regarding the appeal and the distribution and consumption of Reggio ideas may be offered.

We do not confine our analysis here to any particular type of publication or authors. We consider that any publication in the public domain by any author bearing on Reggio Emilia's perspectives and practices is a legitimate source to draw on. We are interested in examining how Reggio is represented in the literature, although we do not claim that our analysis is in any sense definitive – it is inevitably selective. Another analysis of its discourse may well offer different arguments and conclusions, and contest the claims made here. However, we suggest that the approach we are adopting is worthwhile because it invites the reader to engage more critically with what has become a substantial initiative in early childhood education internationally and with a set of writers who are almost entirely in agreement with one another.

Bearing in mind the questions and issues just outlined, the chapter is structured under three key themes as follows:

1.   The exceptionality yet transferability of Reggio.
2.   The sensory, awe-struck, spontaneous child *and* the enculturated child.
3.   The romanticized, idealized community.

In the case of each theme, the rhetorical mechanisms used to bring into being a Reggio version of reality will be highlighted. The two overarching questions already listed above will be revisited in the conclusion of the chapter where speculations regarding the take-up and popularity of Reggio as an international movement will be offered.

The Exceptionality Yet Transferability of Reggio

One is struck by the references in the Reggio literature to how *unique* and *exceptional* and *different* the Reggio approach is represented to be, such that one would expect it to be geographically and contextually bound and unable 'to travel' beyond its original setting. However, this is not the case. Exceptionality and transferability are accommodated, if not easily so, and in this case can co-exist harmoniously, as evidenced by the descriptions of the many journeys, some in pilgrimage style, that British and American practitioners and scholars make to Reggio annually. Educators plan to return to their respective workplaces enthused and inspired and ready to change their home practices in the direction of principles and practices they were exposed to on their Italian visit. Indeed, one could argue that exceptionality and transferability go hand in hand, for the former is precisely what captivates the imagination and makes it seductive to outsiders searching for a holy grail of early childhood care and education. Reggio is at once a discourse of impossibility and a discourse of hope and potential. We try to show this in what follows. We will also show how a key mechanism used to establish both the exceptionality and transferability of Reggio is binary oppositioning and negative comparing with non-Reggio settings.

The style of participation of the very young children attending the Reggio schools is so sophisticated that it is akin more to typical academic, university practice at postgraduate level than to what one might normally expect for young learners. Take the following observation:

> I have the feeling . . . that when I am with the children at the Diana school or even for that matter at the Nido Arcobaleno with the very, very young children, that it is like a seminar at the graduate department of the university, with the same kind of respect, of exchange in talking about what you have just said, and about your former thinking.
>
> (Rinaldi, 2007, p. 58)

A number of points are noteworthy about this brief representation. First, feelings are triggered and potentially engendered in the reader: Reggio onlookers, visitors and writers place enormous emphasis on how much they are moved by what they see and experience. Second, the practice being described is contrasted with what might be deemed ordinary, more typical and expected early-years practice – implicitly in this case – the comparator here is the university graduate seminar. This is the pinnacle of sophisticated dialogue, it is assumed, and these young children, the writer describes, exhibit the same level of sophisticated interaction, reflection and respect for their co-participants. Third, the observer who uttered these words is purported to be Jerome Bruner (who incidentally was conferred with an honorary citizenship by the Mayor of Reggio Emilia in 1997). As an established international authority on learning who is associated with rich theorizing in education over many decades, Bruner's authorial voice has special persuasive power – such a figure is assumed to have interpretive authority. The latter raises a more general point about how Reggio practices are represented and disseminated via the literature which we return to shortly.

Carol Seefeldt's writing (see, for example, *Learn from the Theories of Reggio* and *Creating Rooms of Wonder*, 2002a), based on visits to Reggio Emilia schools and centers, and all aimed at practitioners, are replete with references to how amazing Reggio Emilia practices are. The following likens the children's products to what one might find in a museum of modern art:

> Stunned with the exquisitely intricate art of children in Reggio Emilia, Italy, educators throughout the world stand in awe and wonder . . . after all, everywhere you look, splendid works of art are displayed. Perhaps because of the abstract quality of the artwork, you are in a museum of

modern art. But you are not in an art museum at all. Rather, you are in a city-run child-care center of Reggio Emilia.

(Seefeldt, 1995, p. 39)

Howard Gardner refers to the 'adult standards' the children achieve. In the following quotation from his Foreword (noted above) he affirms Bruner's and Seefeldt's claims to Reggio's exceptionality:

The Reggio schools *stand out* [from other affluent, attractive, well-appointed schools] by virtue of the type and quality of the activities that the children carry out on a regular basis; the deeply caring and respectful ways in which teachers interact with the youngsters and with one another.

(emphases added)

Gardner refers to '*specialized* colleagues' and 'the *astonishing* documentation of student work' (emphases added) thus highlighting the extraordinary nature of Reggio practices. Assuming a desire to reproduce the Reggio Experience elsewhere, Gardner comments on how transferability is made possible by the extraordinary enthusiasm and commitment of Reggio staff – characteristics, he implies, that are not evident among American educators:

What is perhaps most difficult to imitate, Reggio staff members live their work, spending many extra hours in the schools, and enthusiastically putting in many weekends and summers as well. Perhaps not all are married to their work, but the considerable personal sacrifices made by such educators never cease.

The suggestion is that the outstanding provision requires practitioners to forfeit their personal lives, or rather that their personal and professional lives are one and the same, since the ideal practitioner is so loyal and devoted that he or she (usually 'she') must be wedded to the job. And the majority of Reggio practitioners, it seems, can be thus described. This discourse of exceptionality keeps Reggio special, unique, out of the reach of the ordinary, and it hints at the impossibility of imitation, reproduction and accommodation outside of its cultural milieu. A prospective Reggio teacher, whose beliefs about children and learning are inconsistent, or fundamentally at odds, with the Reggio approach 'would not choose to work in such a setting or would quickly be discovered' (Phillips and Bredekamp, 1998). So only those fully committed to Reggio ideals would opt to work there, and anyone who was found to be not so committed would be soon 'discovered' and presumably ejected from the club. The assumption is that all those who work within the system are completely committed to it and that the only factor bearing on their decision to be employed within it or not would pertain to their agreement with its principles. Rinaldi (2007, p. 73) claims that 'we need teachers who feel that they *truly* belong to and participate' and also 'possess the culture of research, of curiosity, of working in a group: the culture of project-based thinking' (emphasis added).

For, as Rinaldi confidently declares, to work in Reggio requires a particular way of thinking about the world, a fundamentally 'different' way of being educated to the impoverished one which we, the readers, are assumed to have experienced:

> More than a methodological proposition, this is a mindset, a different way of thinking from that which many of us are used to, as most of us are survivors from an education system where relations-connections were at best avoided, and at worst, actually forbidden. There was no relationship between what was happening outside school and what was going on inside, nor between what we were studying in history and the knowledge we were gaining in geography, and so on.
>
> (Rinaldi, 2007, p. 46)

The endorsement by already eminent American scholars in the field of education, as well as the invoking of such scholars by other, less acclaimed writers, is, in our opinion, a significant device that supports the promotion of the system beyond its Italian roots. Through this mechanism of 'appropriating a constituency', knowledgeability and credibility are brought into and made part and parcel of the Reggio discourse (MacLure, 2003). Any ambiguities and partiality can be eliminated, or at least minimized. The narrative is 'tidied up' in a 'trust the author' signal. In the early 1990s, the magazine *Newsweek* asserted that the preschools of Reggio were the best in the world. Referring to this article in his book, *The Disciplined Mind*, Gardner pronounced: 'In general I place little stock on such ratings, but here I concur. The twenty-two municipal preschools and thirteen infant-and-toddler day care centers and preschools in this charmed community are unique' (Gardner, 2000, p. 1). That he deviates from his usual practice of ignoring such crude rankings only serves to emphasize his endorsement of Reggio.

The next three paragraphs are taken from Howard Gardner's Foreword (1998a) and a chapter entitled 'What Can we Learn from Reggio Emilia?' by Lilian Katz (1998). We reproduce them here in order to show how Reggio practices and settings are constructed as ideal; not merely that, but also to enable us highlight how textually such an argument is made:

In America we pride ourselves on being focused on children, and yet we do not pay sufficient attention to what they are actually expressing. We call for cooperative learning among children, and yet we rarely have sustained cooperation at the level of teacher and administrator. We call for artistic works, but we rarely fashion environments that can truly support and inspire them. We call for parental involvement, but are loathe to share ownership, responsibility, and credit with parents. We recognize the need for community, but we so often crystallize immediately into interest groups. We hail the discovery method, but we do not have the confidence to allow children to follow their own noses and hunches. We call for debate, but often spurn it; we call for listening, but we prefer to talk; we are affluent, but we do not safeguard those resources that can allow us to remain so and to foster the affluence of others. Reggio is so instructive in these respects. Where we are often intent to invoke slogans, the educators in Reggio work tirelessly to solve many of these fundamental – and fundamentally difficult – issues.

(Gardner, 1998a, p. xvii)

In American schools, children's graphic representations may be treated as mere decorative products to be taken home at the end of the day, most likely never to be discussed or looked at again. In Reggio Emilia, graphic representations serve as resources for further exploration and deepening knowledge of the topic.

(Katz, 1998, p. 34)

In his studies of the Oxford preschools in England, Bruner (1980) showed that the content of the teacher–child interactions was predominantly about managerial issues. He lamented, for example, that of nearly 10,000 units of observation, only 20% contained genuine conversations, and he pointed out that the nursery classes observed were organized so that it was difficult for connected conversations to occur. He also pointed out that 'a high proportion of the adult-initiated interaction with children was given over to the boring stuff of petty management – housekeeping talk about milk time, instruction about picking up, washing, and the like'.

(Katz, p. 36, 1998, citing Bruner, 1980)

These paragraphs are a polemical attack on the state of early-years education in the United States; indeed, it is arguable that they are an attack on education outside Reggio Emelia. The legitimacy of the claims is produced primarily by the use of the binary dynamic: all that is good happens to be found in Reggio, and none of what is negative is found there; the exact opposite is the case in America (and England) and by implication outside Reggio Emilia. A polemical text tends to wear its binaries on its sleeve and the above extracts from two different texts are no exceptions (MacLure, 2003). This is a golden-age story where the assumed inferiority of the American and English systems is invoked to establish the superiority of the Reggio system. The dichotomy is mapped onto the Reggio and non-Reggio distinction, as we have illustrated in Table 1. The intellectual, professional and moral ineptitude of the American and English educator is asserted, indeed needed, in order to reveal the purity, perfection and propriety of the Reggio one.

Table 1: Blatant Binaries

Reggio Settings: Positive	Non-Reggio Settings: Negative
Listening to children.	Ignoring what children say, talking to/at children.
Collegiality, co-operation and co-operative learning.	Lack of staff collaboration.
True support for the arts.	Rhetoric of arts support but lacking in practice.
Close, warm parental involvement.	Reluctance to work in partnership with parents.
Embrace ideal of community.	Reject community values in favor of interest groups.
Discovery learning giving curiosity free rein.	Lacking in confidence and competence to support self- and interest-initiated learning so denying freedom to learn.
Facilitating debate and discussion.	Closing down debate to narrow, dull and rigid interactions with children.
Openness, generosity, selflessness.	Affluence, greed, selfishness.
Authenticity, fit between policies, principles and practices.	Inauthentic, gulf between rhetoric and reality.
Deep engagement with children's products and attentive to children's meaning-making.	Superficial treatment of children's work; trivializing their efforts, denying them their meaning-making.

Our readers might take issue with the suggestion that the third paragraph above from Katz is polemical since it reports evidence to support her claim about what distinguishes the Reggio settings from English ones. However, Katz's text draws on research to support the claim of distinctiveness, and although she later calls for evaluations of Reggio and laments the lack of research evidence about the long-term influence of the Reggio experience on children, this does not deter her from, in the meantime, claiming its superiority.

There is the assumption that American readers will agree with the caricaturing of them and their systems and that they will not be difficult to persuade. It is as if the authors do not have to challenge themselves too much to make their bid for believability. Blatant binaries and polarized contrasts are used liberally to represent Reggio's merits. It is worth noting that these texts are written for particular audiences: early-years practitioners and their educators, although Gardner suggests that anyone with an interest in the education of children should read *The Hundred Languages of Children*. He says that 'few who do [read it] will remain unaffected by the experience'(p. xv). So the reader is primed for and expected to react emotionally to the ideas expressed in the book. Gardner talks about how practitioners involve children 'in long-term engrossing projects . . . carried out in a beautiful, healthy, love-filled setting' (p. xvi). What reader and practitioner could reject such positioning!

Despite the negative positioning of the American practitioner, there is the contradictory discourse throughout most of the Reggio literature that the non-native Reggio educator will be able to be transformed into, or at the very least approximate, the more authentic, selfless, competent, open and generous Reggio-style human being who will listen to children, foster learning by discovery and so on.

Describing the fostering of early literacy through books and imagination, Alga Giacomelli, in conversation with Carolyn Pope Edwards and Lella Gandini, talks about the 'exceptional new concepts and innovations' which she encountered in early childhood education in Reggio. She goes on to suggest that the '[p]eople who visit Filastrocca Preschool are struck by the *special* emphasis on the imagination of children that gives a beautiful and *unique* flavor' (Edwards et al., 1998, p. 9, emphases added). Similarly for those tired of conflicts with children's parents, Reggio Emilia 'offers *a new way of thinking* about the home–school relationship' (pp. 10–11). Dahlberg and Moss (2007, p. 17) claim that 'the importance of Reggio for us lies in its difference, its otherness, its alterity'.

Newness, difference, exceptionality, distinctiveness, originality, innovation, beauty and pioneering practice are all concepts recruited to construct the Reggio philosophy. It is not surprising, then, that it has the potential to solve many contemporary ills, to correct the negative features of what is represented as the dominant, highly inappropriate model of early childhood that has so gripped the western world. The authors Gunilla Dahlberg and Peter Moss (2007, p. 19) say Reggio 'speaks to those of us who long for something else, another belonging'. They claim that Reggio 'gives comfort and hope by being different, by showing the possibility of different values, different relationships, different ways of living' (p. 19). This is how they explain the positive international welcoming of Reggio Emilia thinking on early childhood:

> We think that the worldwide interest in Reggio reflects a reaction to the increasingly dominant discourse about early childhood education . . . This discourse is inscribed with highly instrumental and calculative neo-liberal values and assumptions and managerial practices. It is a discourse that treats early childhood services as sites for applying 'human technologies' to produce pre-defined and normative outcomes, to better govern the child to serve as a redemptive agent who will save us from the uncertainties and inequalities of the world – a technical solution which will avoid us having to confront the political and ethical problems that are ruining our world and its peoples.
>
> (Dahlberg and Moss, 2007, p. 19)

So the assumption is that Reggio has the potential to confront political and ethical problems that are ruining our world and its peoples. This is a grand claim indeed, and one that valorizes the Reggio approach and represents it as full of positive potential for the world and its future. The rhetorical mechanism used by Dahlberg and Moss (and many others) to make such a grand claim is one of oppositional positioning: current thinking, policies and practices on early childhood are assumed to be wholly wrong-headed. The Reggio approach is the corrective that enlightened early-years educators recognize and crave for. By positioning the current and, what is assumed as, the increasingly dominant discourse of early childhood as inhumane and technical, the Reggio approach can then be more easily positioned as humane, ethical and, of course, non-technical. It is *the* alternative after which the enlightened world hankers.

The use of opposing binaries also allows the already convinced author to invoke the (already convinced) readers' emotions of longing: '[Reggio] speaks to those of us who long for something else, another belonging.' The rhetorical device enables the writers to evade the kind of messy accounts of practice and of real participants which would include resistances, problems, power struggles and so on, features that are an inevitable part of human interaction and participation.

In a chapter entitled 'Bridge to Another Culture: The Journey of the Model Early Learning Center', Ann Lewin, Founder and Director of a US Early Learning Center, says it was challenging to implement Reggio thinking into an inner-city setting in the USA. Referring to teachers and families in the local community, she and her contributing author colleagues comment on the difficulties they believed they had to overcome in enacting a Reggio philosophy: 'It was, and still is, not an easy process. It requires *extraordinary* openness and effort . . . It means learning self-esteem, trust, how to collaborate, to believe in what you are doing and in its importance for the well-being not only of the children, but also of the families and their teachers' (Lewin et al., 1998, p. 349). In keeping with the discourse of Reggio's exceptional practices and personnel, these educators, it seems, have to make an *extraordinary* effort to achieve the success they crave. Nothing ordinary will do. How they manage such a feat is never really explained in the chapter – how the necessary self-esteem, trust and ability to collaborate were won is glossed over. The reader is left in no doubt, though, about the success of the *journey* which involved the Center staff studying the sets of Reggio slides, listening to presentations by Ann Lewin based on her study visit to Reggio, and Center discussions of the recommended approaches. The biblical, fervent rhetoric deployed to convey the Center's success is noteworthy:

> Then the children came, and tentatively the teachers began. By the end of the fall, many children were working in small groups on projects that included studying the movement of Coco (the school cat), discovering the trains at Union Station next door, exploring a variety of ways to use paint, making complex block structures, and becoming friends by exchanging messages with one another through the mailboxes. Calm prevailed, the children were engaged and productive, and the teachers were at peace. We were pleased with where we had gone . . .
>
> (Lewin et al., 1998, p. 340)

Lewin comments in her jointly authored chapter that she felt the need to return to Reggio with a list of questions designed to enable herself and her staff to 'understand how to go farther and deeper'. Among the questions she seeks answers to are: How do you decide what projects to do? How do you select children for projects? How do you add children to projects? How do you keep children from fighting over who gets to do what with whom? How long do projects last anyway? So practitioners in this particular US center are represented (represent themselves) as lacking this knowledge, while the questions are assumed to be so profound and challenging that answering them requires their director to travel back to Reggio once more, not an inexpensive expedition.

Reggio works and is transferable, despite its exceptionality. Like several accounts of implementation in other settings outside Italy, this one is silent on the detail of the complexities, the ambiguities, the struggles. There is no room for such complications. Despite assertions of the complexity of children in the Reggio literature, people are not portrayed in the accounts as complex human beings with desires, feelings, opinions, strengths and weaknesses. There are many photographs of the environment and of children working together. What we see in those visuals is the generic child; the actual child is rarely described. We do not see a particular child (or teacher, parent). It could be any child. While the writers are speaking *from the scene*, the scene is nowhere in particular, they assume a distanced position (MacLure, 2003). The reified teachers and learners are represented in ways that suggest complete acceptance of and consensus on the 'new' approaches. This point applies also to the vast array of multimodal materials produced by the company, 'Reggio Children'. Illustrations, slides of children and adults collaborating, photographs of children's artwork, depict actual children, but the reader has far too little detail to enable a rich interpretation of the curriculum enactment, there is little or no detail about how participants themselves experienced the various projects they engaged in. What we get is the decontextualized child and the decontextualized educator. The intention throughout in the materials seems to be to convey 'good practice', to reveal what children and educators do, but the artefacts and illustrations lack the specificity needed to capture the complexity of practice.

The Sensory, Awe-Struck, Spontaneous Child *and* the Enculturated Child

The concept of intertextuality refers to ways in which texts are related to other texts by virtue of the discourses embedded in them (Locke, 2004; Gee, 1999; MacLure, 2003). As one reads the Reggio texts, one's intertextual knowledge is recruited, though the connections mostly remain tacit rather than explicit. Through making some of that inter-textualiy explicit, this section highlights both the enduring and the changing nature of Reggio discourses of the child.

The audiences to which the Reggio texts are aimed, i.e. all those interested in early childhood education and care, are likely to be familiar with the main thrust of child-centered philosophy. They are likely to share an immersion in those earlier texts, thus marking themselves as subscribing to that earlier celebratory discourse, a major component of which was the notion that the child is innocent, naturally good, playful, curious and different from the adult. This construction of the child is revitalized in the Reggio texts. A discursive analysis allows one to see how meanings residing in the Reggio texts have a pedigree which is used to provide additional power and authority. In drawing attention to the intertextuality, we are glimpsing the texture, the weave (MacLure, 2003) and the implicit appeal to other times and other thinkers.

However, texts bleed: they do not necessarily maintain a coherent, stable story throughout; discourses may conflict and contradict. This happens in the Reggio portrayal of the child, especially as a socio-cultural perspective on learning and the self is also claimed, a position which challenges the celebratory discourse of the earlier, child-centered writers. While the parallels with the earlier child-centered discourses of childhood and the young learner are not coincidental, the Reggio texts work in a way that does not mimic them, the subscribing to a socio-cultural orientation ensures that a direct mapping does not occur, hence the claim for newness. Rather, discourses of the spontaneous, sensory child, traceable to early child-centered theorists like Froebel and Rousseau, as well as psychologists like Piaget (who incidentally is invoked but nearly always rejected), brush up against the mediated, enculturated child, influenced by community members of peers, teachers and parents and many others.

Carlina Rinaldi's writings are especially revealing of the discourse of the child as innocent and naturally good. The following is an example:

> The newborn child comes into the world with a self that is joyous, expressive, and ready to experiment and explore, using objects and communicating with other people. Right from the beginning, children show a remarkable exuberance, creativity and inventiveness toward their surroundings, as well as an autonomous and coherent consciousness.
>
> (Rinaldi, 2007, pp. 66–7)

This naturalizing discourse goes back to Rousseau. Rinaldi talks about the 'constant discovery of the child's extraordinary abilities' (Rinaldi, 2007, pp. 38–9) so emphasizing how abilities are discoverable, they are within the child already, awaiting an opportunity to unfold in Froebellian-style emergence. Like many of the well-known early progressive, child-centered theorists, from Froebel to Rousseau, and from Pestallozzi to Montessori, Rinaldi's attention is on the innate nature of the child (naturalness), and so she attends to the child's biology, albeit overlain with the newest scientific discourse of neuroscience: 'We see a child who is driven by the enormous energy potential of a hundred billion neurons, by the strength of wanting to grow and taking the job of growing seriously, by the incredible curiosity that makes children search for the reasons for everything' (Rinaldi, 2007, p. 123).

So a neuroscientific Rousseau might describe a curious Emile. Neuroscience, the most recent scientific justification for traditional practices in early-years education, is recruited to authorize and legitimate Reggio's appeal to the sensory, the practical, the embodied learner who learns through activity, experience, participation and play, but also to produce the competent, amazingly able child who is driven by a search for meaning and understanding. Liz Brooker (2005) observed how the emphasis on sensory learning, interaction with the environment, learning by experience, has a long history going back to Comenius.

Rinaldi's innateness, perception and sensory experience have echoes of the 1960s progressivists so evident in policy texts such as the *Plowden Report* (Board of Education, 1967) in England and Wales, the *Scottish Memorandum* (Scottish Education Department, 1965) and *Curaclam na Bunscoile* (Department of Education, 1971) in Ireland, as well as Dewey-informed policy documents in the United States. The following could have come from any one of those texts:

> Young children demonstrate an innate and extremely high level of perceptual sensitivity and competence – which is polysemous and holistic – in relation to the surrounding space. Their immediate receptors are much more active than they will be in later stages of life, and they show a great ability to analyse and distinguish reality using sensory receptors other than those of sight and hearing. For this reason the utmost attention should be given to designing light and colours, as well as olfactory, auditory and tactile elements, all of which are extremely important in defining the sensory quality of a space.
>
> (Rinaldi, 2007, p. 82)

Compare the above with the following quote from an early-years text by Curtis and Carter (2003, p. 106, cited in Langford, 2006):

> As children work with these materials, they are learning about themselves and their role using physical properties of the world. Children are transfixed by looking at, touching, tasting, and moving and re-arranging things. As they absorb the rich information around them, their brain

pathways are making connections that will be the foundations for a lifetime of experience and learning.

The Romantic child here fits with the new discourse of neuroscience (Langford, 2006). The point of the Curtis and Carter quote is to highlight not only Reggio's intertextual links with previous texts but to show the textual connections with contemporary texts on early childhood.

The rhetoric of the Romantic, sensory child is akin to the 'language experience' rhetoric of the 1960s when lighting candles, playing music, pouring water and burning paper acted as the trigger for spontaneous self-expression in the then less risk-averse creative writing lesson. In this pedagogy, creativity, originality, self-expression, individuality, unique response, authenticity, personal voice, personal growth and ownership were all hallmarks. Not (yet) recognized was the idea that writing always involves borrowing from other texts and genres that authors have been exposed to. The 'linguistic fingerprints' of other, previous texts belie the notion that 'writing is an act of creativity springing fully-blown from the writer's head' (MacLure, 1994, p. 288). The child, the self, is assumed to be the original meaning-maker. This discourse also permits the inordinate emphasis on a perfect, orderly, physical environment – a space that teaches (Gandini, 1998), concretely described here by Gardner:

> If you walk into one of the preschools on a given morning, you will first be struck by the beauty and spaciousness of the building. Reggio buildings are ample, open, streaming with light; potted plants and inviting chairs and couches are strategically placed, adding color and comfort to the surroundings. There are secluded alcoves to which youngsters can retreat, interior gardens and common space where the teachers can meet. Most of the classrooms flow easily into one another and spill out into a large central *piazza*. Passage to the play areas outside the school is also convenient, and in good weather, one will see groups of children playing together on the grounds. On neat shelves are stored literally hundreds of materials – from colored geometric forms to grains of cereal to seashells to recyclable wooden sticks – with which the youngsters may become engaged at some point (or repeatedly) during the year. Everything seems in place; there is no clutter or mess; and yet, the spaces feel inviting and flexible.
>
> (Gardner, 2000, p. 3)

Here are evoked reminders of Froebel's gifts and Montessori's order. Historically, the importance of a pleasurable environment in which to learn, of an environment that invites interaction and the manipulation of mat-erials and learning through the senses, challenged previous notions of learning as just about the head and perhaps morality. Now the 'whole child' is center-stage involving mind, body, spirit, soul and heart. The whole child 'orients to desire' (Gallacher, 2006): motivations, inclinations, pleasures, wishes, feelings and longings are relevant. In Reggio 'Learning must be pleasurable, appealing and fun' (Rinaldi, 2007, p. 81). As before, roman-ticism is alive and well.

The following extended quotation from Gardner's 'The best preschools in the world' (2000, p. 2), expounding the nature of interest-initiated project work, attests to the enduring nature of that early 'progressive' discourse. We reproduce it here primarily to illustrate the intertextuality, the instructive, journalistic rhetoric, and to show how Reggio's choosing, awe-struck child is produced:

Consider how this process works. Suppose that on the second day of school a rainbow appears, which can be observed through a skylight above the central *piazza*. Either a child or a teacher notices the rainbow and brings it to the attention of the others. Youngsters begin to talk about the rainbow and, perhaps at the suggestion of the teacher, a few children begin to sketch it. Suddenly the rainbow disappears. Children begin to talk about where it came from, and whether it has traveled to another site. A child picks up a prism that happens to be nearby and looks at the light streaming through it. She calls over to her classmates and they begin to experiment with other translucent vessels. The next day it rains again and afterwards the sky is cloudy and no rainbow is visible. Henceforth children set up observational posts after a storm, so that they can be sure to spy the rainbow when it appears and capture it in various media. And if no rainbow appears, or if they fail to capture its appearance, students will confer on the reasons why and consider how better to prepare for the next sighting of a rainbow.

A project on rainbows has been launched. In the following weeks, children read and write stories about rainbows, explore raindrops, consider rainbow-like phenomena that accompany lawn hoses and mist, record a sensational double rainbow, and play with flashlights and candles, noting what happens to the light as it passes through various liquids and vessels. No one knows at the start just where the project will eventually land; and while earlier projects clearly influence the 'moves' made by teachers (and, eventually, by students) this open-ended quality is crucial to the educational milieu that has been created over the decades at Reggio.

Implied is the message that this pedagogy is new, fresh and unique to Reggio. Assumed is that all young children are intrigued about the natural world, and that what interests one will interest all. Disagreements, negotiation, resistances do not arise in this orderly, concrete portrayal. There is no need for the reader/practitioner to be concerned about resources, planning, staffing, time, staff–child ratios, or any other constraining influences in their local context. All those things can be taken for granted. Prisms, translucent vessels, flashlights, candles will 'happen to be nearby'. The journalistic style of the present tense enlivens the instructive nature of the text and naturalizes and renders all unambiguous and consensual.

Unlike her predecessors, Rinaldi and several other Reggio enthusiasts (e.g. New, 2007; Moran et al., 2007; Edwards, 1995) also subscribe to the more contemporary socio-constructivist and socio-cultural perspectives on learning and development, orientations that do not sit easily with a biological discourse. This intertextuality is an inevitable part of texts (Bakhtin, 1986) and in this case we get a glimpse of how a given text shows its incoherence. Texts bleed (MacLure, 2003) and containers leak (McDermott and Varenne, 1995). The discourse of the already knowing child who is born innocent and good clashes somewhat with the cultural and enculturated child, whose biology, though not denied, is backgrounded to more significant cultural shaping processes.

In a cultural perspective, learning or development occurs as people engage in collective activities, and it is from this collective learning that individual meanings and learning are created. Experience, participation and opportunity to learn are key, though always problematic because meaning can't be given to individuals, it has to be perceived, and because experiences are not equally available to all. In this perspective, learning is understood not solely in terms of what individuals can do, but crucially, in terms of what it is possible to do in certain situations with certain people. Moreover, the process of learning is not seen as different for children and for adults, nor is the process seen as different in different settings (e.g schools, and 'everyday' settings like home and workplace): all learning involves participation and experience and opportunity to learn (Murphy and Hall, 2008). In addition the self in a socio-cultural perspective is a produced, depersonalized self, as opposed to a self in essence, and the enactment of self is a function of one's agency and identity, aspects that are dynamic, mediated and unpredictable (Hall, 2008).

As already noted in earlier chapters, the notion of the competent, independent able child is fundamental to Reggio thinking – a child who is a social actor, who is at once shaped and shapes the social environment. The child is agentic, making decisions, requiring to be listened to, action- and active-oriented and, of course. investigative. A sense of the mediated, enculturated child is evident from Rinaldi's (2007, p. 83) claim that our conceptions of children and childhood become 'a determining factor in defining their social and ethical identity, their rights and the educational contexts offered to them'. Rinaldi (and other Reggio enthusiasts) variously describe this enculturated child, but the biological discourse remains a preoccupation even when overtures to a more cultural discourse are in the same paragraph:

> Children are *biologically predisposed* to communicate, to exist in relation, to live in relation . . . Listening, then, seems to be an *innate predisposition* that accompanies children *from birth*, allowing their process of acculturation to develop. The idea of an *innate capacity* for listening may seem paradoxical but, in effect, the process of acculturation must involve *innate motivation and competencies*.
>
> (Rinaldi, 2007, p. 66, emphases added)

The idea of competencies being innate and constituting a set of inherited skills contradicts fundamentally a socio-cultural discourse of development (see, for example, Rogoff, 1998b; Wenger, 1998; Lave, 1996). A similar bleeding is evident in the text of Dahlberg (1999) which is quoted by Dahlberg and Moss in the introduction to Rinaldi's *In Dialogue with Reggio Emilia* (2007, p. 8) in making the case that Reggio might be termed 'post-modern':

> Choosing to adopt a social constructionist approach; challenging and deconstructing dominant discourses; realizing the power of these discourses in shaping and governing our thoughts and actions . . . ; rejecting the prescription of rules, goals, methods and standards, and in so doing risking uncertainty and complexity; having the courage to think for themselves in constructing new discourses, and in so doing daring to make the choice of understanding the child as a rich child, a child of infinite capabilities, a child born with a hundred languages; building a new pedagogical project, foregrounding relations and encounters, dialogue and negotiation, reflection and critical thinking; border crossing disciplines and perspectives, replacing either/or positions and an and/also openness; and understanding the contextualized and dynamic nature of pedagogical practices, which problematizes the idea of transferable 'programme'.

The statement 'a child *born with* a hundred languages' (emphases added) and the 'and/also' reference is an indication of the contradictory discourses in operation here. Rinaldi's claims that the 'search for the meaning of life and of the self in life is born with the child and is desired by the child' and her notion that educators have to help children find the meaning in what they do and experience (pp. 63–4) is also difficult to reconcile with the socio-cultural notion that people make meaning from their experiences (Wenger, 1998) although it may not always be the meaning the educator intends.

Our main argument in this section is that the Romantic, sensory discourse clashes with the socio-cultural one. The vast amount of material depicting children engaged in various sensory activities, together with the drawings that adorn virtually every chapter in some Reggio texts, are meaningless from a socio-cultural perspective because the reader knows little or nothing about those depicted – they are not presented as located subjects with histories and contexts. They are usually mere adornment, bearing hardly any relationship to the content of the chapters and the themes discussed. Such depictions can't be 'read off' unproblematically – they need contextualizing and explanation.

The Romanticized, Idealized Community

The theme of community permeates Reggio discourse. The notion of community implied and assumed in Reggio texts is benign, ideal and positive. It is not usually the more problematic, nuanced, critical and complex community associated with socio-cultural theorizing (see, for example, Wenger, 1998) which recognizes issues of power, privilege, constraint, differential experience and treatment, positioning, gender, ethnicity, histories of belonging and not belonging, marginality, identity, agency and so on. This section examines the construction of community in the Reggio literature and attends to the rhetorical devices employed to represent that construction.

Carolyn Edwards (1995, p. 4) says that

> . . . creating community is very difficult to achieve in practice in American schools given that many children, not to mention teachers, are highly mobile and transient, and moreover, many of the organizational elements in schools work toward increased fragmentation and segmentation of knowledge and social relations.

In this view, communities don't already exist, or the assumption has to be that the right kind of community doesn't exist, that community making is difficult when people are 'mobile and transient'. In the same article, Edwards (p. 8) affirms the benign notion of community which she argues is what Malaguzzi sought. She refers to the practice of keeping children together in the same group for up to three years: 'The three years spent together allow the group to construct a history of relationship and a sharing of culture that creates a sense of community and guarantees the quality of life and well-being for children as part of families.' The notion that this arrangement in itself guarantees the well-being of learners and the notion of community implied would be challenged by socio-cultural theorists of community.

The following extended extract is from a chapter in *The Hundred Languages of Children* entitled 'Poppies and the Dance of the World Making' by an American writer and film producer, Paul Kaufman, who came to Reggio to film a project:

The warm, honeyed breath of the Italian spring hangs in the air. A line of children moves quietly into the poppy field. Parting the long grasses – like Moses and the Israelites – they make their way through a blazing sea of red. 'You may pick a few flowers', says the *atelierista*, a handsome woman with Botticellian hair and a 35mm camera.

A boy holds a poppy up to the sunlight, scrutinizes it with obvious discernment, and blows at it. 'This is better than ice-cream', he murmurs. In the sweetest of primeval rituals, two girls groom each other. 'Let me try to put the flower in your hair', one says. She inserts the stem of the poppy delicately into her friend's hair and pats it approvingly. The other girl responds in a soft, husky voice, 'I want to make a cross of flowers in your hair'.

Eeeeee! Shrieks and squeals. A zebra has entered the far end of the field: some of the children have spotted it. Head vigorously bobbing up and down, a bouquet of poppies clenched in its foam-rubber mouth, its stark black and white formal attire clashes deliciously with the country reds and greens. A boy shouts: 'It's the Diana School zebra and *I* know *who* it is!' The children hurry across the field to greet the beast and the teacher's aides crazy enough to bob and sweat under the zebra's skin.

. . . The producer [retires] with a beer to the outdoor table onto the grand *piazza*. It is evening and he watches the men of Reggio Emilia gather as they have gathered for centuries . . . to talk. They stand in little groups just as their fathers and grandfathers before them stood. He wonders what they are discussing. Politics, no doubt. The producer longs to belong in such a ritual, this communion through communication . . . The bells of a nearby church sound and the producer recalls the faces of the children. 'Little saviors of Interpretation,' he muses. 'God knows we need them.'

(Kaufman, 1998, pp. 285–6, 289)

Many points can be made about this extract. It offers a vignette, a concrete illustration to persuade and capture the reader's attention. It is intensely visual and in realist mode; it speaks from the scene (MacLure, 2003) in guidebook style that infers a single, blissful, coherent, stable, ideal, uncontested culture or community. The use of the present tense conveys a sense of the 'everyday', common practice that is unremarkable and taken for granted by the 'natives'. Only the enlightened outside onlooker, the cultural stranger, can notice and impartially describe the exotic nature of this uncontaminated domain. Such an empirical account smuggles in credibility and knowledgeability.

While we are not claiming that this way of positioning boys, girls and so on is typical of Reggio texts, it is worth bearing in mind that this extract features in what is *the* key published resource on the Reggio Emilia approach to education. It appears in a section called 'Reflections on the Interplay of Theory and Practice'. Given the emphasis generally in Reggio on children as active learners, as having rights, and on communities embracing civic values and democracy, its inclusion in the volume is quite staggering. It is surely a Disneyfied version of Reggio and specifically of the Reggio child. The stereotyping of women, men and children is blatant, unaware and therefore unapologetic. Children are seen and not heard (they 'move quietly'); they await an invitation to act ('You may pick a few flowers'); they are at one with nature, spontaneously picking and examining flowers and adorning themselves with them. However, boys are permitted to be active – they run and shout while girls groom each other and display delicate movements. Females are described in terms of their physical attributes ('a handsome woman with Botticellian hair'; 'a husky voice'). Only men appear in the public domain and discuss politics 'like their fathers and grandfathers before them'. The sound of church bells triggers images of children's faces and reminders that only their innocence can save the implied bad, adult world. The yearning for a past golden age is everywhere in this romanticized, sentimentalized and nostalgic depiction.

A small-scale empirical study by Naima Browne (2004) based on observations and interviews in Reggio settings concludes that the Reggio approach is not helpful in addressing gender equity, and she recommends that Reggio policies and practices should be subjected to critical analysis in relation to gender issues.

The Reggio literature seems loath to acknowledge the dynamic nature of communities of practice, though it claims to endorse that discourse (see the 2007 special issue of *Theory into Practice*). On those rare occasions when the notion of a disagreement is hinted at, it is countered and made positive: 'Teachers organize environments rich in possibilities and provocations that invite the children to undertake extended exploration and problem solving, often in small groups, where cooperation and disputation mingle pleasurably'(Edwards, 2002, p. 7). Only positive emotions are noticed: 'A classroom atmosphere of playfulness and joy pervades' (p. 7). Negative, critical emotions are not part of the discourse. Moreover, communities of learners are composed of people of equal status where no one individual has predominant responsibility and where it is assumed all are equally empowered to act: 'In the community of learners, all participants are active: no one has predominant responsibility' (Moran et al., 2007, p. 8).

A similarly benign conception of parents is presented which is also out of line with socio-cultural thinking on communities of practice. Although parents are depicted as having more responsibility now than in the past, there is no such thing as 'a bad parent' – the benign discourse of Reggio couldn't accept such an idea:

> Being a parent today implies, in addition to a very high emotional investment, also a broader range of responsibilities, linked to a widespread awareness of educational issues and problems. It requires an environment of real Socialisation, civil co-responsibility and social solidarity . . . There is no such thing as a good or a bad parent – there are just different ways of being a parent.
>
> (Rinaldi, 2007, pp. 34–5)

'The good home' (Mansson, 2007) is assumed. 'Reggio is assumed to offer those tired of conflicts with children's parents . . . a new way of thinking about the home–school relationship' (pp. 10–11). Conflict, it seems, is just not allowed in the ideal Reggio community; it simply does not fit with the togetherness, belonging, unity and certainty of the Reggio world. The discourse of the innately good person and community conflicts with the socio-cultural discourse of communities of practice.

The notion of community in Reggio is associated only with what is good: the approach builds communities, empowers participants, enables learning, extends capacity among practitioners and parents. It is distinguished by a dominant discourse of positive emotion, benign practices and relationships, and well-intentioned interactions and agendas on the part of all players. Consensus is everywhere. This ever-positive notion of community belies the socio-cultural perspective where differences in power, status and privilege are an inevitable dimension of human participation, although actual power structures in a given context are far from inevitable since they have an emergent quality and so are unpredictable and indeterminate.

Conclusion

In this chapter we set out to explore some of the textuality of Reggio discourse and to show how Reggio texts (like all texts) are fabricated to convince the reader of their authority, their common sense, and their naturalness. MacLure (2003) explains how the meanings that reside in texts arise partly from their linguistic fingerprints, their intertextual links with other, similar texts. Reggio texts descend from other related texts on child-hood and child education. The two questions posed at the beginning of the chapter can be repeated here to frame some concluding comments:

1. What are the powerful and dominant discourses of the Reggio movement?
2. What symbolic resources and rhetorical devices are used to achieve their legitimacy?

On this analysis the twin discourses of exceptionality and transferability characterize Reggio representations. Reggio thinking is presented as some-thing new, different, unusual and exceptional – this is evident in the writing of the key Reggio (Italian) authors and in the writing of many of those who visited Reggio and who describe its features and/or their attempts to implement it in their own settings. Yet, it is assumed to be transportable to other cultural milieus far away from its origins, evidenced by the dissemi-nation industry which takes a variety of formats from slides, videos, books, artwork, samples of artifacts made by children to professional journal articles, book chapters, and authored and edited books.

The discourse of the individual, active, unique, sensory child who is born good with inbuilt capacities is strongly in evidence. This is a biological discourse that is historically associated with early childhood 'pioneers' of progressive education. Reggio revitalizes and invigorates this discourse, claiming it as fundamental to its practices of project work, listening and responding to the child's actions. It manifests itself too in the huge stress on the empirical process of 'documentation' that was discussed earlier in the volume. This is a discourse that foregrounds the natural, spontaneous self-expressing, unique individual who needs to be listened to, responded to, and encouraged to project and develop a creative self through creative arts initiatives, through the engagement of the senses, and through the fostering of the imagination. This is the self as essence. It is a child-centered discourse that has endured over centuries and one in which early childhood educators are deeply embedded. It is far from unique to Reggio. The discourse of the enculturated, mediated child is another, somewhat conflicting child of Reggio. This is a discourse of the child as inseparable from her or his family, school and community and the values informing those institutions. However, two elements militate against a full-blown mediated child: the constant foregrounding of the biological dimension and the notion of family/community as (only) benign.

The discourse of the benign community with its emphasis on sharing responsibility, equal opportunities to participate, and therefore learn, is pivotal in Reggio texts. Such a benign version of community is challenged by socio-cultural perspective. The reluctance of Reggio to adopt a more critical, nuanced notion of community and community of practice means that issues of constraints, differential treatment, differential opportunities to participate and access learning are not examined. Marginalized are accounts that deal with lack of resources, staffing, staff–child ratios, and so on. Issues of gender, class, race, religious and sexual orientation or any other social categories are not made salient in Reggio representations. It is possible that the emphasis on the uniqueness and individuality of the child pushes away from a notion of diversity that recognizes the shaping power of those major social constructions.

The Reggio practitioner is produced as someone who is passionate about children and their curiosity, alert to the individual needs of children, patiently observant of children's endeavors, able to collaborate and be a good team player, who is reflective and prepared to be developed, and who is always willing to suppress his or her own desires in favor of the welfare of others. Most importantly, the Reggio practitioner views their role as educator as deeply complex and requiring enormous self-sacrifice. Foregrounded are emotional dimensions. As others have pointed out (though not referring specifically to Reggio Emilia), this discourse of the good practitioner coincides with traditional female roles (James et al., 1998; Langford, 2006). Indeed, the Reggio construction intensifies this caricature and backgrounds other dimensions like authority, leadership, expertise, knowledge and autonomy. In this sense it is arguable that Reggio reproduces the stereotypical female role – another indication of an enduring, continuing discourse.

Our analysis is based on a particular assumption about the relationship between language and reality, more specifically that language is deeply implicated in the production of the social and cultural world. Moreover, it is based on the notion that meaning is ambiguous, open to contestation and never finally determined or resolvable with reference to some 'external' certain world (MacLure, 1994). In this post-structuralist perspective we have sought to reveal the language maneuvers that Reggio writers have used to convince their readers of the impartiality and authority of their claims. The rhetorical devices that are used to produce the above discourses and constructions and to legitimate and claim authority for them as well as claim their naturalness and taken-for-grantedness include the following: the use of binary opposites and negative comparing; the recruitment of feelings; 'speaking from the scene' manifested in the journalistic, visual and realist, concrete accounts; the inter-textual connections with older discourses (the child as good); and newer scientific genres (e.g. neuroscience). Making the linguistic resources visible and explicit enables one to see the incoherencies, the ambiguities and the contradictions. Such destabilizing enables one to contest the official or preferred reading of the Reggio material and invites the reader to ponder other issues, not featured in Reggio versions of early childhood education.

Before ending, we repeat a point we noted in the introduction to the chapter, which is that we are not claiming that our analysis in any way invalidates the principles and practices of Reggio as enacted in the various schools and centers. Our focus here has been on how people do representations of its enactments. This is important because representations influence social practices. There are many 'Reggios', possibly a Disneyfied version (Wright, 2000). We are not suggesting, as Johnson (1999) does, that the Reggio Emilia approach shows 'limited theoretical traditions' or is 'atheoretical' or adopts an 'anti-intellectual approach to conceptualizing early childhood education'. Quite the contrary, we have shown that representations of Reggio draw on several theoretical orientations and perspectives, sometimes implicitly, how some of these positions are in tension, and how, in representing Reggio experiences and principles, writers deploy particular textual resources to persuade the reader of the credibility, authority and knowledgeability of their claims.

Part 3

The Relevance of Reggio Emilia

Each new generation offers humanity another chance. If we *provide* for the survival and development of children everywhere, *protect* them from harm and exploitation and enable them to *participate* in decisions directly affecting their lives, we will surely build the foundation of the just society we all want and that children deserve.

(Excerpt from *The Rights of the Child*, Fact Sheet #10, UN Centre for Human Rights)

Chapter 6

Reggio Emilia: A Question of Quality

Introduction

For many in the field of early childhood education, Reggio Emilia is synonymous with high quality provision. Its principles and practices have been endorsed by eminent scholars, including Gardner, Bruner, Moss and Katz. Early childhood educators in Europe, the United States and beyond have embraced its principles and methods and have sought to align practices in their own settings with those they have observed in Reggio Emilia or read about in Reggio Emilia literature. Despite the fact that Loris Malaguzzi wrote little about his philosophy of childhood education (but see Malaguzzi, 1998, 2005), there is now a considerable literature on the 'Reggio Emilia Experience' as well as significant interest in its practices, as evidenced by the many study visits made to Reggio preschools and infant–toddler centers (Rinaldi, 2006; Katz, 1998; Edwards et al., 1998). Exchanges with Swedish educators began as long ago as 1979, while in the United States, interest in Reggio emerged following the 1991 *Newsweek* report in which a panel of experts identified the Reggio municipal pre-school system as the best in the world. Subsequently, the Reggio educators received many requests for visits and exchanges, and Reggio-inspired preschools began to be established in many countries including Japan, Australia and Thailand, as well as the United States and Canada.

The interest in and the international reputation of the Reggio preschools have been constantly reinforced and enhanced by statements such as those from Howard Gardner. Gardner, whose Theory of Multiple Intelligences has caused a rethinking of conventional notions of human intelligence, paid tribute to the Reggio Emilia preschools when he wrote, 'To my mind, no place in the contemporary world has succeeded so splendidly as the schools of Reggio Emilia' (Gardner, 1998a, p. xviii). Similarly, Peter Moss, a former co-ordinator of the European Community Childcare Network, has been greatly influenced by the Reggio Emilia Experience and claims that one of its benefits is that it enables us to look critically at our own practice.

In her introduction to the opening of the 'Hundred Languages of Children' exhibit, the mayor of Reggio Emilia, Antonella Spaggiari, wrote: 'Here on the threshold of the twenty-first century, we have an enormous challenge ahead of us in Europe and worldwide: the challenge of providing high quality educational services for young children' (Spaggiari, 1996, p. ix). Reggio preschools appear to have succeeded in so doing. According to respected educationalists from Bruner to Gardner, Reggio preschools have succeeded in meeting this challenge, and are a most accomplished example of quality early childhood education (Katz, 1998; Dahlberg et al., 1999; Bruner, 2000; Gardner 2004; Dahlberg and Moss, 2007). Reggio has been described as 'one of the most important early childhood experiences in the world' (Rinaldi and Moss, 2004, p. 2). It has been argued that Loris Malaguzzi dedicated his life's work 'to constructing an educational experience of quality' (Hoyuelos, 2004, p. 6). Nevertheless, Reggio teachers do not claim to be experts, nor do they make claims about the standard of excellence embodied in their way of working and dealing with children. Despite this, the Reggio preschools and infant–toddler centers are attracting worldwide attention for the perceived quality of the experiences of their children. One reason for this is that quality has now become a dominant issue in early-years provision across countries and continents, in both private and state sectors.

However, Reggio Emilia educators resist the idea that theirs is a model that can be applied universally. As we have seen, they are conscious of their own history; their practice is deeply embedded in their social, cultural and political development. They therefore encourage educators wishing to draw inspiration from them to reinterpret the approach and to ensure that their practice is rooted in their own cultural values and ideals. Neither do Reggio educators (or Malaguzzi in his writings) claim that theirs is a totally original model. Rather, as we have seen in previous chapters, they acknowledge the inspiration they draw from a wide range of educational thinkers and philosophers. We have argued that the Reggio Emilia approach is situated at the child-centered, progressive and emancipatory end of the ideological continuum, encompassing both a social constructivist perspective (where children actively construct their own knowledge in an enabling, supportive environment) and a social constructionist perspective (where culturally situated, powerful, agentic children can challenge and transform through discourse with adults):

All people – and I mean scholars, researchers, and teachers, who in any place have set themselves to study children seriously – have ended up by discovering not so much the limits and weaknesses of children but rather their surprising and extraordinary strengths and capabilities linked with an inexhaustible need for expression and realisation.

(Malaguzzi, 1998, p. 78)

In looking at the literature on Reggio, we have highlighted what we have termed 'the exceptionality, yet transferability of Reggio'. A key assumption for us was that meanings are constructed, not given, and so we have attempted to make visible the meanings implicit in texts produced by and about Reggio. In this way we have attempted to generate new understandings regarding the appeal, distribution and consumption of Reggio ideas.

In this chapter, we will address the question of why the 'Reggio Experience' is perceived as being of such high quality in terms of interactions, relationships and learning opportunities. We show how it can be situated within current discourses of quality in early-years education and care. We establish its position on the quality spectrum in relation to processes, structures and outcomes, and we examine the reasons for this in the light of five main correlates of high quality provision. These indicators, which have been found to correlate positively with pedagogical practice, are: the nature of the curriculum; partnership with parents; children's participation; early-years teacher education; and, finally, the level of financial investment in early-years services (Cunningham, 2008). These have emerged from reviews of international research on quality provision and from the children's rights perspective that has informed policy and practice in many countries worldwide in recent years (Epstein, 2001; Larner and Phillips 1994; Murphy, 2002; Sheridan and Pramling-Samuelsson, 2001; Sylva et al., 2004; UN *Convention on the Rights of the Child*, 1989; Whitebook et al., 1990; Whitebook, 2003).

Quality in Early-Years Education and Care

The notion of quality in early childhood provision is a relatively new concept. It began to be applied to the field of early childhood services in the 1980s, in the form of research and policies for good practice. Today, child-care experts are in agreement that education and care in the early years are connected: 'Education and care are inextricably linked. Quality care is educational and quality education is caring' (Pugh, 1996, p. 153).

To understand recent discourse in relation to quality, one must first look at both past and present societies and the transformations that have taken place in the past 50 years. It was the modernist belief that absolute truths could be found through the use of scientific measuring and human reasoning. Rationalism was at the heart of modernity, where it was believed that, through the use of universal laws and explanations, human nature could be understood. This was a period where the world was considered ordered and knowable, where humans were seen as rational beings, who attained self-realization through the use of knowledge coupled with human reasoning. Furthermore, modern society was made up of standardizations, authoritarianism from the political and religious institutions, and pre-dictability of life cycles and outcomes. Since the 1970s, modernist thinking has been severely criticized as being dominant and oppressive because of the social conformity that it demands, which can lead to domination and exploitation with no regard for individuality or culture. Postmodern thinking 'recognizes, even welcomes uncertainty, complexity, diversity, non-linearity, subjectivity, multiple perspectives and temporal and spatial specificities' (Dahlberg et al., 1999, p. 22). Where modernity sought simple, neat answers, the postmodern perspective recognizes that there are no absolute truths and that nothing is certain:

> We asked what prompted the people of Reggio Emilia to design an early childhood education system founded on the perspective of the child. He [Bonacci, Mayor of Reggio Emilia in the 1960s] replied that the Fascist experience had taught them that people who conformed and obeyed were dangerous, and that in building a new society it was imper-ative to safeguard and communicate that lesson and nurture and maintain a vision of children who can think and act for themselves.
>
> (Dahlberg et al., 1999 p. 14)

This passage reflects the move from modern to postmodern thinking, and the importance placed on developing individualistic thinkers in Reggio Emilia. According to his biographer, Malaguzzi was a troubled individual who fought against 'the limits imposed by pedagogical culture and tradi-tion' and who questioned the rigid 'truths' that curb the possibility of thinking differently (Hoyuelos, 2004, p. 6).

In this postmodern worldview, there are no neat answers to be found in relation to what constitutes quality services: 'Ambiguity is a central compo-nent of post-modern worldviews' (Inglehart, 1997, p. 20). Reggio Emilia practitioners do not follow any one educational theorist or method: rather, 'Reggio is in a constant state of change and renewal, its present always recognized as provisional and contestable. Reggio is not a stable model producing predetermined and predictable outcomes, but a place where questions and uncertainty, change and innovation are welcome' (Rinaldi and Moss, 2004, p. 2). This perspective of ambiguity and uncertainty is frequently expressed in writings by Reggio enthusiasts, who see the world as socially constructed.

It is important then, that when looking at early-years provision, the local knowledge of communities and the values that are of importance to such communities are considered. 'In our increasingly pluralistic society, it is incumbent on those who conceptualize and institutionalize quality to incorporate differing cultural norms and values about the attributes of quality early care and education' (Phillips, 1996, p. 56). A fundamental guiding principle of Reggio Emilia's work is the reciprocity of the relationship between the schools and the wider community, in an acknowledgment of the fact that all good educational approaches must be culturally embedded.

However, the discourse of quality is, by and large, modern in nature. It is now recognized, in the postmodernist view, that many evaluations of early childhood services have come from a modern perspective and that they reflect particular ideologies and understandings of childhood and early childhood services. Allied to this are issues of power and legitimacy, because it is those in positions of power who decide what is right or wrong and true or false in the first place. Looked at in this way, meaning-making comes to the fore in evaluation. Moss refers to Reggio's application of meaning-making as a means of moving beyond evaluation and standards as end-points:

> Through the use of pedagogical documentation . . . it shows how evaluation can be understood as meaning making and making a judgement of value, so providing an alternative to the modernist concept of quality, where evaluation is understood as conformity to norms through the application of universal and stable criteria.
>
> (Moss, 2007, p. 230)

Critics of postmodern thinking would contend that, when viewing early-years services from a postmodern perspective, different participants look to different elements when focusing on quality services. An example of this would be that, while parents might look for standards in relation to their children's happiness, inspectorate teams look for standards in relation to health and safety issues. This makes absolute judgments of quality difficult, if not impossible. The discourse of meaning-making, however, involves a reciprocal interactive approach and critical reflection, as is evident in Reggio Emilia schools: 'Reciprocity implies give and take, a mutual negotiation of meaning and power' (Lather, 1991, p. 57).

Quality Frameworks

The view of what constitutes quality early-years care and education varies enormously, depending on factors such as the social, cultural and political context and the available resources, as well as the preferences of the individual child and family. However, 'No society can permit an entirely relative approach to quality in services; "anything goes" is unlikely ever to be acceptable' (Moss and Pence, 1994, p. 9). This implies a need for a common core of standards and good practices, around which individual services can build their own definition of quality.

Within these sets of standards and good practices, a broad range of criteria is used for defining quality in early-years services. These criteria encompass both static (staff ratios, structural characteristics, etc.) and dynamic or process (interactions, relationships, etc.) characteristics. Overall, the criteria used internationally to evaluate the quality of early-years services may be divided into three broad categories: structures, processes and outcomes. Woodhead (1996), for example, divides the indicators of quality in three categories: first, input, as in building, equipment and staffing; second, process, as in the style of care, range of facilities, learning and teaching, play, discipline and adult relationships; and lastly, outcomes, as in children's health, children's abilities, school adjustments and school achievement. However, quality provision must be viewed holistically:

> As in perceiving a rainbow, perceptions of quality are strongly dependent on perception, which in turn is strongly dependent on context. Consequently, quality should not be seen in a restrictive, prescriptive way, but in a holistic, relativistic way, where the context of human and material resources and social ecology of lifestyles, values and expectations of childhood are acknowledged.
>
> (Woodhead, 1996, p. 90)

Structural characteristics such as physical features, group sizes and qualifications are one element that is universally held to be closely associated with quality, although it is the view of many writers that characteristics such as these cannot guarantee quality. However, it is generally accepted that they are a prerequisite to quality process characteristics, such as good interactions between adults and children. (European Commission Network on Childcare, 1996; Larner and Phillips, 1994; Hayes, 2002). Because structural characteristics are easily measurable and quantifiable, they are generally used as the first stage in evaluating the quality of provision. Larner (1996), for example, argues that 'to judge early care and education settings fairly, professionals need criteria that are concrete, objective and quantifiable, such as child-to-adult ratios, group size and staff training' (p. 22).

Although structural features of good quality early childhood education (which include staff–child ratios, staff training, group size and wages) are important, the main components of quality lie in social interaction and direct experiences of children. These process characteristics, i.e. activities and interactions, have been identified as the key element in the evaluation of early-years services. The quality of the relationships between adults and children, and between children themselves and how these relationships support each child's overall care and education, is a crucial aspect of the overall quality of the service.

Many existing quality frameworks are based on what is considered to be 'developmentally appropriate practice' (NAEYC, 2009). However, Woodhead (1996) argues that what we term 'developmentally appropriate' is in fact embedded in 'the particular cultural niche in which dominant, expert early child development knowledge has been generated' (p. 91). In the last 20 years, there has been a move to consider children as young as three and four as part of the education system (Dahlberg and Asen, 1994). 'The problem is thus shifted to the child, with reference to his or her lack of capability and competence, ignoring the question of whether the demands in and of themselves are wrong or unreasonable' (p. 163). Such evaluation of young children can be damaging in the extreme because it sends a message to children that they have failed to learn, thus instilling in these children a sense of failure.

In contrast, measures of quality that take into account local culture, knowledge and values, provide for more collaborative and inclusive definitions of quality. Phillips (1996) recognized the locally based nature of definitions of quality in early childhood care and education and proposed a community-based and collaboratively planned system similar to the Reggio Experience. Malaguzzi himself insisted that pedagogical ideas cannot be directly exported, though they may inspire others. The local nature of what is considered to be high quality early-years provision is also emphasized by Rinaldi and Moss (2004), when they reiterate that 'the pedagogical thought and practice of Reggio comes from a very particular context and a very particular political and ethical choice' (Rinaldi and Moss, 2004, p. 3).

Towards Defining Quality in Early-Years Services

The consensus in recent years is that all participants in early-years services (children, parents, teachers, administrators, ancillary staff, families, employers, etc.) should be involved in defining the characteristics of quality (Dahlberg et al., 1999; Woodhead, 1996; Moss and Pence, 1994). These and other writers have highlighted the importance of the process of defining quality. They have questioned how this process has been carried out in the past, arguing that it has been dominated by a small group of experts, to the exclusion of others involved in early childhood institutions. It has been argued, for example, that service providers lack input in shaping discussions on the definition of quality in the early years (Phillips, 1996).

Many quality frameworks assume that within early childhood services there is an element of quality which can be determined, standardized and represented. Reggio Emilia schools make no claim of such standardized elements of quality, but 'like in the most sustained deconstructive mode, they seem to avoid assuming master discourses' (Dahlberg et. al., 1999, p. 11). Instead, 'the aim of the schools is to construct public arenas for the production of shared reflection which lets each and every individual's own thinking circulate and grow' (Cagliari et al., 2004, p. 30). Reggio preschools embrace participation by parents and the wider community, not just in the everyday running of the schools but also in planning and reflecting on pedagogy.

Children as Partners

Research into pedagogical practices shows that relatively little attention is paid to the wishes of children in relation to early childhood services (Qvortrup, 1993; Corsaro, 1997; Moss, 1999). However, concern relating to the status of children, particularly following the UN Convention on the Rights of the Child (1989), has led to initiatives to improve their status in this regard and to recognize their rights as citizen and actors:

> The Convention on the Rights of the Child reinforces this viewpoint, encouraging adults to allow a high degree of initiative to young children. A new culture of participation and co-determination is now emerging in areas of life important for young children, including life in early childhood centres . . .
>
> (UNESCO, 2004, p. 1)

Children should be considered as the most important partners in any discussion of quality in early-years services, particularly with the shift in thinking in recent years towards a children's rights perspective. From this perspective, children are recognized as citizens; as social actors; as learners from birth and co-constructors of knowledge and identity. When looking at quality in relation to early childhood services, we should listen to children, because what they have to tell us is important and something that only the children as partners of these services can express: 'These examples show that even young children have strong opinions about their everyday life, and there is evidence that you can improve the life conditions of children by listening to and going along with their opinions about their everyday life' (Langsted, 1994, p. 41).

Sheridan and Pramling-Samuelsson (2001) also suggest that it is vital that children participate in decision-making. They argue that one cannot truly evaluate the quality of early education and care services without listening to the voices of the children. This necessitates a rethinking of children's status in society, where children are no longer seen as adults in waiting and childhood is seen as an entity in itself rather than as a conveyor belt for producing society's future workforce.

Until relatively recently, children's perspectives were not sought, under the belief that children did not have the linguistic skills to be reliable informants (O'Doherty et al., 2002). However, children's participation is a fundamental guiding principle of Reggio schools. Through the practice of co-operation and solidarity, democracy and emancipation are fostered. Hence, civil society is seen as a place 'in which children and adults participate together in projects of social, cultural, political and economic significance' (Moss, 1999, p. 73). They are also considered to be critical thinkers and powerful pedagogues within a pedagogy of relationships (Moss, 1999). The emphasis here is on children as co-constructors of knowledge, through critical thinking and meaning-making, rather than children as recipients of pre-packaged answers to pre-determined education programs.

Malaguzzi's philosophy starts with the child, seeing the child as a possessor of extraordinary potential. Children are viewed as strong, competent and capable, with the ability to express their own ideas and therefore, within a democratic environment, are given the freedom to make independent choices on issues that affect them. Malaguzzi, in an interview with Carlo Barsotti, made the following response to the perception of children being frail, delicate and passive:

Our response to this is one of total contrast . . . we support a vision of the child who is extremely open to the world, strongly equipped from the moment of birth, rich in resources, in abilities and in qualities which urge us to define democracy in a new way. I believe that today this means giving back to individuals their central importance inside society, attributing value to the ability and the will of individuals to act, and be recognised, as free and responsible agents.

(Malaguzzi, 1993c, p. 15)

Parents as Partners

As discussed in Chapter 3, parental involvement is a fundamental element in quality early childhood education and care (Larner and Phillips, 1994; Tijus et al., 1997; Bridge, 2001; Murphy, 2002). Parental partnership is characterized by a shared sense of purpose and an ongoing sharing of information, responsibility, decision-making and accountability (Pugh and De'Ath, 1989). Only recently have parents' views and wishes been given due consideration when defining quality in early-years provision. Prior to this, it was early childhood professionals who controlled what was viewed as constituting quality preschool education. 'The child's knowledge will be crucially dependent upon and filtered through systems over which the ordinary family has little control' (Gammage, 1999, p. 154).

It is clear that quality is a paramount issue for parents in relation to services for their children. They act as advocates for their children's interests within the services. Research shows that it is their perception of their children's experiences, rather than structural standards, that are the deciding factors for parents when choosing services for their children. Larner and Phillips (1994), in their review of research, found that, for most parents, quality services involved 'taking the time for each child' and 'really caring about them and their well being', as well as 'teaching them' and 'being qualified to care for children' (p. 51).

It is notable that the first Reggio Emilia schools were founded by the parents, and that parental participation is at the heart of the pedagogical experience of Reggio schools (Spaggiari, 1998). Malaguzzi (1998) points out that it was from the aspiration of the parents that Reggio Emilia's philosophies evolved, because it was they who wanted legitimate rights and citizenship for their children to be central to the ethos of the schools. As detailed in Chapter 3, parents' involvement in Reggio schools starts when the toddler enters an infant–toddler center and continues throughout the time the child attends the preschool and beyond.

An integral part of the Reggio Emilia experience and ethos is the recognition of the importance of partnership with parents. The partnership involves an ongoing process of dialog with parents and the sharing of documentation of children's experiences and thoughts. This partnership allows teachers to get a better understanding of the children through dialogue with their parents. Furthermore, parents' involvement in the management of the Reggio schools means that parents are involved in decisions affecting their children. Parents are actively involved in decision-making and problem-solving in the everyday running of the school, which demonstrates 'the critical role of parents as protagonists alongside their children and the teachers (Fontanesi et al., 1998, p. 149).

Early-Years Teacher Education

A major research project in early-years services in the UK found that the key to quality rests with practitioners themselves (Blenkin and Kelly, 1997). Quality in working with young children is contingent upon a commitment on the part of practitioners to reflect on and improve their ongoing practice. Pugh (1999) contends that this can only be achieved through staff development, and for this reason the central theme of early-years services must be the commitment to the pre-service and in-service preparation of staff.

Many studies have shown that regulations requiring even a modest level of training for practitioners in day-care centres could have important and positive effects on job performance and the quality of experiences for children. This serves to emphasize the vital relationship that exists between training and quality in early childhood provision (Smith, 1996; Moss and Penn, 1996; Arnett, 1989; Curtis, 1996). Thus, it is agreed that the level of qualification and training of the practitioner has a direct effect on the quality of the service and that one cannot discuss quality without taking into account the qualification of the staff.

Studies in several countries have found that the education of the practitioner directly correlates with the quality of the service (Ruopp et al., 1979; European Commission Network on Childcare, 1996; Sylva et al., 2004). Whitebook (2003) found that practitioners who held a bachelor's degree in early education were 'the teachers who are best equipped to lay the groundwork for an optimistic and rewarding experience in pre-kindergarten and beyond' (p. 4). Indeed, it is argued that teachers with bachelor's degrees in early education are 'more effective in their responsive involvement and in being engaged with children in activities that promote language development and emergent literacy than most teachers without BA degrees' (Howes et al., 2003, p. 118). Reggio Emilia teachers generally have a recognized university degree, with the exception of teachers employed prior to 1998, who normally hold a vocational qualification (Pacini-Ketchabaw et al., 2006).

Other research indicates that there is a need for ongoing training and support, targeted towards practitioners' interactions with children (Early et al., 2007). International studies in nursery education in many European countries found that in-service training was important and a key means of keeping up to date, improving and developing practice. A number of studies have found that following in-service training, staff adopted a more sensitive and supportive role with young children (Arnett, 1989; Cassidy et al., 1995; Penn, 1997; Rhodes and Hennessy, 2000). An American study was undertaken of a state-funded Enhancement Grant project for the professional development of child-care personnel over a three-year period. The study found that, after this period, significant improvements were obtained in a number of areas essential to high quality care for young children (Fontaine et al., 2006).

Indeed Bennett (2004), in a UNESCO Policy Brief, states that well-trained and well-supported staff are an essential precondition of an open framework approach to curriculum, where rigid guidelines are not imposed and practitioners have greater autonomy. As discussed in Chapter 4, the training within Reggio Emilia preschools offers teachers extensive in-service staff development opportunities. It must also be noted that, since 1998, preschool teachers in Italy receive pay parity with their primary school counterparts. This is rare, as numerous studies have found that early-years practitioners are poorly paid (Whitebook et al., 1990; Whitebook, 1999; NIEER, 2004; OECD, 2004; Murphy, 2005; NESF, 2005). According to Whitebook (1999), employment in child care offers low salaries, few job benefits, and very little opportunity for professional advancement. Italy is now one of the few countries in the world which offers preschool teachers remuneration that equals that of other teaching professionals.

The Nature of the Curriculum

In Chapter 4, it was argued that the curriculum in Reggio preschools is social constructivist in nature, with some gravitation towards social constructionism. Underpinning this is a view of the child as an active, empowered citizen. The cumulative body of evidence from child development studies, neuroscience and critical theory, has identified child-centered/ progressive and emancipatory models of curriculum, such as those in Reggio, as key determinants of holistic child development in early-years education and care services.

In Reggio, it is believed that children learn best in a well-resourced, well-prepared environment, with highly qualified practitioners (see Chapter 2). The starting point of all practice in Reggio Emilia schools is that the child has rights rather than simply needs. A core principle is the development of critical thinkers, through opportunities to engage, explore, discuss, represent, hypothesize and problem-solve. What is obvious here is that Reggio schools do not endorse the premature schooling of their children, in the sense of following a traditional curriculum with defined cognitive goals and content. Rather, they embrace a critical pedagogy committed to empowering their children to be reflective thinkers within an equal and democratic society.

The influence of Reggio Emilia on what is considered appropriate practice may be noted in the views expressed, for example, in the UNESCO policy brief on curriculum in early childhood education and care (Bennett, 2004). This briefing notes that many countries now issue broad curricular frameworks which respect and acknowledge the rights of young children and the nature of learning in early childhood. In particular, there is a greater recognition than formerly of the importance of relationships, and of children's initiative and involvement:

> It is recognised, for example, that for deep and more permanent learning to take place, the child's environment should be constructed 'so as to interface the cognitive realm with the realms of relationship and affectivity' (Malaguzzi, in Edwards et al., 1993). In other words, young children's learning is grounded in the affective and social domains. Children learn best within positive relationships – with their parents and families, with their peers and with well-trained early childhood educators.
> (Bennett, 2004, pp. 1–2)

The direct influence of Reggio Emilia and of Malaguzzi can be seen in this quotation; it is by no means untypical of recent documents on curriculum.

Financial Investment

Since 1968, Italy has achieved free universal preschool education for all three- to six-year-old children and is one of few countries in the world that does so. Allied to this, the Italian government fully supports and recognizes the importance of early childhood education through its legislative process. All state-run services are fully funded by the government; funding is transferred from state to municipalities and provinces to manage the expenses of the state services. Funding is allocated as follows: the central government provides funding for administrative costs such as staffing; the regions fund the capital costs and student services such as transport and meals; and the provinces and municipalities fund the costs of maintaining the school buildings (Qualifications and Curriculum Authority, 2005). As we have noted, preschool teachers in Italy enjoy pay parity with primary school teachers, which is not the case in many other countries.

Reggio Emilia preschools are rich in resources, well financed and employ highly qualified teachers, conditions that have been associated with high quality early-years provision. In Reggio, the environment is viewed as the 'third teacher'. As discussed in Chapter 2, the structural characteristics of Reggio Emilia schools are unique in many respects: the relationship between the teachers, *atelierista* and *pedagogista*, the provision of an *atelier* in each school, and in the arrangement of space, light, furniture and play materials. All of this evidences the commitment in Reggio Emilia to maintaining the quality of their early-years provision.

However, it must be acknowledged that there are huge financial benefits accruing to Reggio Emilia schools following their international success. Interest in Reggio-inspired schools has grown internationally, with 80 countries involved in ongoing study tours to Italy to learn more about the approach. These tours are hosted by 'Reggio Children' which organizes courses in professional development, seminars and study meetings in both Italy and internationally. From March 1994 to May 2007, more than 150 groups visited Reggio Emilia preschools, totalling almost 20,000 people (Reggio Children, 2007). In this light, cognizance must be taken of the fact that, in 2009, the cost of participating in a five-day workshop in Reggio Emilia is approximately £1,250 sterling (Sightlines Initiative, 2009). By 2007, over 20,000 participants had undertaken these workshops.

In addition to this, between 1980 and 2007, 'The Hundred Languages of Children' exhibition was hosted in over 120 venues in various cities and countries worldwide. It is worth noting that the Reggio materials used in these exhibitions cost each recipient city or country approximately €15,000 per month, payable to Reggio Children (personal e-mail from Reggio Children, 19 February 2009). Furthermore, this figure does not include the considerable additional costs of housing and running these exhibitions.

An additional income is generated by the sale of publications. By 2007, the Reggio Children association had overseen the publication of over 30 books pertaining to the Reggio Experience. More than 200,000 copies of these books have been sold worldwide and they have been translated into 16 different languages (Reggio Children, 2007). It is interesting to note that, as Reggio Children is a limited company, there is no available access to their financial statements. However, Reggio Children state that from 1994 (the year of its inception) to 2006, they have invested more than €1,700,000 in their early-years centers (Reggio Children, 2007). Company profits are reinvested for the future development of the schools and for educational research. Thus, the Reggio preschools have access to considerable additional funding compared to their counterparts elsewhere. The benefits to the city and the region of so many visitors must also be noted.

Conclusion

We set out in this chapter to locate Reggio Emilia within the contemporary discourse on quality in early-years education and care. As we have found, while quality is widely sought after, it is more difficult to pin down and define. We have emphasized the locally based and culturally specific nature of definitions of quality, and shown that, in these terms, the Reggio Emilia preschools and infant–toddler centers are of very high quality indeed. We have also seen that their reputation is worldwide, and that in spite of the reluctance of the Reggio educators to see themselves as a model, they have influenced thinking on quality provision in many countries throughout the world. This is in spite of (or perhaps partly because of) the very different approach they take to defining quality. As Gardner points out, much of what is special about Reggio Emilia has grown out of promising practices, developed and reflected upon, rather than from a theoretical basis. The interweaving of teaching, learning, documentation, assessment, individual and group learning, also adds to the challenge of understanding Reggio. Finally, Gardner identifies the way in which the Reggio preschools use visual and graphic representations rather than written accounts to document their work as signifying a way of thinking and of being that is very different from the more familiar US model (Project Zero/Reggio Children, 2001).

This last point is significant in the light of the debate about quality. In the introduction to this chapter, we set out three aspects of early-years education and care that have been found to be significant in this regard: structures, processes and outcomes. Throughout this book, we have explored the structures that support the children of Reggio Emilia and their teachers, and we have looked at the processes in terms of curriculum, participation by children and partnership with parents, families and the community. We now come to look at the third element, that of outcomes. As Mooney and her colleagues point out, much existing empirical research on quality has been undertaken in the United States, and it has been highly influenced by developmental psychology. Hence, the emphasis has been on attempting to measure the effects of child care on children's intellectual, social and emotional development (Mooney et al., 2003). This focus on specific developmental outcomes reflects a particular set of values and priorities – just as the Reggio Emilia Experience reflects a very different view of children and of early-years education. For the Reggio educators, the focus is on the present, on the here-and-now. They are concerned with listening to children and their parents, with fostering relationships, with enabling children to express themselves in all of the 'hundred languages'. The notion of the competent child, which has been so much to the fore in the Nordic countries, also permeates practice in Reggio Emilia. It is allied to the principle that children have rights – individual, social and legal – as eloquently expressed in Malaguzzi's 'Bill of Three Rights' (Malaguzzi, 1993a).

There is no doubt that the Reggio Emilia educators are aided in this endeavor by the resources to which they have access, both structural and intellectual. The culture of relationship and listening within which they work emphasizes the importance of belonging and community. The paradox is that in emphasizing the local, culturally situated, nature of their practice, they have inspired countless others worldwide.

Conclusion

The municipal preschools and infant–toddler centers of Reggio Emilia have attracted worldwide attention and many imitators. The principles of children's rights, children as active initiators of their own development in collaboration with adults as listeners, the notion of making learning visible through documentation, the environment as teacher, the significance of parents and community involvement, are all hallmarks that appeal to educators everywhere. In a world that is increasingly preoccupied with measurement, targets, international comparisons, competition, outcomes and productivity, the ideas inherent in the Reggio Emilia Experience represent a refreshing and attractive counter-discourse of process, diversity and attention to relationships and self-expression.

Reggio Emilia educators resist the idea that they follow any particular curriculum model; however, it is apparent that they adopt a particular view of children, of knowledge and of the world. This volume presented and examined the main ideological perspectives underpinning Reggio Emilia preschools. Our analysis leads us to the conclusion that the Reggio Emilia approach is fundamentally child-centered, progressive and emancipatory in curriculum and pedagogic orientation, encompassing both a social constructivist perspective, where children actively construct their own knowledge in an enabling, supportive environment, and social constructionist perspective, where the culturally situated, powerful, agentic child can challenge and transform through interaction with adults and peers.

The Reggio Emilia preschools developed in a particular historical, social and political context. The support for parties of the Left placed this region in an unenviable position during the 1920s, 1930s and the early years of the 1940s when Fascism dominated the Italian political scene. In the case of Reggio Emilia, its anti-Fascist sentiments, its experiences during the Second World War, and its disaffection with the Catholic Church which dominated preschool provision, directly influenced the type of preschools which emerged in 1945 and later years. It was the parents of Reggio Emilia who decided to establish preschools which would reflect their social, democratic and political principles. Their struggles, both financial and political, resulted not only in the end of the Catholic Church's domination of preschool provision, but in a change of government policies in relation to the control, funding and administration of early-years education and care settings, not only in Reggio Emilia, but in Italy itself. This legacy has resulted in early-years provision which is rich in resources, well financed and employing highly qualified staff, all prerequisites of quality services, as we have demonstrated with reference to contemporary debates about quality in early-years education.

A key assumption for us is that meanings are constructed, not given, and so we were interested in making visible how meanings in the published material on Reggio are produced. This approach allowed us to examine and challenge some of those constructions. Subscribing to the view that in describing the world, language simultaneously creates it, we considered how Reggio texts talk, write and draw Reggio thinking into life, into being. Our analysis challenges the conclusion drawn by some that Reggio is atheoretical. We have shown how Reggio Emilia principles and practices are replete with theoretical underpinnings, some of which are in tension and many of which are implicit rather than explicit in the literature.

Along with presenting and critically reviewing the main tenets of Reggio Emilia approaches, we suggest that diversity issues, particularly race and gender, merit greater attention in Reggio practices and research. More generally, we would suggest there is a need for more systematic empirical research on the Reggio Emilia Experience at the level of all participants.

What is fundamental also in our view in terms of Reggio's relevance for early-years education today is the way education is much more favorably supported and funded in this part of Italy than in other parts of the world. The level of investment in human and material resources is in no small way a factor in the international reputation of the quality of Reggio provision.

However, a mindset about children, learning and community triggered this level of resourcing in Reggio Emilia. This mindset which evolved within the community preceded resources. Its philosophical pedagogy, based on children's rights and capabilities, and on educators' focus on fostering relationships and attention to what is salient to children and their communities, is likely to continue to influence educators well into the future.

Appendix

'No Way – The Hundred is There'

Loris Malaguzzi

(translated by Lella Gandini)

The child
is made of one hundred.
The child has
a hundred languages
a hundred hands
a hundred thoughts
a hundred ways of thinking
of playing, of speaking.
A hundred, always a hundred
ways of listening
of marvelling, of loving,
a hundred joys
for singing and understanding
a hundred worlds
to discover
a hundred worlds
to invent
a hundred worlds
to dream.
The child has
a hundred languages
(and a hundred hundred hundred more)
but they steal ninety-nine.
The school and the culture
separate the head from the body.
They tell the child
to think without hands
to do without head
to listen and not to speak
to understand without joy

to love and to marvel
only at Easter and Christmas.
They tell the child
to discover the world already there
and of the hundred
they steal ninety-nine.
They tell the child
that work and play
reality and fantasy
science and imagination
sky and earth
reason and dream
are things
that do not belong together.
And thus they tell the child
that the hundred is not there.
The child says
'No way – The hundred is there'

(Reproduced from *The Hundred Languages of Children*, Carolyn Edwards, Lella Gandini and George Forman (eds). Copyright © 1998 by Ablex Publishing Corporation. Reproduced with permission of Greenwood Publishing Group, Inc., Westport, CT.)

References

Abbott, L. and Langston, A. (2006*), Parents Matter: Supporting the Birth to Three Matters Framework*. London: McGraw-Hill International.

Abbott, L. and Nutbrown, C. (eds) (2001), *Experiencing Reggio Emilia: Implications for Pre-school Provision*. Berkshire: Open University Press.

Abramson, S., Robinson, R. and Ankenman, K. (1995), 'Project work with diverse students'. *Childhood Education*, Summer.

Ankenman, Katie (1995), 'Project work with diverse students: adapting curriculum based on the Reggio Emilia approach'. *Childhood Education*, Summer, 197–202.

Apple, M. (1979), *Ideology and Curriculum*. London: Routledge and Kegan Paul.

—— (1980), 'Curricular form and the logic of technical control', in L. Barton, R. Meighan and S. Walker (eds), *Schooling, Ideology and the Curriculum*. Lewes: Falmer Press.

—— (1982a), *Education and Power*. London: Routledge and Kegan Paul.

—— (1982b), *Cultural and Economic Reproduction in Education*. London: Routledge and Kegan Paul.

Armstrong, T. (1994), *Multiple Intelligences in the Classroom*. Virginia: Association of Supervision and Curriculum Development.

—— (2003), *The Multiple Intelligences of Reading and Writing*. Virginia: Association of Curriculum and Assessment.

Arnett J. (1989), 'Caregivers in day-care centers: does training matter?' *Journal of Applied Developmental Psychology*, 10, 541–52.

Bakhtin, M.M. (1986), *Speech Genres and Other Late Essays*. Austin: University of Texas Press.

Balaguer, I. (2004), 'Social management and participation: heart or head in the childhood schools in Reggio'. *Children in Europe*, 6, 31–2.

Barazzoni, R. (2000), *Brick by Brick: The History of the "XXV Aprile" People's Nursery School of Villa Cella*. Reggio Emilia: Reggio Children.

Barrow, R. (1990), 'Teacher education: theory and practice'. *British Journal of Educational Studies*, 38 (4), 307–12.

Barsotti C. (2004), 'Walking on threads of silk: interview with Loris Malaguzzi'. *Children in Europe*, 6, 10–15.

Bennett, J. (2004), *Curriculum in Early Childhood Education and Care*. UNESCO Policy Brief on Early Childhood, No. 26, September.

Berk, L. and Winsler, A. (1995), *Scaffolding Children's Learning: Vygotsky and Early Childhood Education*. Washington, DC: NAEYC.

Bernstein, B. (1971), 'On the classification and framing of educational knowledge', in M.F.D. Young (ed.), *Knowledge and Control: New Directions for the Sociology of Education*. London: Collier-Macmillan.

—— (1972), *Praxis and Action*. London: Duckworth.

167

—— (1976), 'On the classification and framing of educational knowledge', in M.F.D. Young (ed.), *Knowledge and Control: New Directions for the Sociology of Education*. London: Collier-Macmillan.

—— (1977a), *Class, Codes and Control. Volume 3: Towards a Theory of Educational Transmissions*. London: Routledge and Kegan Paul.

—— (1977b), 'Education cannot compensate for society', in B.R. Cosin, I.R. Dale, G.M. Esland, D. MacKinnon and D.F. Swift (eds), *School and Society: A Sociological Reader*. London: Routledge and Kegan Paul for Open University Press.

—— (ed.) (1971), *Class, Codes and Control. Volume 1: Theoretical Studies Towards a Sociology of Language*. London and Boston, MA: Routledge and Kegan Paul.

Blenkin, G.M. and Kelly, A.V. (1988), *Early Childhood Education: A Developmental Curriculum*: Paul Chapman.

—— (1996), *Early Childhood Education: A Developmental Curriculum* (2nd edn), London: Paul Chapman.

—— (1997), *Principles into Practice in Early Childhood Education*. London: Paul Chapman.

Bloom, B., Englehart, M., Furst, E. and Kratwohl, D.(1956), *Taxonomy of Educational Objectives: The Classification of Educational Goals. Handbook I: Cognitive Domain*. London: Longman.

Board of Education, Central Advisory Council for Education (1967), *Children and their Primary Schools*. Plowden Report. Lady Bridget Plowden, Chairman. London: HMSO.

Bonalauri, S., Filippini, T., Davoli, M. and Ferri, G. (2004), 'The city: images, ideas and theories'. *Children in Europe*, 6, 24–6.

Booth, A. and Dunn, J.F. (eds) (1996), *Family–School Links: How Do They Affect Educational Outcomes?* Mahwah: Lawrence Erlbaum.

Bourdieu, P. and Passeron, J.C. (1977), *Reproduction in Education, Society and Culture*. London: Sage Publications.

—— (1979), *The Inheritors*. Chicago: University of Chicago Press.

Bowles, S. and Gintis, H. (1976), *Schooling in Capitalist America*. London: Routledge and Kegan Paul.

—— (1977), 'Capitalism in education', in M. Young and G. Whitty (eds), *Society, State and Schooling*. Eastbourne: Falmer Press.

Boyd-Cadwell, L. (1997), *Bringing Reggio Emilia Home: An Innovative Approach to Early Childhood Education*. New York: Teachers College Press.

—— (2003), *Bringing Learning to Life: The Reggio Approach to Early Childhood Education*. New York: Teachers College Press.

Bransford, J.D., Brown, A.L. and Cocking, R.R. (eds) (1999), *How People Learn*. Washington, DC: National Academy Press.

Bridge, H. (2001), 'Increasing parental involvement in the preschool curriculum: what an action research case study revealed'. *International Journal of Early Years Education*, 9, 1.

Bronfenbrenner, U. (1979), *The Ecology of Human Development: Experiments by Nature and Design*. Cambridge, MA: Harvard University Press.

Bronfenbrenner, U. and Morris, P.A. (1998), 'The ecology of developmental processes', in W. Damon (series ed.) and R.M. Lerner (vol. ed.), *Handbook of Child Psychology: Vol. 1: Theoretical Models of Human Development*. New York: Wiley, 993–1028.

Brooker, L. (2005), 'Learning to be a child: cultural diversity and early years ideology', in N. Yelland (ed.), *Critical Issues in Early Childhood Education*. Maidenhead: Open University Press, 115–30.

Browne, N. (2004), *Gender Equity in the Early Years*. Berkshire: Open University Press.

Brubacher, J. (1966), *A History of the Problems of Education*. New York: McGraw Hill.

Bruner, J.S. (1963), *The Process of Education*. New York: Vintage Books.
—— (1964), 'The course of cognitive growth'. *American Psychologist*, 19, 1–15.
—— (1966, 1968), *Toward the Theory of Instruction*. Cambridge, MA: The Belknap Press of Harvard University Press.
—— (1972a), 'The course of cognitive growth', in A. Cashden and E. Grugeon (eds), *Language in Education*. London: Routledge and Kegan Paul.
—— (1972b), 'The nature and use of immaturity'. *American Psychologist*, 27, 687–708.
—— (1980), *Under Five in Britain*. London: Grant McIntyre.
—— (1990), *Acts of Meaning*. Cambridge, MA: Harvard University Press.
—— (2000), 'Citizens of the world: excerpt from speech on receiving honorary citizenship from the mayor and City Council of Reggio Emilia', in M. Davoli and G. Ferri (eds), *Reggio Tutta: A Guide to the City by the Children*. Reggio Emilia: Reggio Children, 122–3.
—— (2003), 'Some specifications for a space to house a Reggio preschool', in G. Ceppi and M. Zini (eds), *Children, Spaces Relations: Metaproject for an Environment for Young Children*. Reggio Emilia: Municipality of Reggio Emilia.
—— (2004), 'Reggio: a city of courtesy, curiosity and imagination'. *Children in Europe*, 6, 27.
Bruner, J.S. and Haste, H. (eds) (1987), *Making Sense: The Child's Construction of the World*. London and New York: Methuen.
Buber, M. (1980), in P. Murphy and B. Moon (eds), *Developments in Learning and Assessment*. Milton Keynes: Open University Press.
Cagliari P., Barozzi A. and Guidici, C. (2004), 'Thoughts, theories, and experiences for the educational project with participation'. *Children in Europe*, 6, 28–30.
Campbell, B. (2008), *Handbook of Differentiated Instruction Using the Multiple Intelligences*. Boston: Allyn and Bacon.
Campbell, L. and Campbell, B. (1999), *Multiple Intelligences and Student Achievement*. Virginia: Association for Supervision and Curriculum Development.
Caplan, J.G. (1998) *Critical Issue: Constructing School Partnerships with Family and Community Groups*. Oak Brook, IL: North Central Regional Educational Laboratory. Accessed September 2008 at http://www.ncrel.org/sdrs/areas/issues/envrnmnt/famncomm/pa400.htm.
Carr, W. and Kemmis, S. (1986), *Becoming Critical: Education, Knowledge and Active Research*. London: Falmer Press.
Carsten, F.L. (1967) *The Rise of Fascism*. London: Methuen.
Cassidy D.J., Buell M.J., Pugh-Hoese, S. and Russell, S. (1995), 'The effect of education on childcare teachers' beliefs and classroom quality: Year One of the TEACH early childhood associate degree scholarship programme'. *Early Childhood Research Quarterly*, 10 (2), 171–83.
Catarsi, Enzo (2004), 'Loris Malaguzzi and the municipal school revolution'. *Children in Europe*, 6, 8–9.
Centre for Early Childhood Development and Education (CECDE) (2006), *Síolta: The National Quality Framework for Early Childhood Education Handbook*. Dublin: Centre for Early Childhood Development and Education.
Ceppi, G. and Zini, M. (eds) (2003), *Children, Spaces, Relations: Metaproject for an Environment for Young Children*. Reggio Emilia: Municipality of Reggio Emilia.
Charters, W.W. (1924), *Curriculum Construction*. New York: Macmillan.
Children in Scotland (2004), 'Celebrating 40 years of Reggio Emilia: the pedagogical thought and practice underlying the world-renowned early years services in Italy'. *Children in Europe*, 6.

Ciari, B. (1961), *The New Teaching Techniques*. Rome: Editori Riuniti.

—— (1972), *The Great Maladjusted*. Rome: Editori Riuniti.

Corsaro W.A. (1997), *The Sociology of Childhood*. California: Pine Forge Press.

Costa, A. and Kallick, B. (2000), *Assessing and Reporting on Habits of Mind*. Virginia: Association for Supervision and Curriculum Development.

Council of Europe (2008), *Intercultural Cities: Governance and Policies for Diverse Communities: Reggio Emilia, Italy*. Accessed November 2008 at http://www.coe.int/t/dg4/cultureheritage/Policies/Cities/reggio_en.asp.

Cunningham, D. (2008), *An Exploration of the Perspectives of the Various Stakeholders of Preschool Education in Ireland in Relation to Quality Practice*. University College Cork: unpublished PhD dissertation.

Curtis, A. (1996), 'Do we train our early childhood educators to respect children?', in C. Nutbrown (ed.), *Respectful Educators, Capable Learners: Children's Rights and Early Education*. London: Paul Chapman.

Curtis, D. and Carter, M. (2003), *Designs for Living and Learning*. St Paul, Minnesota: Redleaf Press.

Dahlberg, G. (1999), 'Early childhood pedagogy in a changing world', in J. Robertson and A. Fleet (1999), *Unpacking Observation and Documentation: Experiences from Italy, Sweden and Australia*. Conference Proceedings, North Ryde, Australia, 24–25 September 1999. Downloaded November 2008 from ERIC database, at http://eric.ed.gov/ERICDocs/data/ericdocs2sql/content_storage_01/0000019b/80/1a/8a/42.pdf.

—— (2004), 'Making connections'. *Children in Europe*, March, 21–2.

Dahlberg, G. and Asen, G. (1994), 'Evaluation and regulation: a question of empowerment', in P. Moss and A. Pence (eds), *Valuing Quality in Early Childhood Services: New Approaches to Defining Quality*. London: Paul Chapman.

Dahlberg, G., Moss, P. and Pence, A. (1999), *Beyond Quality in Early Childhood Education*. London: Falmer Press.

Dahlberg, G. and Moss, P. (2007), 'Introduction: our Reggio Emilia', in C. Rinaldi, *In Dialogue with Reggio Emilia: Listening, Researching and Learning*. Abingdon: Routledge, 1–22.

Darwin, C. (1871), *The Descent of Man and Selection in Relation to Sex*. New York: Appleton.

Davies, I.K. (1976), *Objectives in Curriculum Design*. Maidenhead: McGraw-Hill.

de Carvalho, Maria Eulina P. (2001), *Rethinking Family–School Relations: A Critique of Parental Involvement in Schooling*. New York: Lawrence Erlbaum Associates.

Deegan, J.G. (2008), 'Teacher–writer memoirs as lens for writing emotionally in a primary teacher education programme'. *Teaching Education*, 19 (3), 186–96.

Della Peruta, F. (1980), 'At the origins of early childhood assistance in Italy', in I. Sala La Guardia and E. Lucchini (eds), *Asili nido in Italia*. Milan: Marzorati.

Department of Education, Ireland (1971), *Curaclam na Bunscoile Teacher's Handbook Parts 1 and 2*. Dublin: Government Publication.

Department of Justice, Equality and Law Reform (1999), *National Childcare Strategy: Report of the Partnership 2000 Expert Working Group on Childcare*. Dublin: Stationery Office, Government Publications.

DeVries, R. and Zan, B. (1994), *Moral Classroom, Moral Children: Creating a Constructivist Atmosphere in Early Education*, New York: Teachers College Press.

Dewey, D. and Dewey, E. (1962), *Schools of Tomorrow*. New York: Dutton and Co.

Dewey, J. (1913), *Interest and Effort in Education*. Cambridge, MA: Riverside Press.

—— (1938), *Experience and Education*. Kappa-Delta.

—— (1938), *Experience and Education*. New York: Colier-Macmillan.

—— (1966), *Democracy and Education: An Introduction of the Philosophy of Education*. New York: Free Press.

Doyle, W. (1978), 'Paradigms for research on teacher effectiveness', in L.S. Shulman (ed.), *Review of Research in Education Volume 5*. Itasca: Peacock, 163–98.

Early D.M., Maxwell, K.L. and Burchinal, M. (2007), 'Teacher's education, classroom quality, and young children's academic skills: results from seven studies of preschool programs'. *Child Development*, 78 (2), 558–80.

Edwards, C. (1995), 'Democratic participation in a community of learners: Loris Malaguzzi's philosophy of education as relationship'. Lecture prepared for 'Nostalgia del Futuro', an international seminar to consider the educational contributions of Loris Malaguzzi, Milan, October 1995. Accessed September 2008 at http://digitalcommons.unl.edu/famconfacpub/15.

Edwards, C.P. (1998), 'Partner, nurturer and guide: The role of the teacher', in C. Edwards, L. Gardini and G. Forman (eds), *The Hundred Languages of Children*. Norwood, NY: Ablex Publishing, 179–98.

—— (2002), 'Three approaches from Europe: Waldorf, Montessori and Reggio Emilia'. *Early Childhood Research and Practice*, 4 (1). Accessed October 2008 at http://ecrp.uiuc.edu/v4n1/edwards.html.

Edwards, C., Gandini, L. and Forman, G. (1993), *The Hundred Languages of Children: The Reggio Emilia Approach to Early Childhood Education*. Norwood, NJ: Ablex Publishing.

—— (eds) (1998), *The Hundred Languages of Children: The Reggio Emilia Approach – Advanced Reflections* (2nd edn). Westport: Ablex Publishing.

Edwards, C. and Raikes, H. (2002), 'Extending the dance: Relationship-based approaches to infant/toddler care and education. *Young Children*, July, 10–17.

Edwards, C. P. and Gandini, L. (2008), Filastrocca preschool in Pistoia, Italy: Promoting early literacy through books and the imagination: A conversation with Alga Giacomelli. Accessed January 2009 at http://digitalcommons.unl.edu/famconfacpub/59/.

Egan, K. (1998), *The Educated Mind: How Cognitive Tools Shape our Understanding*. Chicago: University of Chicago Press.

Eisner, E. (1993), 'Rethinking what schools are for'. Paper delivered at St Patrick's College of Education, Dublin, 9 October.

—— (1996), 'Curriculum ideologies', in P.W. Jackson (ed.), *Handbook of Research on Curriculum: A Project of the American Educational Research Association*. New York: Simon and Schuster, pp. 302–26.

Elman, J., Bates, E., Johnson, M., Karmiloff-Smith, A., Parisi, D. and Plunkett, K. (1998), *Rethinking Innateness*. Cambridge, MA: MIT Press.

Engels, F. (1888 [2002]), *Preface to the 1888 English Edition of the Communist Manifesto*. London: Penguin.

Epstein, J.L. (1995), 'School/family/community partnerships: caring for the children we share'. *Phi Delta Kappan*, 76 (9), 701–12.

—— (2001), *School, Family and Community Partnerships: Preparing Educators and Improving Schools*. Boulder, and Oxford: Westview Press.

European Commission Network on Childcare (1996), *Quality Targets in Service of Young Children*. Brussels: European Commission Network on Childcare.

Eurybase Italy 2006/07. Accessed November 2008 at www.eurydice.org.

Feldman, D.H. (1980/1994), *Beyond Universals in Cognitive Development* (2nd edn). Norwood: Ablex Publishing.

—— (1998), 'How spectrum began', in J. Chen, J. Viens and M. Krechevsky (eds), *Building* on *Children's Strengths: The Experience of Project Spectrum.* New York: Teachers College Press.

Filippini, T. (1998), 'An interview with Lella Gandini', in C. Edwards, L. Gandini and G. Forman (eds), *The Hundred Languages of Children.* Norwood: Ablex Publishing, 127–37.

Fleetham, M. (2006), *Multiple Intelligences in Practice.* Stafford: Network Continuum Education.

Flett, Marion (2007), 'Supporting mothers. Enriching the learning environment for young children'. *Early Childhood Matters*, 109, 45–50.

Fontaine, N.S., Torre, L.D., Grafwallner, R. and Underhill, B. (2006), 'Increasing quality in early care and learning environments'. *Early Child Development and Care*, 176 (2), 157–69.

Fontanesi G., Gialdini M. and Soncini, M. (1998), 'The voice of parents: an interview with Lella Gandini', in C. Edwards, L. Gandini and G. Forman (eds), *The Hundred Languages of Children: The Reggio Emilia Approach. Advanced Reflections* (2nd edn). Westport: Ablex Publishing.

Forman, G. (1996), 'The "Project Approach" in Reggio Emilia', in C.T. Fosnot (ed.), *Constructivism: Theory, Perspectives and Practice.* New York: Teachers College Press, 172–81.

Forman, G. and Fyfe, B. (1998), 'Negotiated learning through design, documentation and discourse', in C. Edwards, L. Gandini and G. Forman (eds), *The Hundred Languages of Children.* Norwood: Ablex Publishing, 239–60.

Foucault, M. (1980), *Power/Knowledge: Selected Interviews and Other Writings 1972–1977.* Ed. and trans. by Colin Gordon. Brighton: Harvester.

—— (1991), 'Politics and the study of discourse', in G. Burchell, C. Gordon and P. Miller (eds), *The Foucault Effect: Studies in Governmentality* 53–72. London: Harvester Wheatsheaf.

Fraser, S. and Gestwicki, C. (2002), *Authentic Childhood.: Exploring Reggio Emilia in the Classroom.* New York: Delmar.

Freire, P. (1970), *Pedagogy of the Oppressed.* New York: Herder and Herder.

—— (1972a), *Cultural Action for Freedom.* Harmondsworth: Penguin.

—— (1972b), *Pedagogy of the Oppressed.* Harmondsworth: Penguin.

Furlong, J. and Maynard, T. (1995), *Mentoring Student Teachers: The Growth of Professional Knowledge.* London: Routledge.

Gadamer, H.G. (1977), *Philosophical Hermeneutics.* Berkeley: University of California Press.

—— (1979), *Truth and Method* (2nd edn). London: Sheed and Ward.

Gage, J. (1968) *Life in Italy at the Time of the Medici.* London: B.T. Batsford Ltd.

Gallacher, L.A. (2006), 'Block play, the sand pit and the doll corner: the (dis)ordering materialities of educating young children'. Online papers archived by the Institute of Geography, School of Geosciences, University of Edinburgh, at http://www.era.lib.ed.ac.uk/handle/1842/1002.

Galton, F. (1869), *Hereditary Genius: An Inquiry into its Laws and Consequences.* London: Macmillan/Fontana.

Gammage, P. (1999), 'Early childhood education in the post-modern world', in L. Abbott and H. Moylett (eds), *Early Education Transformed.* London: Falmer Press.

Gandini, L. (1994), 'Not just anywhere: making child care centers into "particular" places'. Redmond: *Child Care Information Exchange*, 3, 94.

—— (1997a), 'Foundations of the Reggio Emilia approach', in J. Hendrick (ed.), *First Steps Towards Teaching the Reggio Way.* New Jersey: Prentice-Hall, 14–25.

—— (1997b), 'The Reggio Emilia story. History and organization', in J. Hendrick (ed.), *First Steps Toward Teaching the Reggio Way.* New Jersey: Merrill.

—— (1998), 'History, ideas, and basic philosophy', in C. Edwards, L. Gandini and G. Forman (eds), *The Hundred Languages of Children: The Reggio Emilia Approach. Advanced Reflections* (2nd edn), Westport: Ablex Publishing, 49–97.

—— (2005), 'From the beginning of the atelier to materials as languages', in L. Gandini, L. Hill, L. Cadwell and C. Schwall (eds), *In the Spirit of the Atelier.* New York: Teachers College Press.

Gardner, H. (1983), *Frames of Mind* (2nd edn). London: Fontana Press.

—— (1991), *The Unschooled Mind.* New York: Basic Books.

—— (1993), *Creating Minds: An Anatomy of Creativity as Seen through the Lives of Freud, Einstein, Picasso, Stravinsky, Eliot, Graham and Gandhi.* New York: Basic Books.

—— (1998a). 'Foreword: Complementary perspectives on Reggio Emilia', in C. Edwards, L. Gandini and G. Forman (eds), *The Hundred Languages of Children* (2nd edn). Greenwich: Ablex Publishing, xv–xviii.

—— (1998b), A multiplicity of intelligences, in *Scientific American*, 9 (4), Winter, 19–23.

—— (1999a), *Intelligence Reframed.* New York: Basic Books.

—— (1999b), *The Disciplined Mind.* New York: Simon & Schuster.

—— (2000), 'The best preschools in the world', extracted from Chapter 5 of *The Disciplined Mind.* Accessed November 2008 at http://www.reggioinspired.com/gardneronreggio.htm.

—— (2004), 'The hundred languages of successful educational reform'. *Children in Europe*, 6, 16–17.

—— (2006), *The Development and Education of the Mind.* Oxford: Routledge.

Gardner, H., Kornhaber, M.L. and Wake, W.K. (1996), *Intelligence: Multiple Perspectives.* Orlando: Harcourt Brace.

Gee, J. (1999), *An Introduction to Discourse Analysis: Theory and Method.* London: Routledge.

Ghiardi, Max (2002), 'Our school as part of the Reggio Emilia experience', in Martiri di Sesso Centro Verde Preschool, *Along the Levee Road.* Reggio Emilia: Reggio Children.

Giddens, A. (1993), *Sociology* (2nd edn). Cambridge: Polity Press.

Giroux, H.A. (1981), *Ideology, Culture and the Process of Schooling.* Lewes: Falmer Press.

—— (1989), *Schooling for Democracy: Critical Pedagogy in the Modern Age.* London: Routledge.

Gomez, M.L. (1992), 'Breaking silences: building new stories of classroom life through teacher transformation', in S. Kessler and B.B. Swadener (eds), *Reconceptualising the Early Childhood Curriculum: Beginning the Dialogue.* New York: Teachers College Press, 165–88.

Gramsci, A. (1971), *Selections from the Prison Notebooks.* London: Lawrence and Wishart.

Greenough, W.T., Black, J.E. and Wallace, C.S. (1987), 'Experience and brain development'. *Child Development*, 58, 555–67.

Griffiths, R. (2005), *Fascism.* London: Continuum Books.

Grundy, S. (1987), *Curriculum: Product or Praxis?* London: Falmer Press.

Gunther, J. (1940), *Inside Europe.* New York: Harper and Brothers.

Habermas, J. (1971), *Towards a Rational Society.* London: Heinemann.

—— (1972), *Knowledge and Human Interests* (2nd edn). London: Heinemann.

—— (1979), *Communications and the Evolution of Society.* London: Heinemann.

Hall, K. (2008), 'Leaving middle childhood and moving into teenhood: small stories about agency and identity', in K. Hall, P. Murphy and J. Soler, *Pedagogy and Practice: Culture and Identities*, London: Sage, 87–104.

Hall, K. and Murphy, P. (2003), 'Introduction', in K. Hall, P. Murphy and J. Soler, *Pedagogy and Practice: Culture and Identities*, London: Sage, ix–xiv.

Hall, K., Murphy, P. and Soler, J. (eds) (2008), *Pedagogy and Practice: Culture and Identities.* London: Sage.

Hargreaves, A. (2002), 'Teaching in a box: emotional geographies of teaching', in C. Sugrue and C. Day (eds), *Developing Teachers and Teaching Practice: International Research Perspectives.* London: Routledge Falmer, 3–25.

Hargreaves, A. and Fullan, M. (1992), *Understanding Teacher Development.* New York: Teachers College Press.

Hatch, T. and Gardner, H. (1993), 'Finding cognition in the classroom: an expanded view of human intelligence', in G. Saloman (ed.), *Distributed Cognitions: Psychological and Educational Considerations.* Cambridge, MA: Cambridge University Press, 164–87.

Hayes, N. (2002), 'Quality in early childhood education'. Presentation to the National Children's Nurseries Association Annual Conference, Dublin Castle, 23 March 2002 (unpublished).

Healy, J. (1990), *Endangered Minds: Why Our Children Can't Think.* New York: Simon and Schuster.

Hearder, H. (1991), *Italy: A Short History.* Cambridge: Cambridge University Press.

Heckman, J.J. (2000), 'Policies to foster human capital'. *Research in Economics,* 54 (1), 3–56.

Henderson, Anne T. and Berla, Nancy (1994), *A New Generation of Evidence: The Family is Critical to Student Achievement.* Washington, DC: National Committee for Citizens in Education.

Henderson, Anne T. and Mapp, K.L. (2002), *A New Wave of Evidence: The Impact of School, Family and Community Connections on Student Achievement.* Accessed October 2008 at http://www.sedl.org/connections/research-syntheses.html.

Hendrick, J. (ed.) (1997), *First Steps toward Teaching the Reggio Way.* New Jersey: Prentice Hall.

Hetland, L., Winner, E., Veenema, S. and Sheridan, K. (2007), *Studio Thinking: The Real Benefits of Visual Arts Education.* New York: Teachers College Press.

Hilton-Young, W. (1949), *The Italian Left: A Short History of Political Socialism in Italy.* London: Longmans.

Historical Archives of 'Italian' Communist Left. Accessed November 2008 at: http://www.quinterna.org/lingue/english/historical_en/0_historical_archives.htm.

Hoerr, T. (2000), *Becoming a Multiple Intelligences School.* Virginia: Association for Supervision and Curriculum Development.

Holmes, G. (ed.) (1997), *The Oxford Illustrated History of Italy.* Oxford: Oxford University Press.

Hoover-Dempsey, K.V. and Sandler, H.M. (1997), 'Why do parents become involved in their children's education?' *Review of Educational Research,* 67 (1), 3–42.

Howes, C., James, J. and Richie, S. (2003), 'Pathways to effective teaching'. *Early Childhood Research Quarterly,* 18, 104–20.

Howey, K.R. and Strom, S.M. (1987), 'Teacher selection reconsidered', in M. Haberman and J.M. Bakus (eds), *Advances in Teacher Education Volume 3.* Norwood: Ablex Publishing.

Hoyuelos, A. (2004), 'A pedagogy of transgression'. *Children in Europe,* 6, 6–7.

Hyland, Á. (ed.), (2000), *Multiple Intelligences Curriculum and Assessment Project Final Report.* Education Department, University College, Cork.

Illich, I.D. (1971), *Deschooling Society.* London: Calder.

Inglehart, R. (1997), *Modernization and Post-modernization: Cultural, Economic, and Political Change in 43 Societies.* Princeton: Princeton University Press.

Jacobs, B., Shall, M. and Scheibel, A.B. (1993), 'A quantitative dendritic analysis of Wernicke's area in Humans. II gender, hemispheric and environmental factors'. *Journal of Comparative Neurology,* 327 (1), 97–111.

James, A., Jenks, C. and Prout, J. (1998), *Theorizing Childhood.* Cambridge: Polity Books.

Janik, A. and Toulmin, S. (1973), *Wittgenstein's Vienna.* New York: Simon and Schuster.

Jardine, L. (1996), *Worldly Goods: A New History of the Renaissance*. London: Macmillan.

Jensen, D. (1992), *Reformation Europe: Age of Reform and Revolution*. Lexington: D.C. Heath and Company.

Jensen, E. (1998), *Teaching with the Brain in Mind*. Virginia: Association for Supervision and Curriculum Development.

—— (2006), *Enriching the Brain: How to Maximise Every Learner's Potential*. San Francisco: Jossey-Bass.

Johnson, R. (1999), 'Colonialism and cargo cults in early childhood education: does Reggio Emilia really exist?' *Contemporary Issues in Early Childhood*, 1 (1), 61–78.

Jones, E. (1993), *Growing Teachers: Partnerships in Staff Development*. Washington, DC: NAEYC.

Jungck, S. and Marshall, J.D. (1992), 'Curricular perspectives on one great debate', in S. Kessler and B. Blue Sawdner (eds), *Reconceptualising Early Childhood Curriculum*. New York: Teachers College Press.

Kagan, J.M. (1994), *Galen's Prophecy*. New York: Basic Books.

Kagan, S.L. (1992). 'The strategic importance of linkages and the transition between early childhood programs and early elementary school', in *Sticking Together: Strengthening Linkages and the Transition Between Early Childhood Education and Early Elementary School*. Washington, DC: US Department of Education.

Katz, L.G. (1990), 'Impressions of Reggio Emilia schools'. *Young Children*, 45 (6), 11–12. EJ415420.

—— (1998), 'What can we learn from Reggio Emilia?', in C. Edwards, L. Gandini and G. Forman (eds), *The Hundred Languages of Children* (2nd edn). Greenwich: Ablex Publishing, 27–45.

—— (1999), 'International perspectives on early childhood education: lessons from my travels'. *Journal of Early Childhood Research and Practice*, 1 (1), 1–7. Accessed December 2008 at: http://ecrp.uiuc.edu/v1n1/katz.html.

Katz, L.G. and Cesarone, B. (eds) (1994), *Reflections on the Reggio Emilia Approach*. Urbana: Eric Clearinghouse.

Katz, L.G. and Chard, S.C. (1996), *The Contribution of Documentation to the Quality of Early Childhood Education*. EDO-PS–96–2 April 1996. Accessed September 2008 at http://ceep.crc.uiuc.edu/eecearchive/digests/1996/lkchar96.html.

Katz, L.G. and Chard, S.C. (2000), *Engaging Children's Minds: The Project Approach*. Ablex Publishing.

Kaufman, P. (1998), 'Poppies and the dance of world making', in Carolyn Edwards, Lella Gandini and George Forman (eds), *The Hundred Languages of Children*. Westport: Ablex Publishing, 285–94.

Kelleghan, T., Sloane, K., Alvarez, B. and Bloom, B.S. (1993), *The Home Environment and School Learning: Promoting Parental Involvement in the Education of Children*. San Francisco: Jossey-Bass.

Kelly, A.V. (1989), *The Curriculum Theory and Practice* (3rd edn). London: Paul Chapman.

—— (1995), *Education and Democracy*. London: Paul Chapman.

Kennedy, D. (1994), 'The five communities', *Analytical Teaching*, 15 (1), 3–22.

—— (1996), 'After Reggio Emilia: may the conversation begin!' *Young Children*, 51 (5).

Kinney, L. and Wharton, P. (2008), *An Encounter with Reggio Emilia*. Oxford: Routledge.

Kohlberg, L. (1976), 'Moral stages and moralisation: the cognitive development approach', in T. Lickong (ed.), *Moral Development and Behaviour*. New York: Holt, Reinhart and Winston, 31–53.

Kolb, D.A. (1984), *Experiential Learning: Experience as a Source of Learning and Development*. New

Jersey: Prentice Hall.

Kotulak, R. (1996), *Inside the Brain: Revolutionary Discoveries of How the Mind Works*. Kansas City: Andrews and McMeel.

Kratwohl, D.R. (1965), 'Stating objectives appropriately for programme, for curriculum, and for instructional materials development'. *Journal of Teacher Education*, 16, 83–92.

Krechevsky, M. (1998), *Project Spectrum: Preschool Assessment Handbook*. New York: Teachers College Press.

Lamb-Parker, F., Piotrowski, C.S., Baker, J.L., Kessler-Sklar, S., Clark, B. and Peay, L. (2001), 'Understanding barriers to parent involvement in Head Start'. *Early Childhood Research Quarterly*, 16, 35–51.

Langford, R. (2006), 'Discourses of the good early childhood educator in professional training: reproducing marginality or working towards social change'. *International Journal of Educational Policy, Research and Practice*, 1.

Langsted, O. (1994), 'Looking at quality from the child's perspective', in P. Moss and A. Pence (1994), *Valuing Quality in Early Childhood Services: New Approaches to Defining Quality*. London: Paul Chapman.

Larner, M. (1996), 'Parents' perspectives on quality in early care and education', in S. Kagan and N. Cohen (eds), *Reinventing Early Care and Education*. San Francisco: Jossey-Bass.

Larner, M. and Phillips, D. (1994), 'Defining and valuing quality as a parent', in P. Moss and A. Pence, *Valuing Quality in Early Childhood Services: New Approaches to Defining Quality*. London: Paul Chapman.

Lather, P. (1991), *Getting Smart: Feminist Research and Pedagogy Within/In the Post-Modern*. London: Routledge.

Latour, B. (1988), 'The politics of explanation', in S. Wolgar (ed.), *Knowledge and Reflexivity*, London: Sage, 155–76.

Lave, J. (1996), 'Teaching, as learning, in practice'. *Mind, Culture, and Activity*, 3 (3), 149–64.

Lazear, D. (2004), *Multiple Intelligence Approaches to Assessment*. Wales: Crown House Publishing.

Learning and Teaching Scotland (2004), *A Curriculum for Excellence*. Accessed November 2008 at http://www.ltscotland.org.uk/curriculumforexcellence/index.asp.

Lewin et al. (1998), 'Bridge to another culture: the journey of the model Early Learning Centre', in C.P. Edwards, L. Gandini and G. Forman (eds), *The Hundred Languages of Children*. Norwood: Ablex Publishing.

Lewin-Benham, A. (2006), *Possible Schools: The Reggio Approach to Urban Education*. New York: Teachers College Press.

Lillard, A. S. (2005), *Montessori: The Science Behind the Genius*. Oxford: Oxford University Press.

Locke, T. (2004), *Critical Discourse Analysis*. London: Continuum.

Lowyck, J. (1986), 'Post-interactive reflections of teachers: a critical appraisal', in M. Ben-Perez, R. Bromme and R. Halkes (eds), *Advances of Research on Teacher Thinking*. Lisse, Switzerland: Swets and Zeitlinger.

Lucchini, E. (1980), 'The birth of the new type of infant–toddler centers', in I. Sala La Guardia and E. Lucchini (eds), *Asili nido in Italia*. Milan: Marzorati, 13–38.

Lyons, M.N. and Berlet, C. (1996), *Too Close for Comfort: Right Wing Populism, Scapegoating, and Fascist Potentials in US Politics*. Boston: South End Press.

MacLure, M. (1994), 'Language and discourse: the embrace of uncertainty'. *British Journal of Sociology of Education*, 15 (2), 283–300.

—— (2003), *Discourse in Educational and Social Research*. Buckingham: Open University Press.

Mack Smith, D. (1969), *Italy: A Modern History*. Ann Arbor: University of Michigan Press.

MacNaughton, G. (2003), *Shaping Early Childhood: Learners, Curriculum and Contexts*. Berkshire: Open University Press.

Mager, B.F. (1962), *Preparing Instructional Objectives*. Palo Alto: Fearon.

Malaguzzi, L. (1971a), *Experiences Towards a New School for Young Children*. Rome: Editori Riuniti.

—— (1971b), *Community-based Management in the School for Young Children*. Rome: Editori Riuniti.

—— (1993a), 'A bill of three rights'. *Innovations in Early Education: The International Reggio Exchange*, 2 (1), 9.

—— (1993b), 'For an education based on relationships'. *Young Children*, 49 (1), 9–12.

—— (1993c), 'Walking on threads of silk'. Interview with Loris Malaguzzi by Carlo Barsotti, from the film *L'Huomo di Reggio*. Children in Europe, 6, March 2004, 10–15.

—— (1993d), 'Your image of the child: where teaching begins'. *Child Care Information Exchange* March/April 1994.

—— (1996), *The Hundred Languages of Children: Narrative of the Possible* (exhibition catalogue). Norwood: Ablex Publishing.

—— (1998), 'History, ideas, and basic philosophy', in C. Edwards, L. Gandini and G. Forman (eds), *The Hundred Languages of Children* (2nd edn). Greenwich: Ablex Publishing.

—— (2005), 'The hundred languages of children', in *The Hundred Languages of Children: The Exhibit* (5th edn). Reggio Emilia: Reggio Children.

Mansson, A. (2007), 'The construction of "the competent child" and early childhood care: values education among the youngest children in the nursery school'. Malmo University Electronic Publishing: http://hdl.handle.net/2043/4979.

Mantovani, S. (2006), 'An experience of community', in *Crossing Boundaries: Ideas and Experiences in Dialogue for a New Culture of Education of Children and Adults*. International Conference, Reggio Emilia, 2004. Bergamo: Edizione Junior, 113–36.

Mardell, B. (2001), 'Moving across the Atlantic', in *Making Learning Visible, Children as Individual and Group Learners*. Reggio Emilia: Reggio Children, The President and Fellows of Harvard College and the Municipality of Reggio Emilia.

Marx, K. (1875), *Critique of the Gotha Programme*. London: Lawrence and Wishart.

—— (1996), *The Communist Manifesto/ Karl Marx and Friedrich Engels*; Introduction by Mick Hume. London: Junius.

McDermott, R. and Varenne, H. (1995), 'Culture as disability'. *Anthropology and Education Quarterly*, 26 (3), 324–48.

McDonald, J.P. (1988), 'The emergence of the teacher's voice: implications for the new reform'. *Teachers' College Record*, 89 (4), 471–86.

McDonald-Ross, M. (1975), 'Behaviour objectives: A critical review', in M. Golby, J. Greenwald and R. West (eds), *Curriculum Design*, Milton Keynes: Open University Press.

McLaren, P. (1989), 'Forward: critical theory and the meaning of hope', in H.A. Giroux (ed.), *Schooling for Democracy: Critical Pedagogy in the Modern Age*. London: Routledge, 9–21.

Mendoza, J., Katz, L.G., Robertson, A.S. and Rothenburg, D. (2003), *Connecting with Parents in the Early Years*. Accessed December 2006 at http://ceep.crc.uiuc.edu/pubs/connecting.html.

Montessori, M. (1988), *The Montessori Method*. New York: Schocken Books.

—— (1991), *The Absorbent Mind*. Oxford: Clio Press.

—— (1992), *The Secret of Childhood*. London: Sangam.

Mooney, A., Cameron, C., Candappa, M., McQuail, S., Moss, P. and Petrie, P. (2003), *Early Years and Childcare International Evidence Project: Quality*. London: Department of Education and Science.

Moran, M.J., Desrochers, L. and Cavicchi, N.M. (2007), 'Progettazione and documentation as sociocultural activities: changing communities of practice'. *Theory Into Practice*, 46 (1), 81–90.

Moss, P. (1999), 'Early childhood institutions as a democratic and emancipatory project', in L. Abbott and H. Moylett (eds), *Early Education Transformed*. New Millennium Series. London: Falmer Press.

Moss, P. (2006a), 'Schools as spaces for political and ethical practice', in *Crossing Boundaries: Ideas and Experiences in Dialogue for a New Culture of Education of Children and Adults*. International Conference, Reggio Emilia 2004. Bergamo, Italy: Edizione Junior, 107–10.

—— (2006b), 'Early childhood institutions as loci of ethical and political practice', *International Journal of Educational Policy Research and Practice*. http://www.articlearchives.com/company-activities-management/business-climate/16 (accessed on 23 January 2009).

—— (2007), 'Meeting across the paradigmatic divide'. *Educational Philosophy and Theory*, 39 (3), 229–45.

Moss, P. and Pence, A. (eds) (1994), *Valuing Quality in Early Childhood Services*. London: Paul Chapman.

Moss, P. and Penn, H. (1996), *Transforming Nursery Education*. London: Paul Chapman.

Municipality of Reggio Emilia (2000), *The Municipal Infant Toddler Centres and Pre-Schools of Reggio Emilia: Historical Notes and General Information*. Reggio Emilia: Reggio Children.

Murphy, D. (1986), 'The dilemmas of primary curriculum reform'. *Oideas*, 29, 25–40.

Murphy, P. and Hall, K. (eds) (2008), *Learning and Practice: Agency and Identities*. London: Sage.

Murphy, R. (2002), 'Rethinking parental involvement in early years education and care', in M. Horgan and F. Douglas (eds), *Lessons for the 21st Century: Research, Reflection, Renewal: Proceedings of the OMEP Ireland Conference, Dublin, April 2002*. Cork: OMEP Ireland.

—— (2005), 'The changing face of preschool services: a case study', in N. Hayes (ed.), *Contemporary Issues in Early Childhood Education and Care: Proceedings of the Conference held in St. Patrick's College, Drumcondra, Dublin, April 2005*. Cork: OMEP Ireland.

Musatti, Tullia (2006), 'Intelligence and determination to build up schools of quality', in *Crossing Boundaries: Ideas and Experiences in Dialogue for a New Culture of Education of Children and Adults*. International Conference, Reggio Emilia 2004. Bergamo, Italy: Edizione Junior, 79–81.

NAEYC (2009), *Developmentally Appropriate Practice in Early Childhood Programs Serving Children from Birth through Age 8* (3rd edn). NAEYC Position Statement. Accessed February 2009 at http://www.naeyc.org/about/positions/dap.asp.

National Economic and Social Forum (NESF) (2005), *Early Childhood Education and Care Report*, 25 September 2005. Dublin: National Economic and Social Forum.

National Institute of Early Education Research (NIEER) (2004), 'Policy and research effect on class size' *Policy Matters*, Issue 9, December 2004, accessed at http://nieer.org/resources/policybriefs/9.pdf.

Nespor, J. and Barber, L. (1991), 'The rhetorical construction of "the teacher"'. *Harvard Educational Review*, 61 (4), 417–33.

Neugebauer, B. (1994), 'Unpacking my questions and images: Personal reflections on Reggio Emilia'. *Child Care Information Exchange*, 3, 94.

New, R.S. (1991), 'Early childhood teacher education in Italy: Reggio Emilia's master plan for "master" teachers'. *Journal of Early Childhood Teacher Education*, 12 (37), 3.

—— (1993), *Reggio Emilia: Some Lessons for US Educators*. ERIC Digest EDO-PS-93–3. Accessed September 2008 at http://ceep.crc.uiuc.edu/eecearchive/digests/1993/new93.html.

—— (1994a), 'Culture, child development and DAP: an expanded role of teachers as collaborative researchers', in B. Mallory and R. New (eds), *Diversity and Developmentally Appropriate Practices: Challenges for Early Childhood Education*. New York: Teachers College Press, 65–83.

—— (1994b), 'Reggio Emilia: Its visions and its challenges for educators in the United States', in L.G. Katz and B. Cesarone (eds), *Reflections on the Reggio Emilia Approach*. Illinois: ERIC.

—— (1997), 'Next steps in teaching "The Reggio Way"', in J. Hendrick (ed.), *First Steps Toward Teaching the Reggio Way*. Upper Saddle River, NJ: Merrill, an imprint of Prentice Hall.

—— (1998), 'Theory and praxis in Reggio Emilia: They knew what they were doing and why', in C. Edwards, L. Gandini and G. Forman (eds), *The Hundred Languages of Children*. Norwood: Ablex Publishing, 261–84.

—— (1999a), 'An integrated early childhood curriculum: Moving from the *what* and the *how* to the *why*', in C. Seefeldt (ed.),*The Early Childhood Curriculum* (3rd edn). New York: Teachers College Press.

—— (1999b), 'What should children learn? Making choices and taking chances'. *Early Childhood Research and Practice*, Fall, 1999, 1 (2). Online journal, accessed September 2008 at http://ecrp.uiuc.edu/v1n2/new.html.

—— (2000), *Reggio Emilia: Catalyst for Change and Conversation*. Eric Digest EDO-PS-00–15. Accessed September 2008 at http://ceep.crc.uiuc.edu/eecearchive/digests/2000/new00.pdf.

—— (2007), 'Reggio Emilia as cultural activity theory in practice'. *Theory into Practice*, 46 (1), 5–13.

New, R.S., Mallory, B.L. and Mantovani, S. (2000), 'Cultural images of children, parents and professionals: Italian interpretations of home-school relationships'. *Early Education and Development*, 11 (5), 597–616.

Nutbrown, C. and Abbott, L. (2001), 'Experiencing Reggio Emilia', in L. Abbott and C. Nutbrown (eds) (2001), *Experiencing Reggio Emilia*. Berkshire: Open University Press.

O'Doherty, A., Dorit, W.D. and Shannon, G. (2002), 'Consulting children: factors influencing the interview process', in M. Horgan and F. Douglas (eds), *Lessons for the 21st Century: Research, Reflection, Renewal: Proceedings of the OMEP Ireland Conference, Dublin, April 2002*. Cork: OMEP (Ireland).

Organisation for Economic Co-operation and Development (OECD) (2004), *Education at a Glance*. Paris: OECD.

Pacini-Ketchabaw, V., Berger, I., Kocher, L., Isaac, K. and Mort, J. (2006),*Working Paper: Early Education in British Columbia: Engaging in Dialogue with Reggio Emilia's Early Childhood Project*. University of British Columbia: Early Childhood Education and Research, Faculty of Education UBC.

Painter, S. (1973) *A History of the Middle Ages 284–1500*. London: Macmillan Press Ltd.

Penn, H. (1997), *Comparing Nurseries: Staff and Children in Italy, Spain and UK*. London: Paul Chapman.

Peterson, P. (1988), 'Teachers' and students' cognitional knowledge for classroom teaching and learning'. *Educational Research*, 17 (5), 3–14.

Phillips, C.B. and Bredekamp, S. (1998), 'Reconsidering early childhood education in the

United States: Reflections from our encounter with Reggio Emilia', in C. Edwards, L. Gandini and G. Forman (eds), *The Hundred Languages of Children*. Norwood: Ablex Publishing, 439–54.

Phillips, D. (1996), 'Reframing the quality issue', in S. Kagan and N. Cohen (eds), *Reinventing Early Care and Education*. San Francisco: Jossey-Bass Inc.

Piaget, J. (1932), *The Moral Judgement of the Child*. New York: Free Press.

—— (1942), *The Origins of Intelligence in Children*. New York: International University Press.

—— (1952), *The Language and Thought of the Child*. London: Routledge and Kegan Paul.

—— (1954), *The Construction of Reality in the Child*. New York: Basic Books.

—— (1962a), *Comments on Vygotsky's Critical Remarks*. Boston: MIT Press.

—— (1962b), *Play, Dreams and Imitation in Childhood*. New York: Norton.

—— (1963), *The Psychology of Intelligence*. London: Routledge and Kegan Paul.

Piccone, P. (1983), *Italian Marxism*. Berkeley: University of California Press.

Popham, W.J. (1977), 'Objectives "72"', in L. Rubin (ed.), *Curriculum Handbook: The Disciplines, Current Movements and Instructional Methodology*. Boston: Allyn and Bacon, 605–13.

Postman, N. and Weingartner, C. (1969), *Teaching as a Subversive Activity*. New York: Delacort Press.

Project Zero/Reggio Children (2001), *Making Learning Visible, Children as Individual and Group Learners*. Reggio Emilia: Reggio Children, The President and Fellows of Harvard College and the Municipality of Reggio Emilia.

Pugh, G. (1999), 'Towards a policy for early childhood: a view from the UK'. *New Opportunities for Women, with the Centre for Social and Educational Research*. Dublin: Dublin Institute of Technology.

—— (ed.) (1996), *Contemporary Issues in the Early Years*. London: Paul Chapman, in association with the National Children's Bureau.

Pugh, G. and de'Ath, E. (1989), *Working Towards Partnership in the Early Years*. London: National Children's Bureau.

Putnam, R. (1993), *Making Democracy Work: Civic Traditions in Modern Italy*. Princeton: Princeton University Press.

Qualifications and Curriculum Authority (QCA) (2005), *Education in Italy*. Accessed January 2009 at http://www.inca.org.uk/italy.html.

Qvortrup, J. (1993), 'Nine theses about childhood as a social phenomenon', in J. Qvortrup (ed.) (1993), *Childhood as a Social Phenomenon: Lessons from an International Project, Eurosocial Report No. 47*, Vienna: European Centre for Social Welfare Policy and Research, 11–18.

Rankin, B.M. (1993), 'Curricular development in Reggio Emilia: A long-term curriculum project about dinosaurs', in C. Edwards, L. Gandini and G. Forman (eds), *The Hundred Languages of Children*. Norwood: Ablex Publishing, 215–37.

Reggio Children (2000) *Reggio Tutta: A Guide to the City by the Children*. Reggio Emilia: Reggio Children.

—— (2002), *Along the Levee Road. Our School turns Fifty – from Nursery School to Municipal Centro Verde Preschool, 1945–1997*. Reggio Emilia: Reggio Children.

—— (2005), *ReChild: Reggio Children Magazine*, 7. http://zerosei.comune.re.it/into/rechild/skrc7.htm.

—— (2007), *Reggio Children*. Accessed October 2008 at http://zerosei.comune.re.it/pdfs/foldrerch/RCH_ENGLISH.pdf.

—— (nd), 'The municipal infant–toddler centers and preschools of Reggio Emilia'. Accessed December 2008 at http://zerosei.comune.re.it/inter/nidiescuole.htm.

Regional Educational Laboratories' Early Childhood Collaboration Network (1995), *Conti-*

nuity in Early Childhood: A Framework for Home, School and Community Linkages. Austin: Southwest Educational Development Laboratory. Accessed November 2008 at http://www.sedl.org/prep/hsclinkages.pdf.

Resnick, L.B. (1987), *Education and Learning to Think.* Washington, DC: National Academy Press.

—— (1989), 'Developing mathematical knowledge'. *American Psychologist,* 44 (2), 162–69.

Rhodes, S. and Hennessy, E. (2000), 'The effects of specialized training on caregivers and children in early-years settings: an evaluation of the foundation course in playgroup practice'. *Early Childhood Research Quarterly,* 15 (4), 559–76.

Ricoeur, P. (1979), 'The model of the text: Meaningful action considered as a text', in P. Rainbow (ed.), *Interpretive Social Science: A Reader.* Berkeley: University of California Press.

Richards, C. (1995), *The New Italians.* London: Penguin Books.

Ridgway, M.A. (2002), *Toward the Integration of Teaching, Learning and Assessment: A Study of Junior Classes in Selected Cork City Schools.* University College, Cork: unpublished PhD thesis.

Rinaldi, C. (1993), 'The emergent curriculum and social constructivism', in C. Edwards, L. Gandini and G. Forman (eds), *The Hundred Languages of Children.* Norwood: Ablex Publishing, 101–11.

—— (1994a), 'Staff development in Reggio Emilia', in L.G. Katz and B. Cesarone (eds), *Reflections on the Reggio Emilia Approach.* Champaign: ERIC Clearinghouse on Elementary and Early Childhood Education, 55–60.

—— (1994b), 'The philosophy of Reggio Emilia', *Paper Presented at the Study Seminar on the Experience of the Municipal Infant–Toddler Centres and Pre-Primary School of Reggio Emilia.* Reggio Emilia: June.

—— (1998a), 'Projected curriculum constructed through documentation – *progettazione:* An interview with Lella Gandini', in C. Edwards and L.Gandini and G. Forman (eds), *The Hundred Languages of Children: The Reggio Emilia Approach – Advanced Reflections.* Greenwich: Ablex Publishing, 113–26.

—— (1998b), 'The space of childhood', in G. Ceppi and M. Zini (eds), *Children, Spaces, Relations.* Reggio Emilia: Reggio Children.

—— (1999), 'Visible listening'. *RECHILD,* 3, 7.

—— (2000a), 'The construction of the educational project: an interview with Carlini Rinaldi by Lella Gandini and Judith Kaminksy', in C. Rinaldi (2007), *In Dialogue with Reggio Emilia: Listening, Researching and Learning.* Abingdon: Routledge, 121–36.

—— (2000b), 'Visible listening'. Presentation to UK study group, October, in L. Thornton and P. Brunton, *Understanding the Reggio Approach.* London: David Fulton.

—— (2001), 'Documentation and assessment: what is the relationship?', in C. Giudici, C. Rinaldi and M. Krechevsky (eds), *Making Learning Visible: Children as Individual and Group Learners.* Reggio Emilia: Project Zero and Reggio Children.

—— (2002), 'Teachers as Researchers'. Presentation at ReFocus One Symposium, Kendal, UK in L. Thornton and P. Brunton, *Understanding the Reggio Approach.* London: David Fulton.

—— (2006), 'The child is the first citizen?', in *Crossing Boundaries: Ideas and Experiences in Dialogue for a New Culture of Education of Children and Adults. International Conference, Reggio Emilia 2004.* Bergamo, Italy: Edizione Junior, 101–5.

—— (2007), *In Dialogue with Reggio Emilia: Listening, Researching and Learning.* London: Routledge.

Rinaldi, C., Dahlberg, G. and Moss, P. (2007), 'In dialogue with Carlina Rinaldi: A discussion between Carlina Rinaldi, Gunilla Dahlberg and Peter Moss', in C. Rinaldi, *In Dialogue with Reggio Emilia: Listening Researching and Learning.* Abingdon: Routledge, 178–209.

Rinaldi, C. and Moss, P. (2004), 'What is Reggio?' *Children in Europe*, 6, 2–3.

Ritchart, R. (2002), *Intellectual Character*. California: Jossey-Bass.

Roberts, J.M. (1997), *The Penguin History of the World*. London: Penguin Books.

Rogoff, B. (1990), *Apprenticeship of Thinking: Cognitive Development in Social Context*. New York: Oxford University Press.

—— (1994), 'Developing understanding of the idea of communities of learners', *Scriber Award Address*, New Orleans: American Educational Research Association.

—— (1998a), 'Cognition as a collaborative process', in W. Damon (ed.), *Handbook of Child Psychology: Cognition, Perception and Language* (5th edn), Vol. 2. New York: John Wiley, 679–744.

—— (1998b), 'Observing sociocultural activity on three planes: participatory appropriation, guided participation, and apprenticeship', in K. Hall, P. Murphy and J. Soler (eds) (2008), *Pedagogy and Practice: Culture and Identities*. London: Sage, 58–74.

Rogoff, B., Chavajay, P. and Matusov, E. (1993), 'Questioning assumptions about culture and individuals. Commentary on Michael Tomasello, Ann Call Kruger and Hillary Horn Ratner'. *Behavioural and Brain Sciences*, 16, 533–4.

Ross, A. (2000), *Curriculum: Construction and Critique*. London: Falmer Press.

Rugg, H. (1936), *American Life and the School Curirculum*. Boston: Ginn.

Ruopp, R., Travers, J., Glantz, F. and Coolan, C. (1979), *Children at the Centre: Summary Findings and Their Implications. Final Report of the National Day Care Study*. Cambridge, MA: ABT Assoc.

Rusk, R.R. (1937), *The Doctrines of the Great Educators*. London: Macmillan; University of London Press.

Rymer, R. (1993), *Genie: An Abused Child's Flight From Silence*. New York: HarperCollins.

Salomon, G. (1993), 'No distribution without individuals: Cognition: a dynamic interactional view', in G. Saloman (ed.), *Distributed Cognitions: Psychological and Educational Considerations*. Cambridge, MA: Cambridge University Press, 111–38.

Schön, D.A. (1983), *The Reflective Practitioner*. New York: Basic Books.

—— (1987), *Educating the Reflective Practitioner*. San Francisco: Jossey-Bass.

—— (1990a), *The Reflective Turn: Case Studies in Reflective Practice*. New York: Teachers College Press.

—— (1990b), *The Reflective Behaviour*. New York: Basic Books.

—— (1995), *The Reflective Practitioner: How Professionals Think in Action*. London: Arena.

Scottish Education Department (1965), *Scottish Memorandum: Primary Education in Scotland*. Edinburgh: HMSO.

Seefeldt, C. (1995), 'Art – a serious work'. *Young Children*, 50, 39–45.

—— (2002a), *Learn from the Theories of Reggio Emilia and Put Children's Art to Work*. New York: Gryphon House.

—— (2002b), *Creating Rooms of Wonder: Valuing and Displaying Children's Work*. New York: Gryphon House

Sheridan, S. and Pramling-Samuelsson, I. (2001), 'Children's conceptions of participation and influence in preschool: a perspective on pedagogical quality'. *Contemporary Issues in Early Childhood Education*, 2 (2), 169–94.

Shore, R. (2002), *Baby Teacher, Nurturing Neural Networks from Birth to Age Five*. Kent: Scarecrow Press.

Sightlines Initiative (2009), accessed January 2009 at: http://www.sightlines-initiative.com/.

Síolta, the National Quality Framework for Early Childhood Education in Ireland (2005). Síolta website www.siolta.ie.

Skilbeck, M. (1976), *Three Educational Ideologies – Curriculum Design and Development: Ideologies and Values*. Buckingham: Open University Press.

Slaughter, R.A. (1989), 'Cultural re-construction in the post-modern world'. *Journal of Curriculum Studies*, 21 (3), 255–70.

Smail, W.M. (1938), *Quintilian on Education*. Oxford: Oxford University Press.

Smith A.B. (1996), *The Quality of Childcare Centres for Infants in New Zealand*, Monograph No. 4 of the New Zealand Association for Research in Education, 'State of the Art' series.

Smith, C. (1998), 'Children with "special rights" in the preprimary schools and infant–toddler centres of Reggio Emilia', in C. Edwards, L. Gandini and G. Forman (eds), *The Hundred Languages of Children* (2nd edn). Greenwich: Ablex Publishing, 199–214.

Smith, D. and Lovat, T. (1990), *Curriculum: Action or Reflection*. Sydney: Social Science Press.

Spaggiari, A. (1996), 'A challenge for the future', in T. Filippini and V. Vecchia (eds), *The Hundred Languages of Children: The Exhibit*. Reggio Emilia: Reggio Children.

Spaggiari, S., (1997), 'The invisibility of the essential', in *Shoe and Meter, Children and Measurement*. Reggio Emilia: Reggio Children, Municipality of Reggio Emilia.

—— (1998), 'The community–teacher partnership in the governance of the schools: an interview with Lella Gandini by Sergio Spaggiari', in C. Edwards, L. Gandini and G. Forman (eds), *The Hundred Languages of Children* (2nd edn). Greenwich: Ablex Publishing, 99–112.

Spodek, B. and Saracho, O.N. (2003), 'On the shoulders of giants: Exploring the traditions of early childhood education?' *Early Childhood Education Journal*, 31 (1), 3–10.

Staley, L. (1998), 'Beginning to implement the Reggio philosophy'. *Young Children*, 53 (5), 20–5.

Stenhouse, L. (1975), *An Introduction to Curriculum Research and Development*. Oxford: Heinemann.

Strong-Wilson, T. and Ellis, J. (2007), 'Children and place: Reggio Emilia's environment as third teacher'. *Theory into Practice*, 46 (1), 40–7.

Strozzi, P. (2001), 'Daily life at school: Seeing the extraordinary in the ordinary', in *Making Learning Visible, Children as Individual and Group Learners*. Italy, Reggio Emilia: Reggio Children, The President and Fellows of Harvard College and the Municipality of Reggio Emilia.

Sylva, K., Melhuish, E., Sammons, P., Siraj-Blatchford, I. and Taggart, B. (2004), *The Effective Provision of Preschool Education (EPPE) project. Final Report November 2004*. London: Sure Start.

Taba, H. (1962), *Curriculum Development: Theory and Practice*. New York: Harcourt, Brace and World.

Taylor, P.H. (1982), 'Metaphor and meaning in the curriculum'. *Journal of Curriculum Theorizing*, 4 (1), 18–26.

Taylor, P.H. and Richards, C.M. (1985), *An Introduction to Curriculum Studies*. Windsor: NFER-Nelson.

Thornton L. and Brunton P. (2005), *Understanding the Reggio Approach*. London: David Fulton Publishers.

—— (2007) *Bringing the Reggio Approach to Your Early Years Practice*. London: Routledge.

Tijus, C. A., Santolini, A. and Danis, A. (1997), 'The impact of parental involvement on the quality of day-care centres'. *International Journal of Early Years Education*, 5, 1–7.

Tyler, R.W. (1949), *Basic Principles of Curriculum and Instruction*. Chicago: University of Chicago Press.

UNESCO (2004), *Curriculum in Early Childhood Education and Care*, UNESCO Policy Brief on Early Childhood, No. 26, September.

United Nations (1989), *UN Convention on the Rights of the Child*. New York: United Nations.

Vecchi, V. (1993), 'The role of the atelierista', in C. Edwards, L. Gandini, and G. Forman (eds), *The Hundred Languages of Children*. Norwood: Ablex Publishing.

Vygotysky, L.S. (1962/1986), *Thought and Language*. ed. Alex Kozulin. Massachusetts: MIT Press.

—— (1967), 'Play and its role in the mental development of the child'. *Soviet Psychology*, 5, 6–18.

—— (1978), *Mind in Society: The Development of Higher Psychological Processes*. Cambridge, MA: Harvard University Press.

Walsh, W. H. (1969), *Hegelian Ethics*. London: Macmillan.

Wenger, E. (1998), *Communities of Practice: Learning, Meaning and Identity*. Cambridge: Cambridge University Press.

Wertsch, J.V. (1991), *Voices of the Mind: A Sociocultural Approach to Mediated Action*. Cambridge, MA: Harvard University Press.

Wheeler, D.K. (1967), *Curriculum Process*. London: University of London Press.

Whitebook, M. (1999), 'Child care workers: high demand, low wages'. *The Annals of the American Academy of Political and Social Science*, 563, 146–61.

—— (2003), 'Bachelor's degrees are best: higher qualifications for pre-kindergarten teachers led to better learning environments'. Washington, DC: The Trust for Early Education. Accessed November 2008 at http://www.trustforearlyed.org/docs/WhitebookFinal.pdf.

Whitebook, M., Howes, C. and Phillips, D. (1990), 'Who Cares? Childcare Teachers and the Quality of Care in America. Final Report of the National Childcare Staffing Study.' Accessed November 2008 at http://www.ccw.org/pubs/whocares.pdf.

Wien, C.A. (ed.) (2008), *Emergent Curriculum in the Primary Classroom: Interpreting the Reggio Emilia Approach in Schools*. Columbia: Teachers College Press.

Williams, R. (1976), *Keywords: a Vocabulary of Culture and Society*. London: Fontana.

Wolfendale, S. (2004), 'Getting the balance right: towards partnership in assessing children's development and educational potential'. *Department of Education and Skills Discussion Paper for TeacherNet – Working with Parents*. Accessed January 2008 at http://www.teachernet.gov.uk/docbank/index.cfm?id=7302.

Woodhead, M. (1996), *In Search of a Rainbow. Pathways to Quality in Large-scale Programmes for Young Disadvantaged Children*. The Hague: Bernard Van Leer Foundation.

Wright, S. (2000), 'Why Reggio Emilia doesn't exist: a response to Richard Johnson'. *Contemporary Issues in Early Childhood*, 1 (2), 223–6.

Young, M.F.D. (ed.) (1971), *Knowledge and Control*. London: Collier-Macmillan.

Index

Abbott, L. 36
advisory councils 75
Agazzi, Rosa and Carolina (and Agazzi
    Method) 17
Alaric the Visigoth 14
Alexander VI, Pope 15
American education system 50, 125–7,
    130–1, 138, 147, 161
d'Annunzio, Gabriele 10
Aporti, Ferrante 16
Apple, M. 101
April 25th School 20
Aristotle 15, 93, 108
Armstrong, T. 56–7
Asili Nidi 18
assessment 45, 112
atelierista 45–8, 63, 160

Balaguer, I. 35
Bambini (journal) 28
Barazzoni, R. 19, 22, 30
Barchi, Paula 61, 64
Barrow, R. 113
Barsotti, Carlo 5, 27, 155
Bennett, J. 158–9
Bernstein, B. 92
Binet, Alfred 52
Birth to Three Matters framework 83
Black Death (1348–51) 14
Blanc, Louis 8
Blenkin, G.M. 106
Boccaccio, Giovanni 14
Bonaparte, Napoleon 15

Boni Galeotti, Rosa 20–1
Bordiga, Amadeo 10
Boyd-Cadwell, L. 38, 42, 58–9
brain functioning 98–100, 105, 132–4
Bransford, J.D. 39
Bronfenbrenner, Urie 66–7, 87
Brooker, Liz 133
Browne, Naima 115, 140
Brugnoli-Tita, Leontina 20
Bruner, Jerome 36, 39–40, 77, 123–6,
    148
Brunton, P. 38, 47
Buber, M. 98, 106, 108

Cagliari, Paola 72, 76, 154
Campbell, B. 53–5
Campbell, L. 53
Campoli, Cesare 20
Carr, W. 114
Carter, M. 133–4
Casati Law (1859) 16
Catholic Church 12, 16–17, 21–6, 30,
    163–4
Cavour, Camille di 16
Ceppi, G. 40
Cervi, Genoeffa 41
Cervi School 41
Cesarone, B. 36
Chard, S.C. 82
Charlemagne 14
Charter of Rights for Children 103
Charters, W.W. 93
child-centered education 7–8, 45,

Index